Harm's Way

Harm's Way

Tragic Responsibility and the Novel Form

SANDRA MACPHERSON

The Johns Hopkins University Press
Baltimore

© 2010 The Johns Hopkins University Press

All rights reserved. Published 2010
Printed in the United States of America on acid-free paper

2 4 6 8 9 7 5 3 1

The Johns Hopkins University Press
2715 North Charles Street
Baltimore, Maryland 21218-4363
www.press.jhu.edu

Library of Congress Cataloging-in-Publication Data

Macpherson, Sandra, 1964–
Harm's way : tragic responsibility and the novel form / Sandra Macpherson.
p.   cm.
Includes bibliographical references and index.
ISBN-13: 978-0-8018-9384-1 (alk. paper)
ISBN-10: 0-8018-9384-4 (alk. paper)
1. English fiction—18th century—History and criticism. 2. Law and literature—
Great Britain—History—18th century. 3. Liability (Law) in literature. 4. Justice in
literature. 5. Love in literature. 6. Murder in literature. 7. Agent (Philosophy) in
literature. 8. Act (Philosophy) in literature. I. Title.
PR858.L39M33 2009
823'.509—dc22   2009009803

A catalog record for this book is available from the British Library.

*Special discounts are available for bulk purchases of this book. For more information, please
contact Special Sales at 410-516-6936 or specialsales@press.jhu.edu.*

The Johns Hopkins University Press uses environmentally friendly book materials,
including recycled text paper that is composed of at least 30 percent post-consumer
waste, whenever possible. All of our book papers are acid-free, and our jackets and
covers are printed on paper with recycled content.

For Luke, Roma, and Margo,
the loves of my life

The novel is the most hazardous genre.
—Georg Lukács

Contents

Acknowledgments

The story of this book is (mostly) a comedy. It is a sentimental story, a bildungs-roman about the virtues of love and education. I owe so much to so many, an epic catalogue of teachers. First among those in my grateful heart are my parents, Jack and Barb Macpherson, who did everything—absolutely *everything*—for us. Our happiness was their whole attention. My grandmother, Grace MacKinnon, read us poetry from the day we were born. My brother, Scott Macpherson, was my original and has been my most enduring collaborator; his passion for learning is an inspiration and a chastisement.

The dissertation this book once was has disappeared, but the influence of Ronald Paulson and Frances Ferguson can be felt on every page. From the moment I arrived in graduate school, Ron talked to me as though I had something to say about the eighteenth century. The example of his faith and humility is continually before me as I talk to my own students. The example of his voracious curiosity—the way his scholarship is at once broad and deep—is before me as I write. No one has had as profound an impact on my thinking as Frances. Only imperfectly have I come to understand her brilliant, difficult work; very imperfectly have I attempted to emulate its visionary feminist and formalist ethics. Inimitable, too, is her kindness, the patience with which she moves one toward the counterintuitive thought, the thought that changes everything.

I would not have written *this* book without the enlivening presence of my colleagues at the University of Chicago. Many of them read my work with rare attention; many inspired me by their conversation and by the provocations of their own work. Danielle Allen, Lauren Berlant, John Brewer, Bradin Cormack, Jackie Goldsby, Mark Hansen, Miriam Hansen, Paul Hunter, Oren Izenberg, Janice Knight, Loren Kruger, Laura Letinsky, David Levin, Saree Makdisi, Carla Mazzio, Mark Miller, Tom Mitchell, Janel Mueller, Pam Pascoe, Steve Pincus, Lisa Ruddick, Danilyn Rutherford, Eric Santner, Jay Schleusener, Jackie Stewart, Richard Strier, Robin Valenza, Bob von Hallberg, Iris Young, and especially Elaine Hadley, Debbie Nelson, Josh Scodel, Eric Slauter, and Katie Trumpener—

each of these was a boon to me. Bill Brown shepherded me with great care through the perils and benefactions of tenure. I am grateful for this, and for the example of his genial, generous intelligence. Beth Helsinger was a constant ally, an icon of grace, rigor, and integrity—the person I want to be when I grow up. Jim Chandler did more than anyone to champion and enrich my work. To thank him seems a meager return for the transformations wrought in my life by our friendship and collaboration.

My students at Chicago, in whose company work felt like the exhilarating pleasure of a first-year graduate seminar, continue to amaze me. This book would be a sorry thing without the thinking and rethinking my encounters with Andrew Broughton, Tony Brown, Burke Butler, Neil Chudgar, Noelle Gallagher, Andrea Haslanger, Irene Hsiao, Heather Keenleyside, Joanne Myers, Jeremy Rosen, Francesca Simkin, Catherine Sprecher Loverti, Sharif Youssef, and Abigail Zitin inspired. At the last moment a marvelous group of graduate students at the Ohio State University—Chris Belcher, Meghan Burke, Joshua Gass, Andrew Kopec, Corrine Martin, Lizzie Nixon, Aaron Pratt, Peggy Reynolds, and Adam Stier—have given me similar gifts.

I feel very fortunate to find myself among old and new friends at Ohio State. My thanks go to Valerie Lee for bringing me back and to David Brewer, Henri Cole, Mark Conroy, Frank Donoghue, Jon Erickson, Jared Gardner, Michelle Herman, Beth Hewitt, Ethan Knapp, Marlene Longenecker, Sean O'Sullivan, Pedro Pereira, Jim Phelan, Elizabeth Renker, Clare Simmons, Roxann Wheeler, Susan Williams, and Lisa Voigt for making it feel like home. Again. Still.

The field in which I work abounds with persons clever and kind. Rick Barney, Scott Black, Jill Campbell, Lorna Clymer, Helen Deutsch, Mary Favret, Bob Folkenflik, Jonathan Kramnick, Jayne Lewis, Gabrielle Starr, Helen Thompson, Alex Woloch—each has shared with me counsel and affection. Many years ago now, Gillian Brown took this fledgling scholar seriously. I will never forget her goodness or cease to miss her wry, gentle presence. Jonathan Lamb possesses similar gifts of humility and generosity. Deidre Lynch has animated and catechized my work for nearly a decade. This most recent effort is immeasurably better for her bountiful, incisive attentions.

Audiences at UCLA, Rutgers University, Vanderbilt University, and Yale University helped sharpen my ideas. Fellowships at the Huntington Library and the University of Chicago helped me abandon an old book and embark upon a new. Michael Lonegro took a chance on that book, and his constancy allowed me the time and freedom to mend it. Trevor Lipscombe ushered it through to its maturity. M. J. Devaney has made the book as perfect as it can be; all the remaining infelicities are mine. I am indebted to her and to Andre Barnett for their patience and scrupulosity. Wonderful women in two states loved my children while I was at work: Fabiana Alves dos Santos, Jeannie Britton, Jenny Ludwig, and the Parent Co-op for Early Learning in Chicago; Lindsay Hattery, Anne Langendorfer, Caitlin Seabrook, Indianola Children's Center, and Little Dreamer's Daycare in Columbus, Ohio.

Cherished friends have sustained me over the years in which this book took shape: Natalie Brender, Stephanie Brooks, Mark Canuel, Becky Chandler, Hannah Eigerman, Graham Finlay, Erik Gunderson, Cathy Jurca, Joanne Mancini, Rebecca Morton, Donna Sabourin, Staci Swenson—and especially my chickadees, Cynthia Rogers and Victoria Wohl, who pump me up, talk me down, share my worries and my much more copious joys.

My family has grown in these years, and with it my obligations. I am thankful for the accident of fate that gave me those loving parents, that loyal brother, the grandmother who lived long enough to hear that the book was finally done, but not long enough to see it in print. I am thankful for Raffi Folli, Sofia Grace Macpherson, Judy Mage, Eliza Thomas, Pan-Pan Thomas, Julian Wilson, Tona Wilson, and Stanley and Omar Wilson. Most of all I am thankful for Luke Wilson. He read each of these pages, and under the pressure of his brilliance, skepticism, and modesty they became—as I have become—good. (Or as he would say, good enough.) He makes me smart. He makes me happy. Together we share the gift of two beautiful, moving, astounding creatures—Roma Cady Macpherson-Wilson and Margo Lucy Macpherson-Wilson—who are my last, my best, teachers.

Harm's Way

Injuring Love

Could this person be blamed? . . . The cause, but not the
morally responsible agent.

—Ian McEwan, *Enduring Love*

This was once a book about marriage. And then I began to think harder than I
had done about the following striking account of conjugality: "When any Man
finds any occasion to quit his Wife, if he love her, she Dyes by his Hand." The
man in question takes up his wife, and

> imbracing her, with all the Passion and Languishment of a dying Lover, drew his
> Knife to kill this Treasure of his Soul, this Pleasure of his Eyes; while Tears trickl'd
> down his Cheeks, hers were Smiling with Joy she shou'd dye by so noble a Hand,
> and be sent in her own Country, (for that's their Notion of the next World) by him
> she so tenderly Lov'd, and so truly Ador'd in this; . . . All that Love cou'd say in
> such cases, being ended; and all the intermitting Irresolutions being adjusted, the
> Lovely, Young, and Ador'd Victim lays her self down, before the Sacrificer; while
> he, with a Hand resolv'd, and a Heart breaking within, gave the Fatal Stroke; first,
> cutting her Throat, and then severing her yet Smiling Face from that Delicate
> Body, pregnant as it was with Fruits of tend'rest Love.[1]

Although decapitation might look like a dramatic failure of conjugal affection,
the narrator asks us to see the action as a moving fulfillment of the logic of

marital complaisance and romantic love, a word invoked eight times within the space of three sentences. It seems we are being asked this; and yet there is something about that smile—the way the sentimental vocabulary is set off by the gothic and bathetic image of the severed, grinning head—that makes me wonder: what *is* the narrator's relationship to the claim that murder is the apotheosis of wedded love?

Aphra Behn's *Oroonoko* is with increasing frequency called the first realist novel, a claim that derives in part from the precision with which the narrator describes baskets, birds, and bodies but also from the way the tension between love and duty that had characterized heroic romance is transformed into the "nascent conventions" of a sentimental fiction that makes love itself the highest duty.[2] This linking of the practice of formal realism with the thematic of romantic and conjugal love is a resilient commonplace of criticism on the novel. In *Jane Austen, or The Secret of Style*, for example, D. A. Miller ties the realist novel to what he calls the "boundlessly oppressive imperiums of gender, conjugality, and the Person." Austen's innovation, he argues, is to have "audaciously" established within an imperium that novelists before her relentlessly enforce "something like extraterritoriality."[3] Miller's book is one of the most provocative instances of a decades-long attempt to rethink Ian Watt's influential account of formal realism. Yet despite his own audacious originality, Miller invokes a familiar (though in his ingenious hands, defamiliarized) story about the novel's *eighteenth-century* origins. The story goes something like this: the realist novel emerges as a technology for producing what Miller calls the "Person" or the "subject" and what Watt called the "individual." Novels are realist—indeed, novels are novels—to the extent that they sustain an "ideology of the person" grounded, on the one hand, in the particularity of what Miller variously describes as "personality" or "embodiment" and what Watt famously called "psychology," and, on the other, in an inescapable "conjugal imperative" that reveals that for all their particularity, persons come in twos.[4]

Although this alignment of the rise of the novel with the rise of the psychological subject and of companionate marriage has undergone significant refinement in eighteenth-century historiography since the 1950s when Watt introduced it, it has not withered away. A number of important recent studies of eighteenth-century cultural history complicate but ultimately reassert the claim that over the course of the eighteenth century, privacy, interiority, and companionate affiliation are articulated as the core values of modernity. Ruth Perry, for example, describes a "seismic" shift in family formation in the eighteenth century, one that involves a movement from an axis of kinship based on consanguineal ties or blood lineage to an axis based on conjugal and affinal ties of the marriage couple. That is, the biologically given family into which one was born was gradually becoming secondary to the chosen family constructed by marriage.[5]

Perry carefully charts the development of "conjugal kin formation" out of and away from "consanguineal kin formation": although some eighteenth-century fiction "attempts to celebrate a revived moral responsibility to consanguineal families," she observes, these attempts "were, of course, doomed; the forces of history were against them."[6] For Michael McKeon, in contrast, privacy, interiority and intimacy emerge dialectically out of premodern antitheses that remain central to how these values work. McKeon ends his monumental study of modernity with the novel, and, like Miller, with a discussion of Austen's free indirect discourse, which exemplifies the "conflationary" quality of the modern subject, the way she is constituted by and through her engagement with others. *Pride and Prejudice,* he suggests, "display[s] the politics that inhere within the domestic realm of the family in politically resonant conflicts—between individuals and families, 'connections' and 'connections,' children and parents, upbringing and maturity, feelings and design, subjectivity and subjection, the first person and the third person."[7] Yet the conflated self does not cease to be a self: "Like Adam Smith, Austen would have us understand that both self-knowledge and ethical sociability require the sympathetic internalization of the other's point of view *as if it were* one's own." The singular aspect of modernity, McKeon concludes, involves conceiving of the separation of self and society as a problem that nonetheless "proceed[s] from, even within, the interior."[8] The tension between self and other resolves here into a model of self-consciousness that is dialecticized but not, in the end, abandoned.[9]

But if self-consciousness is the precondition for a peculiarly modern practice of affiliation, one that is formally and thematically integral to that most modern of forms, the novel, why are novel characters so often connected to others *accidentally*? Not because they have chosen them or sympathize with them but because, as in the *Journal of the Plague Year,* one has handed someone a piece of cloth infected with a virus; because, as in the *Memoirs of Miss Sidney Bidulph,* one's horse has run a person down; because, as in *Clarissa,* one had meant to rob a woman of her virtue yet instead has robbed her of her life. How are we to understand the novel's obsessive focus on bodily injury rather than conjugal affection? Indeed, what is at stake in the fact that, as the passage I have quoted from *Oronooko* attests, affection leads to and is conceived of *as* injury? These questions led me to reimagine the book I had set out to write. And answering them—accounting for the accidents that move the plots of the very novels literary critics point to as evidence of a new, agentive and affective relationality—meant abandoning the axis of modernity, interiority, and companionate affiliation along with the premise upholding this obdurate alliance: the premise, at once historical and conceptual, that modernity moves "from status to contract," from a feudal to a liberal-democratic society organized around the freedom of persons to choose their associations.[10]

Harm's Way addresses the centrality of accident and injury to the realist novel by shifting attention away from contract—and from the marriage contract as the paradigmatic form of modern belonging—to liability. In doing so it brings into focus a genealogy of liberalism hitherto obscured by liberalism's equation with individualism, consent theory, and the law of contract; it elucidates a liberal countertradition focusing on harms rather than rights, accident rather than will and its analogues (intention, consciousness, sovereignty, freedom). This countertradition emerges from two locations that bear more than a contextual relationship to one another: from eighteenth-century novels that make questions about agency and responsibility central to their formal innovations; and from contemporary developments in laws of "strict liability"—laws that impose responsibility for accidental injury without requiring that it be shown the wrongdoer acted carelessly or with fault, laws indifferent to mental states and thus to the normative criteria of liberal subjectivity. Both strict liability and the novel undergo significant and rapid transformations from the later seventeenth through the early nineteenth century; and although this provides a historical rationale for bringing them together, it is not the only, or the strongest, link between them. These two forms share what I call a "tragic" logic of responsibility, one that conceives of persons as causes of harms that go against their best intentions but for which they are nonetheless accountable. At least one thinker has suggested that strict liability *is* a tragic form: in his critique of the progressivism of contemporary moral philosophy, Bernard Williams objects to the notion that modernity can be understood as a "shift in basic ethical conceptions of agency, responsibility, shame, or freedom."[11] "To a considerable extent the idea that the Greeks thought very differently from ourselves about responsibility, and in particular more primitively, is an illusion generated by thinking only about the criminal law and forgetting the law of torts," he observes. And he goes on to argue that we retain in "offences of strict liability, which require neither intention nor any other culpable state of mind," an interest in sanctioning persons for "things that they did unintentionally"—an interest that for him is synonymous with tragedy.[12]

Nietzsche was among the first, but has not been the last, to insist that the novel is antithetical to a tragic aesthetic. His claim that "Plato has given to all posterity the model of a new art form, the model of the *novel*," aligns Socratic dialectic with prose and narrative; but more importantly it allies narrative with philosophy's unaesthetic cheerfulness—with its "audacious reasonableness," its investment in explanation, in particular an explanation of causation that dispenses with accident.[13] The novel fulfills for Nietzsche the supreme laws of "*aesthetic Socratism*": "To be beautiful everything must be intelligible"; "knowledge is virtue"; "to be beautiful everything must be conscious"; "to be good everything must be conscious"; and, the most legislative of all laws, "the unshakable faith that thought, using the thread of causality, can penetrate the deepest abyss of being, and that thought is capable not only of knowing being but even of correcting it."[14]

Lukács develops Nietzsche's opposition between tragedy and the novel with an intricacy that has rendered *The Theory of the Novel*—the theory of the novel as antitragic—virtually unassailable. His philosophical history of form turns on a Nietzschean genealogy of "the great and timeless paradigmatic forms of world literature: epic, tragedy, philosophy," in which "Plato's new man, the wise man with his active cognition and his essence-creating vision, does not merely unmask but also illuminates the dark peril the [tragic] hero has vanquished."[15] The "peril" of tragedy is its abstraction: "For the drama, to exist is to be a cosmos, to grasp the essence, to possess its totality," and in it, "a level of being beyond life, full of richly blossoming plenitude, has been reached, to which ordinary life cannot serve even as an antithesis."[16] The dramatic hero is a form of life that is not alive but "assumes the symbolic attributes of the sensuous manifestation of life."[17] In epic, however, "men must be alive," and this "aliveness" is what is bequeathed to the novel *by way of philosophy*. Philosophy reveals "tragic destiny as the cruel and senseless arbitrariness of the empirical"; and the "wise man" whose thought makes meaning out of what is otherwise meaningless, "by surpassing the [tragic] hero, transfigures him."[18] In (real) life, tragic "heaviness" means "the absence of present meaning, a hopeless entanglement in senseless causal connections, a withered sterile existence too close to the earth and too far from heaven, a plodding on, an inability to liberate oneself from the bonds of sheer brutal materiality."[19] And life—an existence freed, through the agency of thought, from a purely material causality—is what novels want, and what they render.

Despite Lukács' description of the novel as "the most hazardous genre," these observations move in one direction: toward an account of the form as a hypostasized escape from hazard, accident, necessity.[20] "Unlike what occurs in the short story or in tragedy," Franco Moretti agrees, "the novelistic episode does not refer back to an objective necessity, but to a subjective possibility. . . . The novelistic plot is marked by this curvature toward interiority which dispenses meaning and thereby creates events."[21] ("The dramatic hero knows no interiority," Lukács had insisted. "The dramatic hero does not set out to prove himself." The novel, in contrast, "tells of the adventure of interiority; the content of the novel is the story of the soul that goes to find itself, that seeks adventures in order to be proved and tested by them, and, by proving itself, to find its own essence.")[22] Although the first chapter of *The Way of the World* is a nuanced *revision* of *The Theory of the Novel*, Moretti follows Lukács in arguing that the novel has "impressed" on Western culture an "anti-tragic" tendency tied to "the triumph of meaning over time" and to the related triumph of character over plot, *sjuzhet* over *fabula*.[23] The "inner form of the novel," says Lukács, is a "process of finding out," and it is a process the hero in some sense controls: "The sphere of the soul—psychology—and the sphere of action no longer have anything whatsoever in common"; the "life of a person with such a soul becomes an uninterrupted series of adventures which he himself has chosen."[24] "The novelistic episode is almost never meaningful *in itself*," Moretti confirms. "It becomes so because someone—in the *Bildungsroman* usually the protagonist— *gives it meaning*": *Bildung* is an " 'experiment' performed with one's self," in which "episode" (plot) is transformed into "experience" (character) once "the individual manages to give it a meaning that expands and strengthens his personality."[25] In Lukács, the adventure of interiority, admittedly, is a *via dolorosa*, and the novel of romantic disillusionment continues to feel tragic for the way it subjects a hero of "increased subjectivity" to the "crushing, equalizing universality of fate."[26] But the novel form reaches its synthetic apotheosis in the "humanism" of *Wilhelm Meister*, a "type of work," like Moretti's bildungsromans, in which "the will toward education, a will that is conscious and certain of its aim . . . creates [an] atmosphere of ultimate security."[27] "History is what hurts," it is the place where "desire must come to grief."[28] History is tragic, but realism is comic for the way it consoles an imagination "tormented by unresolvable contradictions."[29]

One finds in these influential distinctions between tragedy and the novel versions of Watt's claim that the novel rises alongside an epistemological practice devoted to the production of meaning, knowledge, self-consciousness, and an ambivalent fantasy of sovereignty.[30] "The suspicion that there is something inherently untragic about the novel-form is hard to shake off," Terry Eagleton has recently observed; and although he wants to shake this suspicion off—arguing that "the belief that novel form is ipso facto untragic springs largely from generalizing this privileged strain of it [realism] to the genre as a whole," and that *The Counterfeiters, Light in August, Under the Volcano, Lolita,* to name but a few of his postrealist (that is, modernist) exempla, are "unmistakably" tragic—he concedes that realism, like the epistemological ethos with which it is invariably aligned, is invested in "establishing connections between far-flung elements and drawing them into an elaborate yet orderly whole."[31] Thus "in George Eliot's hands," he explains, "the novel can avoid tragedy because its task is to trace the complex chains of causality which weave themselves into the present, thus letting explanation take the place of condemnation. *Tout comprendre est tout pardonner.*"[32] For Eagleton, realism is marked by a concern with causation that is untragically exculpatory: realism's championing of "growth, change, and provisionality" continually offers "the promise of redemption."[33] "Nietzsche thought the metaphysical consolation of tragedy was lost when Socrates set *knowing* as the crown of human activity," Stanley Cavell reflects in his elegant meditation on the ethics of tragedy. "And it is a little alarming, from within the conviction that the medium of drama which Shakespeare perfected also ended with him, to think again that Bacon and Galileo and Descartes were contemporary with those events."[34] Cavell says he doesn't want to say that "it was *because* of the development of the new science and the establishing of epistemology as the monitor of philosophical inquiry that Shakespeare's mode of tragedy disappeared." But he does, in fact, say what Eagleton and Moretti also say: that tragedy disappears with the rise of an empiricism that encourages us to believe "that we can save our lives by knowing them."[35]

It is not the task of this book to revisit the question of the simultaneous rise of empiricism and the novel form or to prove, as I think might be proved, that empiricism is more interested than Cavell imagines in the "cruelly inexorable logic" of tragedy—which is to say, in the logic of unintended consequences.[36] More interesting to me is the pervasive assumption among theorists of the novel that the novel is "antitragic" because it inverts the classical relationship between character and plot.[37] Watt's claim that the story of the novel is a story in which "the Aristotelian priority of plot over character has been wholly reversed," has not been seriously contested—a consequence, perhaps, of the influence of German theories of tragedy on the tale of the novel's cheerfulness.[38] Watt is thinking of the Aristotle who, in the sixth chapter of the *Poetics,* asserts: "Tragedy is essentially an imitation not of persons but of action and life, of happiness and misery." Action does not reveal, or "prove," character as it does for Lukács; characters are included "for the sake of the action," or, to be more precise, are an *effect* of the action: "Tragedy is an imitation of an action, and on account above all of the action it is an imitation of agents."[39] As Williams puts the matter: "The whole of the *Oedipus Tyrannus,* that dreadful machine, moves to the discovery of just one thing, that *he did it,*" that "he is the person who did those things"—Oedipus meets himself in the recognition of what he has done.[40] In Lessing's hands, and again in Hegel's, however, tragedy becomes a drama of character that ceases to preoccupy itself with accidental responsibility. For if in the *Aesthetics* tragic action is not fully intentional, neither is it adventitious: "The occasion for collisions is produced by the moral justification of a specific act, and not at all by an evil will, a crime, or infamy, *or by mere misfortune,* blindness, and the like."[41]

Hegel's model of tragic responsibility is underwritten by a "live conception of *individual* freedom and independence"—both sign and symptom of his preference for *Antigone* over *Oedipus Tyrannus.*[42] So synonymous is *Antigone* with the tragic *as such* that Oedipus's actions are read as if they were as deliberate as those of his righteous granddaughter. "What is at issue here is the right of the wide awake consciousness, the justification of what the man has self-consciously willed and knowingly done," Hegel insists; and though he acknowledges that "our deeper consciousness today would consist in recognizing that since [Oedipus] had neither intended nor known these crimes himself, they were not to be regarded as his own deeds," the Greek, "with his plasticity of consciousness, takes responsibility for what he has done as an individual and does not cut his purely subjective self-consciousness apart from what is objectively the case."[43] Clearly uncomfortable with the possibility that one might be responsible for unintended acts, Hegel redescribes accident *as* self-consciousness, and this profound revision (if not distortion) of Aristotle underwrites the concept of "tragic reconciliation," which in turn leads Hegel to reject the idea that tragedy has "anything to do with guilt or innocence."[44] While it is true that tragic heroes produce "injurious and guilty acts" and that "they do not claim to be innocent of these at all," the development of tragic action "consists solely in the cancellation of conflicts *as conflicts*"—in other words, in the cancellation of responsibility and, perhaps, of tragedy itself: "Only in that case does finality lie not in misfortune and suffering but in the satisfaction of the spirit, because only with such a conclusion can the necessity of what happens to the individual appear as absolute rationality, and only then can our hearts be morally at peace."[45]

"Innocent suffering would inevitably produce in the soul of the spectator mere indignation," Hegel avers, and he opts instead for "the vision of an affirmative reconciliation" that confirms the "equal validity of both the powers that were in conflict." "The most perfect classical example of this we have before us is the eternally marvellous *Oedipus Coloneus*," he concludes, in which the hero's transfiguring death is "a visible reconciliation within his own self and personality"—a "*subjective satisfaction*" that, Hegel admits, "enables us to make the transition to the sphere of comedy, the opposite of tragedy."[46]

Hegel's refusal to ground tragedy in accidental responsibility is a preference attributed to the tragic hero as well as his audience: "No worse insult could be given to such a hero than to say that he had acted innocently. It is the honour of these great characters to be culpable."[47] Benjamin invokes this passage when he, too, insists that tragedy does not and should not represent "the ineluctable chain of causality." Guilt, he objects, "unleashes causality as the instrument of the irresistibly unfolding fatalities: Fate is the entelechy of events within the field of guilt." It is a subtle point, one that highlights the progressive tendency since Hegel to psychologize and agentivize tragic responsibility. "Guilt consists only in the proud consciousness of guilt," Benjamin explains. "In tragic poetry the ancient curse which has been passed down from generation to generation, becomes the inner, self-discovered possession of the tragic character."[48] Hegel's admission that his tragic hero's "subjective satisfaction" (his sense that *if* he is responsible for his actions it is only because he has *meant* to be) moves tragedy closer to comedy helps to explain why for Lukács and those who follow him the novel is antitragic.[49] "In comedy there comes before our contemplation in the laughter in which the characters dissolve everything, including themselves, the victory of their own subjective personality which nevertheless persists self-assured," Hegel observes.[50] The adventure of interiority is in the final analysis a comedy.

Hegel's "affirmative" tragedy is no longer what I would want to call tragic; and it is very far indeed from Williams's conception that tragedy *must* turn on "innocent suffering" and on the tragic hero's recognition that he is responsible *without* being culpable: "That is the point of Oedipus's words at Colonus," Williams observes in his anti-Hegelian reading of *Oedipus at Colonus*. "The terrible thing that happened to him, through no fault of his own, was that he did those things."[51] Classical tragedy, as Williams helps us see, produces character as an effect of the realization that one is responsible without being at fault. And in defiance of novel *theory*, novel *practice* frequently entails anagnorisis. This is what a late habitué of realism, Ian McEwan, understands about the form: that it is less an adventure of interiority than of emplotment—a drama, as Benjamin would call it, of fate. The characteristic McEwanite plot is one in which blithe, well-intentioned protagonists are subjected to the realization that they have caused harm and are responsible for it; and the ruthlessness with which McEwan subverts the project of *bildung* suggests a practitioner who is also a theorist of the novel. McEwan works at a remove from the realist aesthetic he so deftly deploys, and in that space one sees what he sees about it: that the novel, like tragedy, is a form of strict liability.

In the passage from *Enduring Love* that serves as my epigraph, the protagonist, Joe, wants to imagine that although he is a cause of the death of the man he watches drop through the air like "a stiff little black stick" from the side of a balloon—"You could see the acceleration. No forgiveness, no special dispensation for flesh, or bravery, or kindness. Only ruthless gravity"—it is precisely because he is *merely* a cause that he is "not the morally responsible agent" of the accident.[52] Joe assumes that because it *is* an accident, because he is not the agent of the tragedy, he is therefore not responsible for it—an assumption marked by a repetition of the metaphors of inanimateness that pervade the opening description of the action. "If the first person had not let go, then surely the rest of us would have stayed in place," Joe reflects:

> And who was this first person? Not me. Not me. I even said the words aloud. I remember a plummeting mass and the sudden upward jerk of the balloon. But I could not tell whether this mass was in front of me or to my left or right. If I knew the position, I would know the person. Could this person be blamed? As I drank my coffee, the rush hour below began its slow crescendo. It was hard to think this through. Phrases, well worn and counterweighted, occurred to me, resolving nothing. On the one hand, the first pebble in an avalanche, and on the other, the breaking of ranks. The cause but not the morally responsible agent.[53]

The person as mass; the person as position; the person as pebble: Joe aligns the thingness of the dead man with the impenetrable instrumentality of the men involved in attempting, and failing, to save him. For although the "plummeting mass" seems to invoke the victim ("I've never seen such a terrible *thing* as that falling man," Joe says) the antecedent is in fact the ambiguously positioned "first person" who lets go of the rope and falls backward, as they all do, as the balloon jerks upward.[54] One encounters here McEwan's rigorous Aristotelianism: who or what a "person" is is worked out by way of her relationship to and responsibility for the action that engenders her. "The beginning is simple to mark," the novel begins, and even Joe is conscious that the story he is telling

is a story about the emergence of (his) character out of plot: "We turned to look
across the field and saw the danger. Next thing, I was running toward it. The
transformation was absolute: . . . What idiocy, to be racing into this story and its
labyrinths, sprinting away from our happiness among the fresh spring grasses
by the oak." The danger is not, or not only, the accident that is the novel's story
but the quasi-ontological, transforming power of plot itself.[55]

As Joe attempts to "think through" the issue of emplotted personhood, he
emphasizes the instrumentality of this person in order to deemphasize her responsibility. But his suggestion that responsibility requires intentional agency
is a "well-worn" cliché, we're told, and as the plot unfolds Joe's responsibility
is insisted on as emphatically as his instrumentality. The novel multiplies the
harms that stem from this one action (the action of letting go, the single action
of plot *as such*), culminating in a scene in which Joe shoots the man who, unbid-
den, yet in the name of love, has hounded him since the accident. The charge
that the police fasten on him for this act, "malicious wounding with intent,"
seems precisely wrong.[56] "Surprise was making me stupid," Joe reflects of the
encounter. "It was so extraordinary, such a reverse, that he was not about to
attack Clarissa [Joe's wife] or me that the fact he was about to slit his throat in
front of us presented itself with numbing slowness." "I managed to say, 'Drop
the knife and we'll talk,'" he tells us, and in what he describes as a kind of pa-
ralysis, he aims a gun he hadn't meant to use at the man's side: "In the enclosed
space the explosion seemed to wipe out all other senses, and the room flashed
like a blank screen. Next I saw the knife on the floor and Parry slumped back
with his hand to his shattered elbow, his face white and his mouth open in
shock."[57] Joe aims, but he is not seen firing; the explosion has an agency all its
own, and yet this is not the only reason the policemen's emphasis on "malice"
and "intent" seems wrong. As Clarissa points out in a letter to Joe following the
shooting, there is a sense in which Joe's and Parry's actions are continuous with
the fatal action that sets the plot in motion: "That evening after the accident,"
she recalls, "you were very troubled by the thought that it might have been you
who let go of the rope first. It was obvious you needed to confront that idea,
dismiss it, make your peace with it, whatever." "Isn't it possible," she asks, that
Parry and his incomprehensible affection "presented you with an escape from
your guilt?"[58]

It is not incidental that the character who asks this question—who inter-
rogates Joe on his need to escape responsibility for things he has not meant
to do—is named Clarissa. It is quite common to point to *Clarissa* as an exception to the rule that the novel is antitragic. "In the very bosom of modernity,

with English civilization apparently at its most blithely self-assured," observes Eagleton, "Samuel Richardson writes the astonishing *Clarissa,* in which tragedy and the commonplace are inseparable."[59] "Clarissa is one of the great tragic figures of English writing," he says, but he declares that "Aristotle would not have found her so. She is too innocent."[60] Like Joe—like Hegel—Eagleton has difficulty conceiving of the possibility that one might be innocent and to blame; but this possibility is precisely what is at stake in *Clarissa* and what makes it among the most Aristotelian of tragedies. Eagleton ignores what for Williams is important about the tragic hero: that his predicament is attributable "not to depravity but to a serious error" "performed in ignorance."[61] After she is forcibly abducted by Lovelace from her family's home, Clarissa writes to tell Anna Howe that she feels responsible for the event "and yet cannot charge" herself "with one criminal or faulty inclination." "Do you know, my dear, how this can be?" she asks, invoking the conundrum of faultless wrongdoing that perplexes Eagleton. "I can tell you how, I believe," she continues. "One devious step at setting out!—That must be it: which pursued, has led me so far out of my path that I am in a wilderness of doubt and error; and never, never shall find my way out of it: for although but one pace awry at first, it has led me hundreds and hundreds of miles out of my path."[62] By "devious" Clarissa means to mark not any duplicity on her part but the impenetrability of emplotment, a point underscored by the text she invokes to explain her "unhappy yet undesigned error":

> To you, great gods! I make my last appeal:
> Or clear my virtues, or my crimes reveal.
> If wandering in the maze of life I run,
> And backward tread the steps I sought to shun,
> Impute my errors to your own decree;
> My FEET are guilty; but my HEART is free.[63]

The text is Dryden and Lee's *Oedipus: A Tragedy* (1678), and it provides Clarissa with a way to perform an action that the realist novel is supposed not to perform: to "trace complex chains of causality" in the interest of *condemnation* rather than pardon.[64] "Clarissa was not drawn absolutely perfect," Richardson once wrote, "but as having something to blame herself for, tho' not in Intention."[65] This detachment of blameworthiness from intentionality—"feet" from "hearts"—bewilders a modern readership steeped in what Williams calls the "bad philosophy" of the will and the corresponding assumption that it is unjust to sanction people for things they have not meant to do.[66] Yet if it is true (and I do not dispute it) that *Clarissa* is an iconic moment in the history of modernity, we need to see more clearly than we have done what modernity, and justice, might entail: the demand that one take responsibility for crimes she has caused though sought to shun.

⚶

The realist novel is a project of blame not exculpation. This is the grand, formalist claim of *Harm's Way;* but it is a claim that comes into focus only by confronting the historical and conceptual specificity of strict liability as precisely as the novelists who pursue the same "devious" path as Richardson. For the tragic model of emplotted personhood so central to the early realist novel unfolds by way of an obsessive and explicit interest in strict liability. In chapter 1, I show how late seventeenth-century developments in laws covering innkeepers, common carriers, and masters and servants are invoked in and help to explain the logic of blame and agency at work in Defoe's *Journal of the Plague Year* and *Roxana.* These novels are striking for the way they mobilize the most strenuous category of indictment there is—"murderer"—to describe persons who have unwittingly and sometimes as a result of the deepest affection (a kiss on the lips, a pull at the breast) killed those they love. Defoe's interest in accidental harm has received little attention in a critical tradition focused on his providentialism—a logic that, like tragedy, is concerned with unintended acts and consequences and is a way of thinking of persons as rigorously emplotted but in which the accidents of fate are necessarily felicitous and, moreover, are something for which no one is responsible. (God occasions events, but he is not blamed for them.) *Roxana* has been described as gothic for the way it subverts the sovereigntism otherwise pervasive, it is said, in Defoe's oeuvre. "Gothic" is supposed to mark the subversion of agency, the haunting of the self by those with whom she does not want to be affiliated, as a problem, something Defoe, and we, ought to be terrified of. But I argue that Defoe uses the law—in particular a newly refined doctrine of agency making masters vicariously liable for the acts of their servants—to reimagine and revalue providentialism as a tragic ethos, one that connects us to and makes us responsible for the strangeness of our acts and the strangeness of others.

Defoe's upping the ante on accidental harms by calling them murder is a thought experiment about the possibilities of strict liability. Legal developments in the 1730s and 1740s make Lovelace's indictment for murder near the end of *Clarissa,* despite, as he insists, having merely raped the eponymous victim, a different kind of gesture. In chapter 2, I argue that Richardson self-consciously invokes a new criminal model of strict liability called "felony murder" to think through the issue of responsibility that so preoccupies *Clarissa*. The doctrine (articulated, among other locations, in the six-volume edition of *State Trials* Richardson printed in the late 1740s) made persons responsible not only for the unintended consequences of their own felonious acts (such as rape) but also for the consequences of acts that were not their own. Linked to the doctrine of agency, felony murder is similarly indifferent to questions of motive and individuation, holding principals accountable for the acts of accessories and accessories accountable for the acts of principals, ruthlessly tying individuals to outcomes they could not have anticipated and to others from whom, and from whose acts, they might want to be distinguished. There is a genuine sense in which felony murder conceives of acts and agents as indistinguishable from one another—conflating them into a single action, the action, one might want to say, of *plot*. The logic of felony murder makes possible Richardson's indictment of Lovelace and his accessories and, more uncomfortably, Clarissa's self-indictment. If Clarissa is the exemplary modern moral subject, the legal context helps us to see that it is because she is less a subject than a cause—because she accepts responsibility for a tragic plot that much as we might want to believe exceeds and is distinct from character, in fact, embodies it. Clarissa is the person who did those things.

Fielding is the first to notice Richardson's commitment to strict liability. His anti-Pamelist satires work by marking as Richardsonian an obsession with the body's propensity to injury and a corresponding interest in the law of damages. In chapter 3, I argue that the famous distinction between Richardson and Fielding hinges on the question of liability, as in *Joseph Andrews* and *Tom Jones* Fielding repeatedly and explicitly rejects the consolations of civil law in favor of the rough justice of his heroes' fistfighting. If Defoe turned to the laws governing common carriers to imagine a form of obligation that would extend to strangers, Fielding's invocations of carrier liability are designed as an attack on a generic investment that is already in focus for him—the novel's investment in the depersonalizing and instrumentalizing logic of strict liability. Fistfighting is a rigorously embodied—and in Fielding's hands, sentimental—alternative to such a logic, one that turns the injured male body into a sign of agency and, paradoxically, a form of *caritas*. Miller astutely distinguishes the impersonality of Austen's narrator from Fielding's "noisy personality"—the bumptious particularity, the de facto masculinity of his all-too-human cast of characters.[67] He is right to do so. But Miller conflates Fielding's avowedly contrarian strain of realism with realism *tout court*, missing what is at stake in the "comic epic in prose"—namely, that it is a relentlessly cheerful, which is to say exculpatory, substitute for a tragic realism devoted to the project of blame.

In Fielding, men are not injured; indeed what looks like injury is in the comic epic form inevitably recuperated as happiness: comedy means never having to say you're sorry. This is no doubt why Frances Sheridan dedicates the *Memoirs of Miss Sidney Bidulph*—a novel that follows *Joseph Andrews* in its interest in male rape—to the "author of *Clarissa*." Unlike Fielding, Sheridan takes the possibility of male rape seriously and in doing so complicates a sentimental model of culpability that insists on the innocence of victims and the perfidy of villains. Can a man be a victim of rape at a woman's hands if he has penetrated and impregnated the woman in question? Sheridan asks; do men move their bodies or do their bodies move them? In chapter 4, I show how Sheridan turns to the law of deodand or "thing liability" to think through the question of masculine inanimateness and the instrumentalism of desire, indeed of action itself. Thing liability evolved to take account of injuries to persons by things; but it also made persons responsible *for* the actions of things and did so by turning them *into* things—by thinking of persons as matter in motion that causes bodily harm. This is a model of liability in which the usual criteria for blameworthiness—intentionality, malice, forethought, foresight—are rendered superfluous because of a prior decision about the mental life of things and animals (that they don't have a mental life). When liability is transferred from nonhumans to humans, so too is the superfluity of the mental life: thing liability detaches (legal) personhood from the quality that has always seemed to ensure the special status of the human person: consciousness. Sheridan conflates persons and things in order to make deodand, quite explicitly, an answer to the problem of rape. By making states of mind irrelevant to the question of harm and compensation, deodand avoids the depredations of consent and makes all harms—even harms complicated by the presence of affection, desire, or consent, even harms produced by good people and experienced by bad—count as harm.

❦

As these brief chapter summaries are meant to suggest, attending to the logic of strict liability at work in these texts requires us to rethink the question of the person in the history and theory of the novel. It also requires us to rethink the question of the nonperson. Recent work on realist characterization has, like Sheridan, been intrigued by the possibilities of depersonalization. Resisting the old humanist consensus that tied the rise of the novel and the rise of the liberal individual to their capacity to escape and exceed typology, McKeon, Miller, Catherine Gallagher, Deidre Lynch, and Alex Woloch have shown that what is called "externality," "impersonality," "disembodiment," "typography," and "allegory," respectively, remain central to the consolidation of liberal and literary subjects.[68] I am profoundly indebted to this body of work but am ultimately more committed than they to abandoning the claims of the person.[69] When Woloch, for example, suggests not only that minor characters fail to achieve the status of "imagined human beings" and "implied persons" but also that they are thereby "alienated," "subordinated," "compressed," "reduced," "suffocated," "proletarianized," there is more than a hint of a worry that might plausibly be called "humanist."[70] Woloch implies that the failure to particularize characters by attending to the content of their form—by entering into the interior, into their "case," which is say into those moments of (self-) consciousness that make them persons rather than mere personalities—entails a more profound failure: the failure of political representation. The argument is of course more properly described as "materialist," directed as it is toward the way the relationship between form and content, structure and reference, "is grounded in the problematic elimination or functionalized compression of real persons in the actual world."[71] The "asymmetric structure of realist characterization," Woloch asserts, "reflects actual structures of inequitable distribution."[72] This is no simple equation of formal abstraction with dehumanization, for form has the potential to attend to underrepresented beings: "The novel's sense of the potential to shift narrative attention is intertwined with a specific notion of human right," he observes, and attention is a "democratic impulse."[73] But to say this is to align justice with what looks like the interiority thesis—with the claims of a person individuated by the contingencies of her experience and by her capacity to give an account of herself that differs from her social emplotment.

In the genealogy of realism I am tracing, depersonalization is literalized in the instrumentalizing logic of strict liability: persons are conceived of as mindless things ("masses," as McEwan puts it), and in being things they are forced to be humane. This paradox is not something to which many people have acceded or might want to accede. Strict liability is notoriously unpopular precisely for its indifference to the claims of the individual (or what amounts to the same thing, the human person). " 'Strict liability' is generally viewed with great odium," observes H. L. A. Hart in *Punishment and Responsibility*, a book committed to the philosophical justification of such opprobrium.[74] The odium is shared by lawyers, legal historians and philosophers of law, and in particular by analytic philosophers (like Hart) committed to delineating the unique contours of human action.[75] "Why, then, do we value a system of social control that takes mental conditions into account?" Hart begins by asking. "What precisely is the ground of dissatisfaction with 'strict liability'?"[76] It seems clear even at this early stage in Hart's argument that the problem with strict liability must be that it does not take mental conditions into account. And indeed strict liability violates the "moral principal" that is the "necessary condition (unless strict liability is admitted) for the moral propriety of legal punishment and no doubt also for moral censure": the principal that "no one should be punished who could not help doing what he did."[77] Strict liability fails to provide the "minimum link between mind and body" that is indispensable for responsibility, and if Hart's central concern is criminal responsibility, at stake in the argument is the immorality of holding persons accountable for accidents *as such*.[78] Insisting on the "relevance of the mind to responsibility," Hart argues that the "principle that a voluntary act should normally be required as a condition of liability to punishment" is predicated on "universal ideas of fairness or justice and of the value of individual liberty."[79] The law, Hart says, "may make responsibility strict, or even absolute, not even exempting very young children or the grossly insane from punishment; or it may vicariously punish one man for what another has done, even though the former had no control of the latter; or it may punish an individual or make him compensate another for harm which he neither intended nor could have foreseen as likely to arise from his conduct." It may do this, but it would be "barbarous and unjust" and move legal responsibility away from what ought to be its grounding in morality: "The hypothesis that we might hold individuals morally blameworthy for doing things which they could not have avoided doing, or for things done by others over whom they had no control, conflicts with too many of the central features of the idea of morality to be treated merely as speculation about a rare or inferior kind of moral system," Hart concludes. And though he admits that it "may be an exaggeration to say that there could not logically be such a morality or that blame administered according to principles of strict or vicarious responsibility . . . could not logically be moral blame," he nonetheless proceeds to say that the admission of a "strict" principle of blame would require a "profound modification" in the concept of morality.[80]

It is this kind of argument to which the revisionist energies of Williams's *Shame and Necessity* are directed: for Williams, the tragic principle that persons must accept responsibility for things they could not avoid doing is at the very heart of ethics. I agree with him that tragedy and strict liability are ethical principles. Yet their alignment puts pressure on the very terms by which he modifies the concept of morality, replacing the bad philosophy of the goodness of the will with an ethics of recognition—with ethics *as* recognition—a move that strict liability itself does not permit. Williams is among a number of scholars influenced by Cavell's argument that suffering makes a claim on our sympathy and that we "acknowledge" that suffering equally in indifference as in caring. Cavell gives us a way to think of ethics as a response to the separateness and strangeness of other persons, one predicated on our own strangeness to ourselves.[81] It is a skeptical and antisentimental ethics; but Williams helps us to see that it is not therefore an anti-individualist or antihumanist one. Acknowledgment requires consciousness and self-consciousness: this is why Cavell repeatedly insists that we cannot and need not acknowledge dummies and dolls, though we may have to acknowledge robots and other forms of artificial intelligence.[82] And it is why Williams finally turns his attention away from "the response that the public or the state or the neighbours or the damaged parties demand of the agent, [to] what the agent demands of himself."[83] Responsibility might be demanded by others; but *recognizing* responsibility requires that a person "express his responsibility for actions when no one else would have the right to make a claim for damages or be in a position to."[84] Recognition, that is, requires persons—and persons conceived ultimately the way Hart conceives them, as beings who think and as beings whose responsibility resides in the reflective, retrospective interstice between thought and action.

If strict liability is a tragic—and therefore ethical—form, however, it is also profoundly indifferent to the possibility and the practice of recognition. The point about strict liability, as Hart observes, is that it is not negligence: if the law does not ask whether the wrongdoer might have foreseen the injury she has caused, it also does not ask or expect her to amend her conduct, nor does it ask her to accede to the responsibility it imposes. Although Williams doesn't put it in these terms, the shift from the demand of the other to the demand on the self at the end of his essay "Recognising Responsibility"—the shift, that is, from strict liability to recognition—is a shift from compensation to amelioration. Recognition is implicitly ameliorative, tied to the ethical work of shame, which makes one reflect on "who one is and [on] what one hopes to be," on "how it will be for one's life with others if one acts in one way rather than another."[85]

In *The Secret of Style*, Miller describes something like this process as central to the ideologies of personhood and conjugation that underwrite the realist novel. "Emma's bravura performance of the Person," he says, is a "sentimental spectacle of an injured subject whose injury makes her exultant, triumphant with all the power of that second injury which, by means of this very performance, *she has given herself*"—the "self-inflicted wound," that is, of shame.[86] The recognition of fault makes Emma a person and also an individual—the bearer of failings that she (and we) come to see as peculiarly her own. It also makes her marriageable: marriage is the reward for one's commitment to amelioration. Recognition leads Emma to the hope that she will become "more rational, more acquainted with herself," and thus more deserving of him whose "intentions and judgments had been ever so superior to her own."[87] Personhood and marriage thus function as paradigmatic instances of what, following Leo Bersani, Miller calls "our culture of redemption," a culture invested, once again, in the notion that we can save our lives—and the lives of others—by knowing them.[88]

Miller, for his part, is captivated by the possibility of failing to be a person, and he insists that we take the impersonality of Austen's narrator literally: this narrator is "No One," resolutely *not* a person.[89] Like Austen, Miller is attracted to the "austere abstraction of structure," to impersonality understood as a way of escaping norms of particularity that are especially oppressive to women and queers. But it is an ambivalent attraction, for as in Woloch, abstraction is a kind of alienation: "Nowhere else in nineteenth-century English narration," Miller asserts, "have the claims of the 'person,' its ideology, been more completely denied." On the one hand, that personhood is ideological suggests that there are utopian possibilities entailed in its refusal. On the other hand, that "Austen Style is decidedly neuter" marks the melancholy, compensatory quality of impersonality—the way it attracts "marginal or malformed subjects who need to take shelter in an image of universality and absoluteness."[90]

The consolations of impersonality are not, in the end, available to persons—neither to the characters nor to the human subjects who are persons. "Austen Style finds its most congenial expression in the Novel, where it splits into two mutually exclusive, and definitive states of being: (godlike) narration and (all-too-human) character," Miller argues. The opposition between narration and character is an opposition between impersonality and what is variously called "roundness," "personhood," "subjectivity," "human being": "free indirect style gives a virtuoso performance, against all odds, of the narration's persistence in detachment from character." Characters cannot be *im*personal because they must be persons; and to be a person means giving up the "inhuman" indifference of "Style": "The melancholy of Style in Austen depends upon the author's firm refusal to give (her) Style a human face."[91] The melancholy is Miller's as well: style is a dispensation from the injury and imperfection involved in being a self, which is to say in being a person involved with others. It's a dispensation that human beings do not really want, for choosing style over self is choosing to be alone. Form is "self-negation"; redemption comes from "being particular *with another* *person.*"[92] If the stylothete is "inflexible" in her "renunciation of the Person," this is because impersonality offers "immunity" from rejection: "The beauty of Style . . . lies in the way it shuts out the world that would otherwise shut out the stylothete." Impersonality is a "fantasy of autarchy" and self-sufficiency available, finally, only to things—like the bejeweled snuffbox that adorns the cover of *The Secret of Style* and like the crystalline sentences contained within it.[93]

Like Miller and Bersani I am interested in what it might look like to conceive of relationship and subjectivity in nonredemptive, impersonal ways. In the chapters that follow I show that what it looks like, pace Miller, is the realist novel before Austen. By shifting attention from (marriage) contract to (strict) liability, *Harm's Way* offers a new account of how the novel thinks about persons and their connections to others. And if we would still want to call this liberalism, then we must change how we talk about the modern dispensation. For if modernity moves anywhere at all in the eighteenth century, it moves from contract to *status*—but status defeudalized, detached from a narrowly socioeconomic understanding of class and made the ground of a more capacious form of belonging.[94] Social contract theory and the law of contract, those dominant models of Enlightenment and even post-Enlightenment thought, are theories of *limited* liability: they presume that subjects are responsible only for relationships they have meant to pursue and to which they have consented. Even when agency and consent are acknowledged to be ambiguous, even when they are made a feature of groups rather than individuals (as in representative democracy or the general will), they remain necessary to mark and ratify association. In laws of strict liability, by contrast, association does not emerge through assent. Strict liability is "strict" because it is *unlimited*—because it is nondisclaimable, because there is no way to escape from obligation. It begins historically as a way to govern status (which is to say, adventitious) relationships such as those between innkeepers and guests, coach drivers and passengers, masters and servants. In the eighteenth century it becomes a way of dealing with *all* accidental encounters between persons; it becomes what can plausibly be called a theory of obligation, one that transfers the law's indifference to the subjective particularity of the innkeeper or his guest onto other categories of persons and other kinds of relationships. In the new articulations of strict liability that emerge in the long eighteenth century (the doctrine of agency, felony murder, products liability) harm alone matters: a preoccupation with the material fact of harm outweighs any interest in the character or interiority of those involved in a crime or accident. As a theory of justice and belonging, strict liability thus combines the abstraction of classical liberalism with the materialism of its most devastating critiques. It conceives of the person as a material abstraction—as the bearer of a harm that is substantive but not particularized, as the perpetrator of a harm that is causal but not agentive. Relationship on this model is not an effect of recognition or affection: one is obliged to another whether or not she likes her, whether or not she knows her, whether or not she acknowledges her.

In its focus on the question of injury, *Harm's Way* is influenced by feminist scholarship likewise skeptical about the historical and theoretical claims of liberal consent theory. In their different ways, writers such as Carole Pateman, Susan Staves, Claudia Johnson, Catharine MacKinnon, Andrea Dworkin, to name just a few, have argued that the liberal model of the self permanently enshrines the injury of gendered inequality.[95] No one argues this point more strenuously, perhaps, than MacKinnon and Dworkin, whose *In Harm's Way*—a book in which "women speak for the first time in history of the harms done to them through pornography" (the most grotesque injury perpetrated by liberal sovereigntism and consensualism, according to them)—my book explicitly invokes.[96] Unlike some feminists, I am interested in what MacKinnon and Dworkin have to say about pornography (that it is a tort) and in their practical strategies for limiting its production (by holding producers civilly liable for harms caused by their products). But I want to put pressure on the redemptive energies of critiques of liberalism such as theirs, on the fragile but persistent belief that if it were possible to rid the world of gender inequality, consent would be fully transparent and contract truly equitable.[97] I am cynical about this aspiration, not only because the eradication of (gender) inequality seems to me unlikely but because such a hope persists in aligning a fantasy of safety with a fantasy of reformed subjectivity and affiliation. "In harm's way": the prepositional phrase invokes a future when we will be out of the way of harm, when harm itself will cease to exist; "harm's way": the modification suggests that harm might be a method of rather than an obstacle to affiliation.

Harm's Way is not, therefore, a book about amelioration—or, to put it another way, it is not a book about utilitarianism nor is it itself a utilitarian project committed to a reduction in harm and corresponding increase in the quantum of pleasure. For Wendy Brown, the problem with such an ameliorative politics is that it looks to the state to redress the injury of domination and disenfranchisement. She is troubled by "recent progressive theoretical and political indifference to state domination, appeals to expand state benefits, and ever increasing reliance on the state for adjudication of social injury"—that is, by the effort to "replace liberalism's abstract formulation of equality with legal recognition of injurious social stratification."[98] Brown objects to how a liberalism organized around injury and its remediation "discursively entrenches the injury-identity connection it denounces" and is particularly dismayed by efforts such as MacKinnon's and Dworkin's to "pursue legal redress for injuries related to social subordination."[99] Such an effort, she says, "delimits a specific site of blame for suffering by constituting sovereign subjects and events as responsible for the 'injury' of social subordination. It fixes the identities of the injured and the injuring as social positions, and codifies as well the meaning of their actions against all possibilities of indeterminacy, ambiguity, and struggle for resignification or repositioning."[100] The law of damages renders injury "intentional and individual," Brown claims, obscuring the culpability of institutional or corporate agents; it thus represents a "marked turn away from freedom's pursuit."[101]

Brown's work is invaluable for bringing into focus a strain of liberalism organized around the problem of injury.[102] But she imagines this to be a recent development in the history of liberalism and as a result establishes a homology between the project of "legal redress for injury" and the project of amelioration, and between agency and responsibility, that is fundamentally mistaken. Brown's deconstructive commitments ironically make it difficult for her to conceive of responsibility in the absence of intentionality. If the brilliance of the deconstructive enterprise was to insist on the accidental quality of agency, the frisson of deconstruction was underwritten by an assumption powerfully at work in Brown's account of liability law: the assumption that accident subverts responsibility, that responsibility requires delimited acts and discrete subjects, that the project of blame is one and the same as the project of meaning.

Patchen Markell has recently criticized Brown for how her invocation of "resignification," "repositioning," and "freedom" retains for the subject a sovereignty and intentionality she otherwise critiques. There is something to this, but I am more interested in the fact that Markell's revision of Brown turns on an attempt to think about the coexistence of accident and responsibility. Markell looks to tragedy in order to recast democratic aspirations "in a way that does not confuse justice in relations of identity and difference with mutual transparency, or with security from risk, or with the overcoming of all experiences of alienation or even hostility in our relations with others."[103] Mobilizing Williams and Cavell to distinguish between "recognition" (knowing) and "*tragic* recognition" (acknowledging), Markell seeks to imagine a liberalism predicated on risk and injury rather than on the escape from risk and injury. This "politics of acknowledgment" would acknowledge first and foremost the lessons of tragedy: that "the very conditions that make us potent agents—our materiality, which ties us to the causal order of the world, and our plurality, which makes it possible for our acts to be meaningful—also make us potent beyond our own control, exposing us to consequences and implications that we cannot predict and which are not up to us" and that action's unpredictability entails the "ineliminable possibility of suffering."[104]

I am sympathetic to this tragic model of liberalism, not least for how it seeks to describe justice as something other than redemption or amelioration. But the "politics of acknowledgment," like "acknowledgment" itself, remains focused on the individual and on self-consciousness in ways that distinguish Markell's commitments from mine. "Acknowledgment is in the first instance self- rather than other-directed," Markell admits; its object is a recognition of "one's basic ontological condition or circumstances, particularly one's finitude." It is a *coming to terms with,* rather than vainly attempting to overcome, the risk of conflict, hostility, misunderstanding, opacity, and alienation that characterizes life among others."[105] If this is not an ameliorative rhetoric, it remains a humanist one—committed, in the end, to the adventure of interiority. For all his sensitivity to the tragic emplotment of persons, that is, Markell's overriding concern is not plot but character, and character understood the way historians of the novel understand it: as *bildung.*

Harm's Way uncovers, in a novel form persistently associated with the historical and conceptual production of self-conscious personhood, a way of thinking of our life among others that *is* other-directed—that treats human subjects (victims and wrongdoers alike) as that most alien of others, the object. In the fictions of harm canvassed in the chapters to come, I unearth a literary and legal genealogy that conceives of persons as matter in motion; and if this is quite literally dehumanizing, it is not, therefore, inhumane. The legal person on this account is a formal person—a person whose content as represented by the state of her interior (or mind) is irrelevant to the question of her responsibility and thus to the question of what or who she is. The law of strict liability therefore functions as the site of a different way of thinking of persons and their obligations than is represented by the tradition of political philosophy in which Markell is working, with its emphasis on the problem of sovereignty and the desideratum of consent. But this difference also marks an alternative *theory* of political and ethical subjectivity, one in which form, and formalism, is not opposed to but is a species of justice.

It is a version of liberalism that is constantly under attack by a conservatism committed to "tort reform" and to a related dismantling of the status obligations central to any progressive politics. Conservatives demonize the law of damages by aligning it with "the special interests"; but this profoundly, perhaps cynically, misrepresents the logic of liability. In its strictest formulation, liability law is a way of thinking about obligation that cannot but be indifferent to the self-directed, prudential calculations suggested by the term "interest": for how can we know in advance whose interests will be served by an accident whose variables can't be predicted? When accident happens, as it must, strict liability does not wait for us to recognize responsibility before ruthlessly imposing it, making connections among distant others who do not know and do not care about one another. In a historical moment rife with anxiety about incomprehensible others and when the very fate of the earth is at risk from a corporate protectionism that takes the form of limitations on liability for toxic among other torts, it is important to be reminded that this model of belonging exists. It is important to be reminded that liberalism is itself a fiction of harm. *Enduring Love:* McEwan's insight—an insight derived from an immersion in the practice of realism—is that relationship (as the slant homophone implies) is injuring, something to be endured.

CHAPTER ONE

Matrimonial Murder

It is an enactment not of fate but of responsibility, including
the responsibility for fate.
—Stanley Cavell, *Must We Mean What We Say?*

It is striking how often Defoe invokes the word "murder" to describe harms
that would seem to be accidental. In the *Journal of the Plague Year*, a mother who
unwittingly passes the plague to her nursing infant is likened to a murderer;
so too is the father whose affection for his family kills them when he kisses his
wife and children on the lips before he knows he is infected. The man in *Conjugal Lewdness* who seduces a young woman who dies of a venereal disease he
didn't know he had is a "Murtherer"; and more improbably, any person whose
marriage causes harm to another is guilty of "Matrimonial Murther."[1] Moll Flanders is a murderer because she has given her child to a wet nurse, and the wet
nurse (it is implied) has let the infant die from neglect. And Roxana holds herself accountable for the murder of *her* daughter, despite the fact that her servant,
Amy—acting without Roxana's knowledge or consent—has killed the girl.

Defoe criticism has tended to call accident something else: Providence.[2] "In
the Puritan religious tradition that informs both H. F.'s view of reality and Defoe's fiction generally," argues Everett Zimmerman, "historical events have a
spiritual meaning: the world is providentially ordered and the ultimate reality
is metaphysical."[3] The notion that providentialism recasts accident as a divine

and happy intentionality is central to broader claims about the effect of Puritan ways of thinking on English literary form. Michael Witmore traces a shift in the category of the accidental from Aristotle's view of the accident as an event that "def[ies] human powers of calculation and foresight" to "the Christian conviction that all events, even accidents, were designed by God." "The idea that accidents put individuals in touch with only the slenderest knowledge of circumstances will be reversed in the early modern period when Calvin and his interpreters assert that accidents reveal the astonishing sweep of God's providence," he observes. In the sixteenth and seventeenth centuries, accidents become a *means* of calculation and foresight: in Calvin, a way for persons to glimpse God's "pervasive presence"; in Bacon, a vehicle for discovering "a hidden order in nature that would otherwise go unnoticed."[4] For Martin Battestin, "the idea of Providence," of "Chance as Direction, of Time as a movement from Genesis to Apocalypse comprehending every contingency under the eye of God" underwrites the formal aspirations of eighteenth-century literary innovation: mock-epic, the novel—each is committed to reproducing in the sphere of art the "rational, foreseeing Power that governs the world."[5] And while recently Christian Thorne has distinguished between Providence and "*fortuna*," arguing that "it is one of the signal projects of eighteenth-century narrative to purge itself of its inherited providential conventions" and that Defoe's narratives "are in fact a single-minded onslaught on providence," in the end the romance of fortune demands what Calvinist and Baconian Providence demands: "a pose of perpetual vigilance" that teaches readers to "narrate causally and prudentially" to produce for themselves a story "that can make sense of the past."[6]

In Defoe one *does* encounter a version of providentialism committed to foreseeing and managing accident. About the risks of harm peculiar to women's position in the marriage market, for example, Moll Flanders reflects:

> As for Women that do not think their own Safety worth their Thought, that impatient of their present State, resolve *as they call it* to take the first good Christian that comes, that run into Matrimony, as a Horse rushes into the Battle, I can say nothing to them but this, that they are a Sort of Ladies that are to be pray'd for among the rest of distemper'd People.

"I would fain have the Conduct of my Sex a little Regulated in this particular," she concludes, "which is the Thing, in which of all the parts of Life, I think at this Time we suffer most in."[7] In the preface to *Moll Flanders* Defoe describes the new form in which he is working as a vehicle for procuring this sort of prudence. "All the Exploits of this Lady of Fame in her Depredations upon Mankind, stand as so many warnings to honest People to beware of them, intimating to them by what Methods innocent People are drawn in, plunder'd, and robb'd, and by Consequence how to avoid them," he famously asserts. "Her robbing a little innocent Child, dress'd fine by the vanity of the Mother, to go to the Dancing School, is a good Memento to such People hereafter; as is likewise her picking the Gold-Watch from the young Ladies side in the *Park.* . . . [A]ll give us excellent Warnings in such Cases to be more present to ourselves in sudden Surprizes of every sort."[8] The hope that "mementos" of harm might prevent harm from recurring is at work in the *Journal of the Plague Year* as well: "I desire this account may pass," says H. F., "rather for a Direction to [others] to act by, than a History of my actings."[9]

But in the midst of such optimism about vigilance and prudential calculation, Moll's alignment of the risk-prone woman first with a horse and then with an infected (perhaps mad) human being puts serious pressure on the "rational, foreseeing power" she and her author would seem to recommend. For if the action of persons is like the action of horses—a creature, Moll's simile suggests, who once set along a path of motion will keep moving in that direction, even unto the breach—then what can it possibly mean to ask such an automaton to be "present" to herself? And if to be a person at risk is to be as one "distemper'd," H. F.'s elaborate account of the "complicated distress" (140) that is the plague reveals at every turn the impossibility of anticipating, and managing, harm.

I am not alone in noticing the challenge the plague poses to what might be called the "comic" strain of Defoe's providentialism—his belief that by learning to read signs of futurity persons can approximate the foresight of gods, his faith that what looks like catastrophe is, in the end, felicity. "The plague is an extended moment of total uncertainty," John Richetti trenchantly observes, "an exaggerated, nearly metaphysical version provided by history of the random destructiveness of an environment." This rather bleak analysis does not prompt Richetti to abandon a comic reading of the *Journal,* however: "Having endured disorder, having looked steadily into it," he continues, "the saddler discovers that the plague is the source of an order greater than that which prevailed before the plague struck. That pattern stands from our perspective on Defoe's narratives as a remarkable epitome of their imaginative strategies."[10] A similarly comic account of providential foresight and novelistic retrospection (and of their interpenetration) underwrites John Bender's provocative analysis of the *Journal* as well:

The only unimpeachable method of survival cited in the entire *Journal* is in fact total self-imposed isolation based on foresight, rational planning and storage of provision, and relentless vigilance. . . . The mental life of Defoe's narrator illustrates the sustaining power of reflective isolation, which is validated within the fiction by the narrator's acceptance of authority, and maintained within the larger novelistic construct as a principle of absolute representational order diffused throughout the whole text.[11]

Despite their differences, Bender's and Richetti's arguments share an important, complex assumption: that Defoe's novels are committed to an account of the person and of the novel that values "relentless vigilance," a hermeneutics of self-conscious retrospection and foresight in which accidents cease to be accidental and are recuperated instead as acts of intention or of intention's other—omission.[12] It is possible to see Defoe's use of the word "murder" in this way, as a gesture that redescribes accidental harms as intentional or as deriving from a culpable failure of foresight. But this is not, in fact, how the term functions. In the *Journal,* where many of these accidental crimes occur, H. F. vocally rejects the idea that the agents of such harms are "willful" murderers:

Men went about apparently well, many Days after they had taint of the Disease in their Vitals, . . . and . . . all the while they did so, they were dangerous to others. . . . It must not be omitted, that when I speak of those People who were really thus dangerous, I suppose them to be utterly ignorant of their own Condition, for if they really knew their Circumstances to be such as indeed they were, they must have been a kind of *willful Murtherers* if they would have gone Abroad among healthy People, and it would have verified indeed the Suggestion, *which I mention'd above, and which I thought seemed untrue, (viz.)* That the infected People were utterly careless as to giving the Infection to others. (157)

If these "dangerous" persons are not "willful Murtherers," what kind of murderers are they? The law had long ago reached a consensus that murder was a crime of "prepensed," or intentional, malice: there was no other kind of murderer than a "willful" one.[13] What does it mean that Defoe imagines that there is?

In what follows I argue that Defoe's providentialism marks a legal as well a theological interest in accident, one that calls into question the comic model of providential thinking described above.[14] Maximillian Novak, one of the few critics for whom disorder persists *as* disorder in the *Journal,* has suggested that the "main impulse" behind the book is a "demonstration of human pity and fellowship in the worst of disasters": the intransigence of the disaster, the fact that it cannot be prevented or ameliorated, means that H. F. (and, Novak implies, Defoe) "resists all temptation to blame."[15] The claim that Defoe "resists" blame is in obvious tension with my suggestion that he applies the most strenuous category of indictment there is to acts that do not appear blameworthy. And yet Novak is onto something when he notes that pity and blame are key concerns of the *Journal* and "central to the development of the novel."[16] Novak imagines that pity and blame are antithetical responses to disaster and that Defoe chooses pity over blame. But Bernard Williams is closer to the mark when, in *Shame and Necessity*, he describes pity as a *species* of blame: "Pity is the minimal, least vengeful[,] . . . least punitive acknowledgement of things done involuntarily."[17] Williams is talking about tragedy: pity is not a psychological but a formal response—at once legal and literary—to the problem of accidental harm. I suggested in the introduction that historians of the novel ought to be talking about tragedy as well, for Defoe's understanding of accident is what Williams would call "Greek": "As the Greeks understood, the responsibilities we have to recognize extend in many ways beyond our normal purposes and what we intentionally do."[18]

Shame and Necessity is itself a project of recognition, an analysis of the persistence of Greek models of personhood, agency, and responsibility in a modernity that is supposed to have overcome them. Williams rejects the notion that modernity can "best be understood in terms of a shift in basic ethical conceptions of agency, responsibility, shame or freedom." "What is alive from the Greek world is already alive and is helping (often in hidden ways) to keep us alive," he insists.[19] What helps to keep us alive is the Greek commitment to blaming persons for involuntary harms:

> Progressivist writers refer to a concept of moral responsibility that we supposedly enjoy and the Greeks lacked, but it is unclear what they have in mind. Their thought seems most typically to be that the Greeks, or at least archaic Greeks, blamed and sanctioned people for things that they did unintentionally. . . . We are thought not to do this, or at least to regard it as unjust.[20]

His analysis of *why* we are thought not to do this brings us back (or is it forward?) to the Enlightenment and to Defoe—to a historical terrain and an "epitome" similarly mired in debates over progress. "To a considerable extent," Williams says, "the idea that the Greeks thought very differently from ourselves about responsibility, and in particular more primitively, is an illusion generated by thinking only about the criminal law and forgetting about the law of torts."[21] Williams points in particular to "offences of strict liability, which require neither intention nor any other culpable state of mind." Under rules of strict liability . . . people can be held criminally liable not only for outcomes they did not intend . . . but in some cases for outcomes they did not even cause. Thus people can be sanctioned for breaches of rules that their employees have committed against their intentions. . . . The idea seems to be that there is a prior and general assumption of responsibility; it is part of what is undertaken, for instance, by one who conducts a certain kind of business that he or she will be liable for certain faults of employees.[22]

Laws governing liability for undertakings (what is now called "enterprise liability") were undergoing significant changes in the late seventeenth century and are explicitly at work in the way Defoe and his culture thinks about Williams's triad of personhood, agency, and responsibility. These changes extended status models of liability governing innkeepers and guests, masters and servants, and carriers and passengers to other kinds of relationships and other types of persons. Indeed, the legal "doctrine of agency" making principals strictly liable for the undertakings of their agents becomes a generalized *theory* of agency over the course of the eighteenth century—one that sees agency as dispersed over a structure, shared by persons rather than located in an individual. Such an individual is different from the one we are used to thinking emerges in the period. For on this view, the person is individuated solely *by* responsibility, and responsibility conceived against the criteria by which we tend to define individuals—against interiority, against intentionality, even, paradoxically, against agency itself. On this view, "persons" are characterized by an unknowing instrumentality as profound as a horse's or an infected, nonsymptomatic nursing mother's. This understanding of agency and of personhood helps to explain the "tragic" quality of Defoe's providentialism, his preoccupation with "things done involuntarily" and his sense that such things are not felicitous—that they demand blame and responsibility rather than quiescence. And it is the claim of this chapter, and this book, that a preoccupation with tragic, involuntary action is the defining feature of Defoe's fictions of harm and of the novel form those fictions bring into being.

᷂

Defoe is obsessed with enterprise liability. The *Essay upon Projects* (1697), his first published work, energetically sorts persons into categories organized around what he calls "contingency"—forms of occupational practice defined by a propensity for injury. In an essay on friendly societies, organizations based on a "Mutual Compact" between members to "Help one another, in case any Disaster or Distress fall upon them," Defoe argues that "if Mankind cou'd agree, as these might be Regulated, all things which have Casualty in them, might be Secur'd." "One thing is Particularly requir'd," he says, for "securing casualty":

> None can be admitted, but such whose Circumstances are, at least in some degree, alike, and so Mankind must be *sorted* into Classes; and as their Contingences differ, every different Sort may be a Society upon even Terms; for the Circumstances of People, as to Life, differ extremely by the Age and Constitution of their Bodies, and difference of Employment.[23]

The type of person with whom Defoe is most concerned in the *Essay* is the merchant sailor, an "enfant perdu," he calls him, whose very being is structured by the risk of harm: "They are Fellows that bid Defiance to Terror, and maintain a constant War with the Elements; who by the Magick of their Art, Trade in the very confines of Death, and are always posted within shot, as I may say, of the Grave."[24] Defoe worries about how these grave fellows will be compensated for the accidents to which their work consigns them and argues that compensation can be guaranteed only if *all* seamen enter their names, addresses, and voyages at a central insurance office, whose premiums would be adjusted according to official statistics on occupational risk and mean sick time.[25]

This intervention is made necessary by the fact that merchants limit their liability for harms incurred by employees to those stipulated in advance by the initial labor contract. In order to ensure seamen a more extensive and reliable level of compensation, the contractual sovereignty of employers *and* employees must be curtailed. "All discounting of Wages, and Time, all Damages of Goods, Avarages, stopping of Pay, and the like," Defoe recommends, ought to "be adjusted by stated and Publick Rules, and Laws in Print, establish'd by [an] Act of Parliament."[26] With statute law governing terms of hire, labor conditions, and wages, contractors would no longer be able to engage in private agreements with one another; sailors would be "the King's hired servants, and receive their Wages from him, *whoever employ'd them*," and merchants will be forced to "hire them of the King, and pay the King for them."[27] In 1705 Defoe submitted a version of this project to a parliamentary committee investigating the manning of the fleet. Published in 1728 as *Some Considerations on the Reasonableness and Necessity of Encreasing and Encouraging the Seamen*, the pamphlet argued that all sailors should be registered in the Royal Navy and assigned to military or merchant ships according to national policy considerations, that they should be prohibited from entering foreign service, and that they should be required to accept a fixed

wage: "All hiring and payment," Defoe recommends, "would be done by the government." According to its author, the proposal was "at last declined only upon
some Scruples about Liberty and Compulsion."[28]

Critics with their own scruples about liberty and compulsion have noticed Defoe's enthusiasm for "executive power," have remarked his sometimes strenuous
resistance to a model of personal and contractual sovereignty his work was once
taken to promote.[29] The argument for Defoe's contractarianism was enshrined
in Ian Watt's *The Rise of the Novel*, from whose cold-war perspective Defoe's
"economic individualism" emerged as the defining feature of Anglo-American
(liberal) politics and aesthetics. It was reiterated by intellectual historians of the
eighteenth century such as J. G. A. Pocock, who called Defoe a "modern, writing to defend the Junto Whigs [and] the Bank of England" (and who thus made
modernity synonymous with whig politics and a credit economy), and Richard
Ashcraft, who described Defoe's thought as "distinctly Lockean and radical"—
contractarian and therefore radical; radical and therefore modern.[30] Literary
historians have been more skeptical about claims for Defoe's "radicalism" and
contractarianism.[31] John Zomchick, for example, argues that *Moll Flanders* and
Roxana are structured by a desire to "strike the most advantageous bargains regardless of others' needs" and that together they depict "the emergence of the
free juridical subject, self-conceived as subjected only to its own desires and society's positive laws." But he concludes that Defoe is ultimately anxious about the
possibility that such freedoms might be merely "fantastical." And Sandra Sherman questions Pocock's unambiguous association of Defoe with Lady Credit by
arguing that Defoe is concerned about the way credit threatens the embodied
quality of the face-to-face, contractual relationships he values.[32]

The "new economic criticism" on Defoe complicated but did not fundamentally revise the narrative of Defoe's contractarianism; and subsequent criticism
has suggested that what looks like "anxiety" is in fact outright hostility to freedom of contract.[33] This hostility tends to be attributed to a "conservative-royal-
ist" thread in Defoe's political imagination, a suggestion that is consistent with
recent eighteenth-century historiography that counters progressivist readings
such as Ashcraft's by insisting on the period's "premodernity."[34] Premodernity
is marked in these histories by the persistence of feudal, status-based forms of
identity and community of the sort that Defoe gives expression to in the *Essay*.
Thus Dror Wahrman argues that the eighteenth century is not, as Watt imagined, the moment in which individualism emerges but a period governed by an
"ancien-régime of identity" that conceives of persons in "collective" rather than
"individual" terms.[35] And Wolfram Schmidgen reveals an "intricate persistence

of premodern communal forms in the eighteenth century" indexed by a conflation of persons and things that similarly belies a depth model of Enlightenment
subjectivity.[36]

Defoe's tendency to describe identity in terms of status—in particular occupational status—supports Wahrman's general claims for the period; and as we
shall see, this tendency often results in the kind of materialist understanding
of the person that interests Schmidgen. These scholars are right that interiority (or depth) is not conceptually central to eighteenth-century representations
of identity and community.[37] But to emphasize the period's "premodernity" is
to reinforce the equation of modernity with interiority, affect, and assent—with
contract rather than status. Wahrman is quite explicit about this equation: the
overarching claim of *Making the Modern Self* is not that selfhood doesn't happen
or doesn't look the way we've imagined it looks—"personal, interiorized, essential, even innate"—but rather that it doesn't happen when scholars have tradi-
tionally argued it happens. Instead, it emerges as a "sea change in the last two
decades of the eighteenth century."[38] Schmidgen's argument is different: for him
there is striking continuity between the eighteenth century's premodernity and a
"postmodernity" characterized by (quoting Jameson) "the 'waning of affection,'
the 'depthlessness' of cultural forms," and the interpenetration of subjects and
objects.[39] In between is "modernity"—a "long *nineteenth* century" represented
by "structures of feeling" and "organized around notions of depth, interiority,
and time."[40] Once again, change happens, and when it does it involves an escape
from status.

There is a sense in which the apparent distance between Watt and Schmidgen, marked by the debate between whig and revisionist historiography of the
eighteenth century, is not much of a distance at all: modernity is moved forward
and backward along a scale of historical temporality, but the contours of modernity, its characteristic transcendence of status, remain the same.[41] The specifically
legal way that Defoe thinks about status, however, helps one to see that when
change happens—and I am agreeing that it does—status is the *vehicle* rather
than the object of modernization. To equate Defoe's interest in status models of
identity, attachment, and obligation with a "retrograde" paternalism or monar-
chialism is to assume a necessary connection between contractualism and liberalism that I want to suggest is historically as well as conceptually mistaken.[42] It is
to miss the precise way that, as Pocock asserted, Defoe is a "modern."

In *Every-Body's Business is No-Body's Business* (1725), perhaps his most rigorous attack on freedom of contract, Defoe calls for japanners, whose cheap shoe
shines divert servants sent on errands through London streets, to

be immediately under the commands and inspections of such task-masters as the government shall appoint, and that they be employ'd, punished, and rewarded according to their capacities and demerits. . . . Nor should any person clean shoes in the streets but these authoriz'd shoe-cleaners, who should have some mark of distinction, and be under the immediate government of the Justices of the Peace.

Indeed, "anyone carrying a basket in the market," he continues, must be "under some such regulation as coachmen, chairmen, carmen."[43] Defoe's recommendations have their basis in an Elizabethan statute establishing legal remedies for harms to servants: "An Action of Tresspass will lie for taking an Apprentice out of his actual Service," the statute reads, "and for enticing such out of their Master's Service, or detaining a hired Servant, an Action on the Case will give Remedy."[44] (Defoe's pamphlet follows closely the text of 43 Eliz. c. 2, cited extensively in Giles Jacob's popular legal commonplace, *The Compleat Parish-Officer*. It's quite likely this is Defoe's source: the book had reached a third edition by 1725.) But by invoking "coachmen, chairmen and carmen" in the context of actions of "trespass" and "case," Defoe does something very interesting with and to the law—something that by 1725 has a new and increasingly influential body of precedent supporting it.

The laws governing coachmen, chairmen, and carmen (whom legal historians call "common carriers") were of relatively recent provenance, emerging in the early seventeenth century in common-law actions of trespass. Writs of trespass, as J. H. Baker describes them, were "not concerned with the vindication of rights, but with punishment and amends for past transgression"; they "embodied a complaint rather than a demand."[45] Legal historians see cases involving common carriers as one of the major grounds on which the "war" between contract and tort, demand and complaint, is played out. Interestingly, this war is reproduced in the legal historiography itself, which continues to disagree about which form of liability is in the ascendancy in the modern era. The debate between whig and revisionist historiography reemerges as a debate between those who think that "judicial opinion of the [eighteenth century] shifted towards Contract" and those who think that the history of the common law is one in which tort takes over from contract.[46] Scholars agree, however, that cases concerning common carriers and the "running down cases" (or traffic accidents) with which they were aligned were concerned less with the distinction between contract and tort than with differences between the two tort actions of trespass and case. The difference, as Blackstone described it, was between harms that were conducted "with force of arms" (*vi et armis*) and "against the king's peace" (*contra pacem*

Regis) and ones that were not; but the distinction was jurisdictional rather than metaphysical.[47] The "eighteenth-century rationalization" of the distinction, Baker says, "made the test one of directness"—a test M. J. Prichard describes as the "immediate/consequential test." It was a test that emerged from the felt need among jurists to arrive at standards of liability for unintentional, remote, and third-party harms as well as for harms to strangers.[48]

Cases against common carriers were adjudicated according to a standard of strict liability derived from laws governing innkeepers. Known as the "custom of the realm," this standard was designed to keep innkeepers, who were structurally bound to accept travelers, from failing to carry out their "common duty" with respect to those travelers. The standard was applied to all persons in the context of "escapes," dangerous forces such as fire, animals, and water, which persons had a common duty to control. Here, Baker observes, "custom prevented the defendant from relying on an act of God"; it defeated providentialist explanations (and exculpations) of accidental harms, allowing common lawyers to "impose a stricter liability than would otherwise attach."[49] A case against a common carrier from 1703 clarifies the legal principles at stake in the custom of the realm. In *Coggs v. Barnard* the plaintiff, John Coggs, complained that the defendant, William Barnard, "undertook to take up safely and securely various casks of brandy belonging to him" and move the casks from one cellar to another. The defendant

> so negligently and improvidently managed the said casks of brandy in laying them down in the cellar last mentioned that for want of the good care of the said William, his servants and agents, one of the same casks of brandy was then and there staved and a great quantity (namely 150 gallons) of brandy in the said casks was by that means spilled on the ground and lost.[50]

The jury found for the plaintiff, and Chief Justice Holt gave the following explanation of the decision: "The reasons are, first, because in such a case a neglect is a deceit to the bailor. For when he entrusts the bailee upon his undertaking to be careful, he has put a fraud upon the plaintiff by being negligent: his pretence of care being the persuasion that induced the plaintiff to trust him." If a man "enters upon [an undertaking]," he concludes, and "miscarries in the performance of his trust, an action will lie against him."[51]

Historians see such actions for harms or losses to carriage passengers as the "first signs of a tort of negligence."[52] Although as I've said, negligence in the performance of an undertaking, calling, or office had been known for centuries—negligence, that is, in the context of prior relationships—"the emergence of liability for what we may call non-relationship negligence is properly associated with the running-down actions on the case that started in the last quarter of the seventeenth century."[53] Initially, running-down cases were actions in trespass rather than case. Negligently driving a horse or cart or ship into someone was seen as "trespass with force," but there were reasons why an action of trespass was disadvantageous: the accident might be shown to be the fault of the horse or the wind, and a jury might find a defendant not guilty or reduce damages if the injury were unintended. Declarations in case, on the other hand, had the advantage of focusing attention on the defendant's fault even in the absence of intention and even in the presence of natural causes. Around 1700, actions on the case established that a master, who was previously liable for a servant's acts only if he had commanded them, "could be made vicariously liable for acts which he did not command, provided that they were for his benefit and in the course of employment."[54] According to Baker, such amplifications of liability meant that pleaders began to look for ways of converting trespass actions into actions on the case: "By 1700," he asserts, "lawyers were beginning to perceive a new general principle: that a man was 'answerable for all mischief proceeding from his neglect or his actions, unless they were of unavoidable necessity.' "[55]

The principle Baker cites comes from *Mason v. Keeling* (1700), a case in which the defendant's knowledge of his dog's dangerous propensities "fixed him with a strict liability for any damage which the animal caused, damage for which he would not otherwise be liable."[56] But the leading case in the development of this "new principle" was *Mitchell v. Allestry* (1676), in which a master was held liable for damages incurred when the plaintiff was kicked by horses being broken in by his servant in Lincoln's Inn Fields. The action was brought by James Mitchell on behalf of his wife, Mary, who was injured when William Allestry's coachman Thomas Scrivener,

> improvidently, rashly and without due consideration of the unsuitability of the place for the purpose, drove and exercised two wild and untamed mares pulling a coach . . . and then and there ran upon her the said Mary and there threw her to the ground with great force and ran over her with the aforesaid coach, so that the same Mary was so seriously crushed and broken in her body and limbs that by reason thereof she became lame and mutilated and cannot now be restored to perfect health.[57]

Allestry did not attempt to defend himself by pointing to his own absence from the scene of the action—to the fact that he had not acted at all. Rather, he argued that the accident occurred against "his" (that is, Scrivener's) will and despite repeated efforts to avoid it. At least one of the King's Bench judges hearing the case, Justice Simpson, agreed: "For it appears by the declaration that the mischief which happened was against the defendant's will, and so *damnum absque injuria*." Sir Peyton Ventris's *Reports* (1701) records Simpson's argument and the ensuing responses—by Justice Wilde, who invoked the recent precedent of *Mason v. Keeling* to argue that "if a man hath an unruly horse in his stable, and leaves open the stable door, whereby the horse goes forth and does mischief, an action lies against the master," and Justice Twisden, who objected that "if one hath kept a tame fox, which gets loose and grows wild, he that kept him before shall not answer for the damage the fox doth after he hath lost him and he hath resumed his wild nature."[58] In the end, however, Allestry was not, by virtue of his good intentions or his inability to have foreseen the dangerousness of the horses, "indemnified against the injury." Finding was for the plaintiff.

According to Baker, the landmark status of *Mitchell v. Allestry* was recognized only after 1700: "The breakthrough appeared to later generations," he says. "At the time there was no awareness that a new principle of liability was in the making."[59] The significance of the case is difficult to describe, and not even Baker does so adequately. On the one hand, its novelty consisted in the fact that liability did not derive from a *scienter* action, that is, did not derive from the defendant's having foreknowledge of the dangerous propensities of the animal that would make him strictly liable for its harms. Baker observes that the horses "had no abnormally vicious characteristics," a fact that explains Twisden's objections on behalf of the defendant. On the other hand, it was not an action for negligence since the evidence showed that the defendants had "done all they reasonably could to prevent the accident."[60] The essence of the wrong had to do with the strict standards of liability attaching to public places: "The law does preserve places frequented, and punishes more severely anything done to disturb them," observes Chief Justice Raynsford. "If one throws a stone into a market and kills one, it is murder."[61] Murder. This inflation of benign practices to homicidal ones explains why Defoe turns to laws governing "coachmen, chairman, [and] carmen" for his strident vision of social security. Baker claims that *Mitchell v. Allestry* shows how negligence standards could be applied in the absence of custom of the realm: "No one thought of arguing that negligence was not actionable without an undertaking or custom of the realm."[62] But it seems to me that the idea of relationship liability underwriting custom of the realm is being extended to types of undertakings and types of persons not formerly covered by the expectation of "common duty." Implicit in the case is a theory of action based on the presumption that to act at all is to be engaged in an "undertaking" and a model of responsibility in which agents could not claim indemnity for injurious acts by appealing to Providence, by showing that they could not have foreseen the harm that came to pass or had no intent to harm—or even, as Baker admits, by proving they were not negligent.

Prichard describes custom of the realm as "interesting" because "it was not limited to a prior relationship type of case": "Actions involving custom of the realm are the start of a development of liability in negligence that was independent of trespass, yet independent also of any prior relationship between the parties other than that brought about by the injury."[63] What's interesting to Prichard, and to me, is how relationship is *brought about by* injury: injury grounds connections between persons, underwriting in turn a generalized social obligation predicated on strangeness. The question of an agent's obligation to distant others receives its fullest articulation in the running-down cases, shooting cases, and "escape" actions emerging from *Mitchell v. Allestry.* The finding for the plaintiff in *Mitchell v. Allestry* required justices to refine a distinction between felonious and tortious liability that had originated in *Weaver v. Ward* (1616), a case in which the defendant, George Ward, was held liable for injuries received by the plaintiff when Ward "accidentally and by misfortune and against his will" discharged his musket in the air.[64] In his 1641 *Reports,* Chief Justice Hobart observes that in *Weaver v. Ward* it was "agreed" that

> if men tilt or tourney in the presence of the king, or if two [prizefighters] playing
> [for] their prizes kill one another, that this shall be no felony—or if a lunatic kill a
> man, or the like—because felony must be done *animo felonico;* yet in trespass, which
> tends only to give damages according to hurt or loss, it is not so. And therefore if a
> lunatic hurt a man he shall be answerable in trespass. And therefore no man shall
> be excused of a trespass (for this is in the nature of an excuse, and not of a justifica-
> tion *prout ei bene licuit*) except it may be adjudged utterly without his fault. As, if a
> man by force take my hand and strike you.[65]

The case clarified that "no man shall be excused of a trespass"—that, as Oliver Wendell Holmes puts it, "a man is answerable for all the consequences of his acts, or, in other words, that he acts at his peril always, and wholly irrespective of the state of his consciousness upon the matter."[66]

Holmes (for reasons I will discuss in more detail in chapter 4) is invested in the idea that in *Mitchell v. Allestry* "we have entered the sphere of negligence."[67] But he acknowledges that in late seventeenth- and eighteenth-century cases stemming from *Mitchell v. Allestry* and *Weaver v. Ward*—*Dickenson v. Watson* (1682), *Bessey v. Olliot* (1682), *Gibbon v. Pepper* (1695), *Underwood v. Hewson* (1723), *Scott v. Shepherd* (1773), *Leame v. Bray* (1803)—claims that "damage was done accidentally and by misfortune, and against the will of the defendant, were held insufficient."[68] These were cases in which distance was not a question of affiliation (being a stranger) but of the spatiality and temporality of action—in which an action was quite literally instrumentalized in the form of pistols, horses, "lighted squibs," and others' intervening acts and yet in which the defendant's inability to foresee or control the consequences of her act did not exculpate her.[69] Holmes considers the cases, and the historical milieu they inhabit, to manifest an unfortunate commitment to strict liability. Arguing that the rule of "absolute responsibility" is "inconsistent with admitted doctrines and sound policy," Holmes insists that "the common law has never known such a rule, unless in that period of dry precedent which is so often to be found midway between a creative epoch and a period of solvent philosophical reaction."[70] The "dry" period to which he contemptuously refers is the period from 1676 through Justice Grose's claim in *Leame v. Bray* (1803) that if an injury "be done by the act of the party himself at the time, or he be the immediate cause of it, though it happen accidentally or by misfortune [*per infortunium*], yet he is answerable in trespass."[71] Throughout the eighteenth century, Holmes says, but especially in the decades after *Mitchell v. Allestry*, judges looked at decisions where their predecessors had "dealt pretty strictly with defendants" and moved from "the premise that defendants have been held trespassers for a variety of acts, *without mention of neglect*, to the conclusion that any act by which another was damaged will make the actor chargeable." "A more exact scrutiny of the early books," he counters, "will show that liability in general, then as later, was founded on the opinion of the tribunal that the defendant ought to have acted otherwise, or, in other words, that he was to blame."[72]

Holmes sees eighteenth-century jurisprudence as indifferent to the question of negligence: for him it matters whether something happens "accidentally or by misfortune," and if it does—if a defendant has not acted negligently—then she is not at fault and cannot be blamed.[73] In the case law influenced by *Mitchell v. Allestry*, however, persons are blamed without having done anything wrong: blameworthiness and faultlessness are improbably aligned. Or rather, as Justice Grose puts it, fault becomes a question of *causation* rather than culpability: if an agent is the cause of harm to another, she is responsible for that harm even if she herself is a victim of the grossest misfortune. To understand persons as causes in this way is to make (legal) subjectivity an effect of the sheer materiality or instrumentality of bodies. And in this, one begins to see how the laws governing "coachmen, chairmen, [and] carmen" influence the way Defoe thinks about persons in *Every-Body's Business is No-Body's Business*, as bodies simultaneously empty and overly full of meaning—as matter in motion, but also as status beings characterized by the "business" they undertake. In the subtitle to the pamphlet, "Private Abuses, Publick Grievances," Defoe revises Mandeville's fable of the interpenetration of privacy and publicity by eradicating the distinction on which the argument about interpenetration depends. In *Every-Body's Business is No-Body's Business*—and in the novels that share its tragic logic of blame—persons are never private, and harmful acts can never be converted into benefits unless they are marked *as* harms for which their unfortunate agents are strictly liable.

❦

It is significant, given the legal history I have just sketched, that one of the exemplary persons in the *Journal of the Plague Year* is a common carrier. H. F. devotes a disproportionate amount of space to the story of a waterman, a *"poor desolate Man,"* as he describes himself, who is not yet visited by the contagion *"tho' my family is, and one of my Children dead."* When H. F. asks how he has managed to escape infection, the man points to a boarded house, saying: *"There my poor Wife and two Children live . . . if they may be said to live; for my Wife and one of the Children are visited, but I do not come at them"* (88). H. F. is initially scandalized by the man's abandonment of his *"own Flesh, and Blood,"* until it is explained to him that not going near one's family is an act of generosity rather than indifference. The man, it turns out, lives on his boat and supports himself and his family by ferrying provisions between the mainland and merchant ships anchored in the Thames. In order to protect himself and his clients from infection, he does not *"go up the Ship Side"* but delivers what he brings to a lifeboat from whence the inhabitants *"hoist it on board."* Nor is he any danger to them, he insists, *"for I never go into any House on Shore, or touch any Body, no, not of my own Family"* (89). *"But I fetch Provisions for them,"* he explains, and *"what I get, I lay down upon that Stone,* says he, shewing me a broad Stone on the other Side of the Street, a good way from his House, *and then, says he, I halloo, and call to them till I make them hear; and they come and fetch it"* (89, 88).

The story is offered as evidence of the value of vigilance: H. F. commends the waterman's "true Dependency, and a Courage resting on God"; and yet he notes that "he used all possible Caution for his Safety" (90). This is not the waterman's account of things, however; reflecting on the imminent demise of his wife and a second of his children, he asserts: "It is infinite Mercy, if any of us are spar'd; and who am I to repine" (88). Yet something like vigilance is at issue in the direction the encounter between H. F. and the waterman takes. "When he said he was going over to *Greenwich*, as soon as the Tide began to come in," H. F. continues, "I ask'd if he would let me go with him, and bring me back, for that, I had a great mind to see how the Ships were ranged as he had told me" (91). "Well, Sir," the waterman replies, "as your Charity has been mov'd to pity me and my poor Family; sure you cannot have so little pity left, as to put yourself into my Boat if you were not Sound in Heath, which would be nothing less than killing me, and ruining my whole Family" (92). H. F. registers this as a "sensible Concern" and agrees to "lay aside [his] Curiosity"; but at the last minute the waterman relents and carries H. F. to Greenwich as a sign of his confidence that H. F. "had no more Distemper upon [him] than the freshest Man in the World" (92).

It makes sense to see the waterman's vigilance as a consequence of a professional life structured by the possibility of strict liability. His heightened conscientiousness about what and whom he will transport is less a sign that he is a "good Man" (as H. F. describes him) than that he is a *water*man—a common carrier liable to be liable for the unforeseen and unforeseeable consequences of an undertaking. (H. F. notes that among the lord mayor's orders published in late June 1665 was one covering common carriers: "That care be taken of Hackney-Coach-men, that they may not [as some of them have been observed to do] after carrying of infected Persons to the Pest-House, and other Places, be admitted to common use, till their Coaches be well aired, and have stood unemploy'd by the Space of fir or six Days after such Service" [41].) As a result, the waterman's decision to allow H. F. onboard when he has scrupulously avoided human contact registers as uncharacteristically risky—negligent, even, given how closely the welfare of others is tied to his own. When he warns H. F. that if he has lied about his "freshness" he will have "killed" the waterman and his family, he ties responsibility to intentionality in a way that contradicts the logic of his own occupation and of the story at hand. For H. F. observes, "It was not the sick People only, from whom the Plague was immediately receiv'd by others that were sound, but THE WELL" (150). "By the Well," he explains,

> I mean such as had received the Contagion, and had it really upon them, and in their Blood, yet did not shew the Consequences of it in their Countenances, nay even were not sensible of it themselves, as many were not for several Days: These breathed Death in every Place, and upon every Body who came near them; nay their very Cloaths retained the Infection, their Hands would infect the Things they touch'd.

"These were the dangerous People," he concludes, "these were the People of whom the well People ought to have been afraid; but then on the other side it was impossible to know them. And this is the Reason why it is impossible in a Visitation to prevent the spreading of the Plague by the utmost human Vigilance, (viz.) that it is impossible to know the infected People from the sound; or that the infected People should perfectly know themselves" (51). If persons cannot know themselves, one must assume that H. F., like any other body— including, significantly, nonsentient bodies (clothes, hands)—is breathing death upon the world; if he is not quite a murderer, he is, as the Waterman worries, a "killer" nonetheless.

The way the agency of persons is aligned with the agency of things in the preceding passage suggests that it's not merely "willful murther" (172) that is an inappropriate category during plague time, but willfulness, perhaps sentience *as such*. It is striking how frequently H. F.'s descriptions of persons as "dismal objects," "frightening objects," or "miserable objects of despair" (65, 86, 80)—as object lessons—become descriptions of persons *as* objects.[74] After recounting how persons would, without warning, "just sit down and die," he reflects: "These Objects were so frequent in the Street, that when the Plague came to be very raging. . . there was scarce any passing by the Street, but that several dead Bodies would be lying here and there upon the Ground" (67). And later he notes that villagers who carried food to infected inhabitants would "find the poor Wretches [lying] dead, and the Food untouch'd. The Number of these miserable Objects were many" (83). It might be objected that in these examples H. F. seems to reserve the term "object" for *dead* persons—persons whose reduction to soulless bodies turns them into things. But elsewhere he uses "Body" to designate living persons, as when H. F. observes how "whole Families were so entirely swept away, that there was no Remembrance of them left; neither was any Body to be found to possess or shew any Title to that little they had left" (179). "Such abandon'd Effects came to the King as the universal Heir," he continues, and "the King granted all such as Deodands to the Lord Mayor and Court of Aldermen of London, to be applied to the use of the Poor" (180).

By invoking the legal category of "deodand" here, Defoe literalizes and clarifies the equation he has been developing between persons and things. In a chapter titled "Of Casual Death and of Deodands," in his *Treatise of the Pleas of the Crown* (1716), William Hawkins defines deodand in a manner that reproduces (and is perhaps a source for) Defoe's characteristic alignment of accidental killing with murder. "Offenses against the Life of a Man come under the general Name of Homicide," Hawkins begins, but before I treat hereof, it may not be improper to consider the killing of a Man merely *per Infortunium,* occasioned by some Animal or Thing without Life, without the Default or Procurement of another Man, as where one is killed by a Fall from a Horse or Cart, &c. which, though it be not properly Homicide, nor punishable as a Crime, *yet is taken Notice of by the Law as far as the Nature of the Thing will bear, in order to raise the greater Abhorrence of Murder,* and the unhappy Instrument or Occasion of such Death is called a Deodand and forfeited to the King, in order to be disposed of in pious Uses by the King's Almoner; as also are all such Weapons whereby one Man kills another.[75]

It is interesting that Hawkins associates killing *per infortunium* with "animals or things without life"; in contemporary report books such misfortune tends to be associated with human agents, whose liability for things they did not mean to do generates a great deal of pathos.[76] It makes sense that he does so, however; for as we have seen, to cause harm *per infortunium* is to be seen to act with the mindless instrumentality of things. Deodand (what legal historians call "thing liability") is a technology for compensating harms to persons *by* things: "If a horse, or ox, or other animals, of his own motion, kill as well an infant as an adult," explains Blackstone, "or if a cart run over him, they shall in either case be forfeited as deodand." But forfeiture is grounded in an "additional reason": "that such misfortunes are in part owing to the negligence of the owner, and therefore he is properly punished by such forfeiture." Deodand thus also makes persons responsible *for* things—and does so, as we shall see in more detail in chapter 4, by thinking of them *as* things. Blackstone uses "negligence" much the way it is used in the cases of instrumental harm coming out of *Mitchell v. Allestry*—not as a sign that a human agent has failed to think or act well but as a formal index of his relationship to the thing and thus to the harm it (and so he) has caused. "It matters not whether the owner were concerned in the killing or not," Blackstone observes, "for if a man kills another with my sword, the sword is forfeited as an accursed thing."[77]

In the *Journal of the Plague Year,* persons and objects are alike "accursed things." By describing the "abandoned effects" of plague victims as "deodand," Defoe assumes that those effects, and their owners, have caused harm to someone. It is a plausible assumption given how frequently objects *are* agents of infection in the text and how similar their agency is to the agency of persons. "Coaches," for example, "were dangerous things, and People did not Care to venture into them, because they did not know who might have been carried in them last" (84). "Our Manufactures, as well as our People, were infected," H. F.

recounts, and he worries that those who run a clandestine trade might thereby be responsible "not only [for] carrying the Contagion into their own country, but also [for] infecting the Nations to whom they traded with those Goods" and thus for the loss of countless other lives (169). Other merchants, he notes, had a similar worry: "They were as much afraid of our Goods, as they were of our People; and indeed they had reason, for our woolen Manufactures are as retentive of Infection as human Bodies, and if pack'd up by Persons infected would receive the Infection, and be as dangerous to touch, as a Man would be that was infected" (167). Animals are similarly dangerous. "We were ordered to kill all the Dogs and Cat," he recalls; "But because as they were domestick Animals, and are apt to run from House to House, and from Street to Street; so they are capable of carrying the Effluvia or Infectious Steams of Bodies infected, even in their Furrs and Hair" (99). Nor are animals the sole "domestick" creatures liable to run from house to house: H. F. admonishes human persons to "stand stock still where they are, and not shift from one End of the Town, or one Part of the Town to the other; for that is the Bane and Mischief of the whole, and they carry the Plague from House to House in their very Clothes" (99).

It is not just that persons and things are like one another—wool like skin, animal fur like the coverings in which humans clothe themselves. The correspondence is closer, based on a shared ontology of action in which agents (human or inhuman) move "insensibly," "instrumentally," "involuntarily" (127, 61). The logic of deodand and the logic of trespass combine in the *Journal* to tie persons to their "abandoned effects"—to the consequences of their actions—as firmly as they are tied to the more literal things they own and cannot disown. Holmes observes that in deodand, "the fact of *motion* is adverted to as of much importance": "So it was said [in Fitzherbert's *Abridgement* (1577)] that 'omne illud quod movet cum eo quod occidit hominess deodandum domino Regi erit, vel fcodo clerici.' The reader sees how motion gives life to the object forfeited."[78] Because in cases of deodand the agent of harm is presumptively nonsentient, it is easy to see how liability attaches solely to the "fact of motion." It is less easy to see this when the agent of harm is presumptively sentient. But in the cases of trespass discussed above, the liability of persons is likewise a consequence of their mobility. In his fruitless desire for persons to "stand stock still," H. F. registers something like this fact: that dogs, cats, rats, and persons are dangerous in precisely the same way—because they "move to the death," because they are *"noxae deditio"* (noxious things).[79]

"One of the most deplorable Cases, in all the present Calamity," H. F. reflects, "was, that of Women with Child" (95): "Where the Mother had the Distemper, there no Body would come near them, and both sometimes perish'd: Sometimes the Mother has died of the Plague; and the Infant, it may be half born, or born but not parted from the Mother. Some died in the very Pains of their Travel, and not deliver'd at all" (96). Defoe's image highlights at once the irresistible instrumentalism of the body and the impossibility of disowning one's connection to others. Throughout the *Journal*, the reproductive body functions as an emblem of the extensiveness of action and relationship during plague time. "I could tell here dismal Stories of living Infants being found sucking the Breasts of their Mothers, or Nurse, after they have been dead of the Plague," continues H. F.; "whether the Child infected the Nurse-Mother, or the Mother the Child was not certain" (98). Defoe frequently turns to nursing to mark the difficulty of determining where agency and responsibility begins and ends. "The Misery of those that gave Suck, was in Proportion great" (97), H. F. intones:

> Many hundreds of Poor helpless Infants perish'd in this manner. Not starved (but poison'd) by the Nurse, Nay even where the Mother has been Nurse, and having receiv'd the Infection, has poison'd, that is, infected the Infant with her Milk, even before they knew they were infected themselves. (97)

The use of the word "poison'd" is one instance of Defoe's "tendency to blame." Deploying the active form of the verb the second time around seems to ascribe deliberation and culpability to a bodily function that from the infant's point of view is necessary and from the mother's quite involuntary. It also links nursing mothers to the nurses, wet nurses, and midwives whom Defoe elsewhere in this text, and indeed throughout his oeuvre, calls "murderers."

Just as pregnant women are icons of dependency (they cannot escape their connection to the fetus; they cannot easily escape their need for another to get it out), nurses are icons of service. These women occupy what can only be described as "status" positions, and the way Defoe treats them reveals an anxiety about service and dependency that approaches paranoia. H. F. recounts "frightful stories" of "Nurses, who attended infected People, using them barbarously, starving them, smothering them, or by other wicked Means, hastening their End, *that is to say*, murthering them" (70). Catalogues of self-murder move seamlessly into a description of "Mothers murthering their own Children" (69)—an ellipsis of self and other that confirms the logic of reproduction encountered in the later, grotesquely literal image of the inextricability of mother and child (the infant "half born or born but not parted from" the mother [96]). That image is itself preceded by two stories that again conflate mothers and nurses. A tale of "distressed Mothers, raveing and distracted, killing their own Children," is quickly followed by an account of women "reduc'd to the utmost distress" by their dependence on unskilled midwives: "Some were deliver'd and spoil'd by the rashness and ignorance of those who pretended to lay them. Children without Number, were, I might say murthered by the same, but a more justifiable ignorance, pretending they would save the Mother, whatever became of the Child; and many Times, both Mother and Child were lost in the same Manner" (95–96). "I cannot but remember to leave this Admonition upon Record," H. F. reflects, "that all Women that are with Child or that give Suck should be gone, if they have any possible Means out of the Place; because their Misery if infected, will so much exceed all other Peoples" (97).

If the misery of women engaged in the business of reproduction exceeds that of other people, so too does their responsibility. In *Moll Flanders*, the midwife called "Mother Midnight" argues that her business ridding women of the "unwelcome Burthen of a Child" has "sav'd the Life of many an innocent Lamb, as she call'd them, which would otherwise perhaps have been Murder'd." Moll agrees this would indeed be a useful occupation "provided the poor Children fell into good hands afterwards, and were not abus'd, starv'd, and neglected by the Nurses that bred them up."[80] But when it comes time to part with her own child, she frets about "having it murther'd, or starv'd by Neglect and Ill-usage (which was much the same)." The relationship between the clauses set off by the comma and the conjunction "or" reveals an explicit interest in the relationship between murder and a kind of destruction Moll *wants* to call murder but that she admits is only similar. What follows is an astonishing disquisition on the difference, if there is one (there is not), between negligent and intentional killing. "I wish all those Women who consent to the disposing their Children out of the way," Moll reflects,

> would consider that 'tis only a contriv'd Method for Murther; that is to say, killing their Children with safety. It is manifest to all that understand any thing of Children that we are born into the World helpless and uncapable either to supply our own Wants, or so much as make them known; and that without help we must Perish; and this help requires not only an assisting hand, whether of the Mother, or some Body else; but there are two Things necessary in that assisting Hand, that is, Care and Skill, without both which, half the Children that are born would die. . . . Since this Care is needful to the Life of Children, to neglect them is to Murther them[.] . . . '[T]is even an intentional Murther, whether the Child lives or dies.[81]

Moll's argument here is underwritten by the logic of custom of the realm. Wet-nursing is an undertaking governed by an imperative of carefulness or "common duty" and a corresponding standard of liability so strict that to violate it, she scandalously suggests, is to be guilty of "intentional murder." What can this phrase mean, and what can it mean to say one is guilty of such a crime "whether the child lives or dies"? The answer has to do with the formalism of the idea of negligence in custom of the realm, the way the possibility of negligence is built into the structure of a certain kind of act. To be guilty of negligence is not, on this account, to be a bad person—a bearer of suspect character or malicious motives—but merely to be the type of person one is (a wet nurse). Certain status positions entail a formal presumption of liability. For Defoe, wet-nursing is this kind of occupation: in its very nature it is a trespass (or tort)—an act predicated on neglect and characterized by a formal intentionality to commit harm. It's not clear that the intentionality of such an act is located in any one individual, however. Roxana observes that while "Men are . . . deliver'd from the Burthen of their Natural Children," women are quite literally forced to bear the consequences of reproduction: mothers have a "dreadful Affliction, either of being turn'd off with her Child, and be left to starve, &c. or of seeing the poor Infant pack'd off with a Piece of Money, to some of those She-Butchers, who take Children off of their Hands, as 'tis called; that is to say, starve 'em, and, in a Word, murther them."[82] The entire system of reproductive heterosexuality is shot through with negligence, and woman's structural inability to escape the teleology of reproduction (once set in motion) means that she cannot escape responsibility for its consequences. One has the sense reading Defoe's work that occupations such as midwifery, wet-nursing, and motherhood itself are encompassed by a more overarching status category: "woman." To be a woman is to be engaged in an undertaking—reproduction—so dangerous that one is never delivered of its burdens: the burden of care and the corresponding burden of liability.

This is in part a consequence of the profound helplessness of infants. But in the *Journal of the Plague Year*, we discover that we are all quite helpless—that, as Moll puts it, "without help we will perish." In this memoir of Being-under-crises, the relationship between mother and child—characterized by radical vulnerability on the one side and radical obligation on the other—comes to emblematize the ontology of relationship as such. Moll says that to neglect helpless creatures is to murder them. For Holmes, negligence involves a failure to have foreseen something that might have been foreseen, a failure to avoid something that might have been avoided. The negligent person, he says, "ought to have acted otherwise." But if helplessness and liability are built into the reproduction of species, if persons are compelled by the force of biology as well as ethics to be tied to others, how can responsibility stem from negligence as Holmes describes it? How can one avoid something that cannot be avoided? How can one ever "act otherwise" than negligently? And if negligence is an unavoidable feature of the agency, perhaps the ontology of human persons, in what sense does it remain a sign of "failure" and of fault?

Defoe sometimes sees responsibility the way Holmes sees it, as an effect of having acted poorly. "There were Cases," H. F., tells us, "wherein the infected People were careless of the Injury they did to others . . . and having been driven to Extremities for Provision, or for Entertainment, had endeavoured to conceal their Condition, and have been thereby Instrumental involuntarily to infect others who have been ignorant and unwary" (61). The word "careless" suggests that "involuntary instrumentality" is a category of negligence; and indeed, H. F. repeatedly and explicitly invokes that term. "Nothing was more fatal to the Inhabitants of this City," he says, "than the Supine Negligence of the People themselves, who during the long Notice, or Warning they had of the Visitation, yet made no Provision for it" (64–65). The watchmen overseeing the "provisions," who had at last been put in place by the government to control the contagion, were not as vigilant as they might have been and were "severely punish'd for their Neglect" when they fell victim to the disease themselves (131). The heads of households who were to report any infection therein found "ways to evade this, and excuse their Negligence" (134). "In this great and dangerous Case of Health and Infection," H. F. concludes, the people of England were "entirely negligent" (179).

But as we have also seen, H. F. vigorously dismisses accounts of the calamity that argue for a "seeming propensity, or a wicked Inclination in those that were Infected to infect others" (124). The plague, he insists, is for the most part propagated "insensibly, and by such Persons as were not visibly infected, who neither knew who they infected, or who they were infected by" (127). Nor is this insensibility solely the property of female bodies. "Fathers *and* Mothers," H. F. tells us, "have gone about as if they had been well, and have believ'd themselves to be so, till they have insensibly infected, and been the Destruction of their whole Families" (158; emphasis mine). He recounts a story of a family "thus infected by the Father," who "as soon as he found out that his Family had been poison'd by himself, he went distracted." The passive construction makes it appear as though the father's self-indictment is inappropriate. But H. F. takes up the project of indictment in the active voice—a voice that I have been suggesting is characteristic of his, and his author's, "tendency to blame." Calling the man a "walking Destroyer," H. F. concludes: "He had ruin'd those, that he would have hazarded his Life to save, and had been breathing Death down upon them, even perhaps in his tender Kissing and Embracings of his own Children" (158–59). In

the *Journal of the Plague Year*—as in the laws that influence its logic of blame—
we are responsible for what we "insensibly" do. We are responsible to those we
harm, even if harm is an effect of the most grotesque misfortune or the deepest
affection. We are responsible, though we are not at fault.

⟨

When in *Roxana* the eponymous heroine calls her daughter Susan "my plague"
(302), the description registers how this novel of inescapable reproductive liability exploits the tragic logic of relationship first articulated in the *Journal of
the Plague Year*. "I wanted as much to be deliver'd from her," Roxana recalls, "as
ever a Sick-Man did from a Third-Day ague; and had she dropp'd into the Grave
by any fair Way, as I may call it; I mean had she died by any ordinary Distemper, I should have shed but very few Tears for her: But I was not arriv'd to such
a Pitch of obstinate Wickedness, as to commit Murther, especially such, as to
murther my own Child" (302). At this point in the narrative, Susan's pursuit of
her mother has reached a fever pitch, and Roxana's maid Amy has vowed to kill
the girl in order to protect her master from exposure. In her compelling account
of the novel, Terry Castle reads Amy's murder of Susan allegorically—explicitly,
as an allegory of the trauma of subjectivity; implicitly, as an allegory of sexuality.
About the final paragraph, in which Roxana recounts how, "after some few Years
of flourishing, . . . the Blast of Heaven seem'd to follow the Injury done the poor
Girl, by us both," Castle observes: "The catastrophe befalling her and Amy is not
to be 'Related.' . . . It, like the actual murder of Susan, is unspeakable."[83] Earlier
Castle has called this unspeakable relationship "intimacy": "Defoe's onomastics,"
she ingeniously suggests, captures "the psychological complexity involved in the
type of intimacy the narrative reveals. Amy is of course the *amie*—the perfect
friend, the familiar. Likewise, she is also, perhaps, a 'me'—an oddly displaced
and altered version of the speaker herself."[84] Seen from this perspective, she
concludes, the "murder is then a simple effect of the structure of relationship we
have already seen between Roxana and her maid. Amy is doubling for her and
protecting her."[85] Murder is not so much murder as love.

Castle's reading is invaluable for the way it foregrounds the homoeroticism
and doubling that are so central to *Roxana*. She is quite right that this is a novel
about relationship but wrong, I think, that it is about "intimacy." Roxana frequently mentions Amy's affection for her: after the landlord "rescues" her we're
told that "the Girl was half distracted with the Joy of it; a Testimony still of her
violent Affection for her Mistress, in which no Servant ever went beyond her"
(32). Castle assumes that such affection is excessive—that it must be transfer-

ence, or mother love, or desire, because it cannot be what Roxana calls it: service. And yet, the logic of service *is* a logic of the double—or rather, it is a logic of identification that Castle describes as "doubling" but that is more precisely a kind of conflation. Castle, among others, has observed the complexities of agency in this novel—Amy's frenetic activity and Roxana's apparent passivity, her "Aversion" to bonds (184). Her seeming indifference to relationship has lead to a critical consensus that Roxana is averse to filial or reproductive obligation and seeks to replace unsolicited bonds with those derived from "equitable contract."[86] What goes unnoticed in the argument that makes this a book about contractual or affective obligation, however, is how relentlessly Roxana imagines herself responsible for the effects of actions she has not consented to and that are not her own. Castle claims that throughout the novel Roxana attempts to avoid "adult responsibility" and never more so than when she "projects" and "transfers" her own agency onto Amy. But the notion that Roxana wants to be freed of obligation is contradicted by the important final clause of the final paragraph of the novel—one Castle does not cite: "The Blast of Heaven seem'd to follow the Injury done the poor Girl, *by us both;* and I was brought so low again, that my Repentance seem'd to be only the Consequence of my Misery, as my Misery was of *my Crime*" (330; emphases mine).[87]

Roxana feels that she too has murdered Susan—and she is right. The novel self-consciously ties its interest in agency (understood as a philosophical problem) to a legal doctrine of agency that, as we have seen, had recently made a master "vicariously liable for acts which he did not command, provided that they were for his benefit and in the course of employment."[88] What Castle and others describe as the gothic, paranoid quality of *Roxana* derives from the way Defoe exploits the practical and conceptual implications of the idea of vicarious liability.[89] Indeed, the doctrine of agency—a doctrine in which responsibility travels recursively from agents back to principals—is explicitly invoked by Susan, who responds to Amy's attempt to shield her mistress by saying "she wou'd not have her think she was so ignorant, as not to know that what she (*Amy*) had done, was by her Mother's Order; and who she was beholden to for it: That she cou'd never make Instruments pass for Principals, and pay the Debt to the Agent, when the Obligation was all to the Original" (312). Susan insists that her pursuit of Roxana is meant to clarify her *own* responsibilities. But Amy immediately recognizes that what's at stake is Roxana's responsibility—and she responds by invoking the specter of an act designed to limit her mistress's liability by dramatically enhancing her own. "Amy wish'd her at the Bottom of the Thames," Roxana recounts, "and had there been no Waterman in the Boat, and no-body in sight, *she swore to me,* she wou'd have thrown her into the River" (312). Roxana repeatedly and emphatically distances herself from her servant's "wishes." Amy has a "fatal and wicked Design in her Head, against [Susan]," we're told, "which indeed, I never knew till after it was executed, nor durst Amy ever communicate it to me; for as I had always express'd myself vehemently against hurting a Hair of her Head, so she was resolv'd to take her Measures, without consulting me any-more" (311). And when Amy speaks of "throwing [Susan] into the River, and drowning her," Roxana is "so provok'd at her, that all my Rage turn'd against *Amy,* and I fell thorowly out with her": "I cou'd not bear the Mention of her Murthering the poor Girl, and it put me so beside myself, that I rise up in a Rage, and bade her get out of my Sight, and out of my House; *told her,* I had kept her too long, and that I wou'd never see her Face more" (312–13).

Roxana's dismissal of Amy is the culmination of a series of escalating disagreements about her daughter's pursuit of a "Principal." From the beginning, Susan's search for her mother is couched in the language of agency, and this conflation of reproduction and service is underscored by the fact that Susan is at once Roxana's servant and her child. Initially only Amy knows that there is another person in Roxana's employ who shares Amy's own filial bond with her employer. "Amy did not tell me this Story for a great-while," Roxana observes, "but as she had Authority to manage every-thing in the Family, she took Occasion some time after, without letting me know any-thing of it, to find some Fault with the Maid, and turn her away" (197). Thereafter, Roxana says, "Amy manag'd my daughter too, very well, tho' by a third hand" (198). In this novel of action by other hands, however, things done by "Instruments" have a way of coming home to roost.[90] An accidental encounter produces a scene of anagnorisis in which Amy is revealed as Susan's benefactress—a revelation that "had like to have blown up the whole Case, and herself and me too," Roxana reflects, for "the passionate Creature flew out in a kind of Rage, *and said to* Amy, that if she was not her Mother, Madam *Roxana* was her Mother then, for one of them, she was sure, was her Mother; and then all this that Amy had done for her, was by Madam *Roxana's* Order" (270). Susan's insight—an insight that "provokes" Amy to thoughts of murder—is that even when she is not acting, Roxana is nonetheless a cause. The distinction Castle observes between Amy's frenetic management and Roxana's "deepening inertia and powerlessness" is real but also irrelevant.[91] For despite her strenuous repudiation of Amy's actions—"I reproach'd her with her knowing that I abhorr'd it, and had let her know it sufficiently, in that I had, *as it were,* kick'd her out of Doors" (324)—Roxana knows what Susan knows: that her maid is always upon her "general Commission" (215). Commission: the word captures the ambiguities of agency, the way the implied subject does and does not act for herself (she "commits" an act whose causality lies elsewhere). "I was, for want of Amy, destitute; I had lost my Right-Hand," Roxana muses after sending Amy from her door but not, significantly, from her service; she "did all my Business; and without her, indeed, I knew not how to go away, nor how to stay" (318). It is not that Amy acts *instead of* Roxana, or that she acts, in any simple sense, *for* her. Her undertakings *are* Roxana's—and the "injury," when it comes to poor Susan, comes, as Roxana acknowledges, from them both.

Defoe's interest in the doctrine of vicarious agency and liability pervades *Roxana*. When Roxana describes the "useless thing" (96) that is her brewer husband, we find that he, too, is a being who causes injury without acting and merely as an instrumental effect of his status as husband. Roxana's description sets up an opposition between his instrumentality and her own managerial efficiency:

> By this Management I found an Opportunity to see what a most insignificant, unthinking Life, the poor indolent Wretch, who by his unactive Temper had first been my Ruin, now liv'd; how he only rose in the Morning, to go to-Bed at Night; that saving the necessary Motion of the Troops, which he was oblig'd to attend, he was a meer motionless Animal, of no Consequence in the World; that he seem'd to be one, who, tho' he was indeed, alive, had no manner of Business in Life. (95)

Unlike Roxana, the husband has no "Business," and this makes him a "meer motionless Animal"—motionless not because he doesn't move but because his motility is an effect of someone else's undertaking. "Yet this *Nothing-doing Wretch* was I oblig'd to watch and guard against," Roxana admits, "as against the only thing that was capable of doing me Hurt in the World" (95). The husband "does hurt" while "doing nothing," causing harm simply by continuing to persist *as* a husband. At this early moment in the narrative Roxana wants to, and imagines she can, distinguish such "unthinking" agency and "necessary Motion" from her own. But the momentum of the novel works against this distinction, and Roxana increasingly finds that she too is a "wretch" responsible for harms she has not meant to produce.

There's Susan's murder, which Roxana continues to insist she "had no Knowledge of, and indeed abhorr'd" (328), right up to the moment she calls it "*my Crime*" (330). But there's another, less frequently discussed murder in the book: that of the jeweler husband, who is killed by highwaymen "because of the Disappointment they met with, in not getting his Case, or Casket of Diamonds, which they knew he carry'd about him" (53) and would have had in his possession had not Roxana persuaded him to leave it behind. Roxana calls her graphic anxiety that "some Harm wou'd attend him" "Second-Sight" (52, 55):

I thought all his Face look'd like a Death's-Head; and then, immediately, I thought I perceiv'd his Head all Bloody; and then his Cloaths look'd Bloody too. . . . I saw him as plainly in all those terrible Shapes, as above, *First*, as a Skeleton, not Dead only, but rotten and wasted; *Secondly*, as kill'd, and his Face Bloody; and *Thirdly*, his Cloaths bloody. (52–53, 55)

Yet in this moment Roxana does not so much foresee as help to bring about the death of her husband; for he responds to the "strange Terror upon [her] Mind" by giving her, in addition to the Casket, "the fine Ring, and his Gold Watch" (52)—booty that would have saved his life. Roxana recounts that when the highwaymen do not find the casket or other clearly visible effects on his person, they "stabb'd him into the Body with a Sword," "pull'd him out of the Coach and search'd his Cloaths more narrowly, than they cou'd do while he was alive." The diminutive size of the objects they discover is emphasized: "They found nothing but his *little* Ring, six Pistoles, and the Value of about seven Livres in *small* Moneys" (53; emphasis mine). The smallness of these effects *requires*, calls into being, the "narrow" search, and their insignificance is thus an ironically disproportionate cause of the man's violent death.

The suggestion that Roxana might be complicit in this crime helps to explain the direction the narrative takes, the excessive response of the prince to whom the jeweler was traveling that fateful day. Although the prince tells Roxana that "he was no way accessory to the Disaster," he announces that he has "resolv'd however, to make me some Reparation; and with these Words, put a silk Purse into my Hand, with a hundred Pistoles, and told me, he would make me a farther Compliment of a small Pension" (58). Roxana "gravely" absolves the prince of responsibility, assuring him that the jeweler met his end because it was known that he "always carry'd a Casket of Jewels about him, and that he always wore a Diamond Ring on his Finger, worth a hundred Pistoles, which Report had magnified to five Hundred" (58). Roxana implies that her husband's habitual practice has killed him, but the reader recalls that it is the *violation* of that practice, prompted by Roxana, that motivates the ire of the "disappointed" robbers. The prince's anxiety that he might, however improbably, be to blame for this event, is contrasted with Roxana's imperviousness to her own, far less improbable, responsibility. Roxana's refusal of vicarious liability goes against its increasing normative authority in the novel's plot. And when the "Jew" emerges

calling for her to be "charg'd with the Robbery and Murther" (114) of her husband when she is found in possession of his jewels, his appearance is motivated
not by extradiegetic racial hatred but by a formal and thematic imperative that
Roxana acknowledge *herself* "accessory to the Disaster."

This she does not do—not yet. The Jew's attempt to "bring a Process against
me for the Murther" is attributed to the fact that "he does not understand *English*
at-all" (114) and does not know the laws of England, where if a person "wou'd
offer such an Injury to any one, they must prove the Fact, or give just Reason
for their Suspicions" (117). The Dutch merchant reminds Roxana that she is not
in England but in France, where she will be "put to the Question, that is, to the
Torture, on Pretense of making you confess who were the Murtherers of your
husband" (118). What follows is an exchange that on its surface concerns Catholic justice (inquisitorial oppression) yet is in fact a meditation on common-law
justice—on what it means to *do something oneself.*

> Confess! *said* I; how can I confess what I know nothing of?
> If they come to have you to the Rack, *said* he, they will make you confess you did
> it yourself, whether you did it or no, and then you are cast. . . .
> Did it myself! *said* I; that's impossible. (118)

The merchant misunderstands the object of Roxana's outraged skepticism, imagining she rejects the possibility that she could foreswear herself: "No, Madam,
says he, 'tis far from impossible; the most innocent People in the World have
been forc'd to confess themselves Guilty of what they never heard of, much less,
had any Hand in" (118–19). But Roxana doesn't for a moment doubt she can be
forced to confess: her doubt bears instead on the content of that confession, on
the possibility that she might be guilty of what she had not heard of and had not
herself done.

The merchant equates such stringency with Catholic culture, but Roxana sys-
tematically portrays Catholicism as a practice and a logic of exculpation. When
she famously proclaims herself a "Protestant Whore" and says she "could not act
as if I was Popish, upon any Account whatsoever" (69), acting "Popish" is acting
on the "absurd" assumption that "Heaven would not suffer us to be punish'd
for that which it was not possible for us to avoid" (69). "As I had none of the recourse, so I had none of the Absolution, by which the Criminal confessing, goes
away comforted," Roxana reflects; "but I went about with a Heart loaded with
Crime" (265). Acting "Protestant," it follows, is punishing oneself for crimes
"not possible for us to avoid": Protestantism *is* strict liability. And if Roxana seeks
to absolve herself of responsibility for the jeweler's murder, this desire for abso-

lution goes against a more pervasive tendency to blame herself even for those harms—like Susan's murder—in which she has had "no hand."

What is called "paranoia"—Roxana's obsessive worrying over the remote and accidental consequences of thoughts and actions—is thus more properly understood as a Protestant ethic and the spirit of capitalism. Robert Clayton's "Table of Encrease" in which Roxana is exhorted to add "every Year the additional Interest, or Income of the Money to the Capital" (167)—in which capital's distant effects are continually reattached to the principal—is the comic version of the novel's tragic logic of responsibility. If Roxana masters the felicitous miracle of compound interest, she cannot control the "encrease" represented by the children who usher from her reflexively reproductive body and who return to her charge despite efforts "not to discover myself to them, in the least; or to let any of the People that had the breeding of them up, know that there was such a-body left in the World, as their Mother" (188). No wonder, then, that she has "such a constant Terror upon my Mind, as gave me every now and then very terrible Shocks, and which made me expect something very frightful upon every Accident of Life" (260). She reports that she "dream'd continually of the most frightful and terrible things" and that "in the Morning, when I shou'd rise, and be refresh'd with the Blessings of Rest, I was *Hag-ridden* with Frights, and terrible things, form'd meerly in the Imagination" (264). That "meerly" is meant to diminish the omnipotence of her thought, to describe as overwrought melancholia the expectation that catastrophe follows "upon every Accident of Life." But in the episode with the jeweler husband, Roxana's presentiment of his bloodied face and rotting body is felt to have brought those harms into being. And while she continues to think of that prescience as affectionate concern rather than contributory negligence, when it comes to Amy's thoughts about Roxana's obligations to her children, matters fall out rather differently.

Roxana strenuously indicts Amy merely for desiring Susan's annihilation. "But you shan't, *says I,* you shan't hurt a Hair of her Head," Roxana describes herself telling Amy. "Why you ought to be hang'd for what you have done already; for having resolv'd on it, is doing it, as to the Guilt of the Fact; you are a Murtherer already, as much as you had done it already" (273). The claim that having resolved on doing something *is* doing it, that Amy is a "murderer already" simply for having imagined Susan's death, has no basis in law. "There must also be an actual killing to constitute murder," says Blackstone, and Holmes observes that "intent to commit a crime is not itself criminal. There is no law against a man's intending to commit a murder the day after to-morrow. The law deals only with conduct."[92] The famous exception is the law of treason, which indicts one who *"doth compass or imagine the Death of our Lord the King, or of my Lady his Queen, or of their eldest Son and Heir."*[93] But even here, Baker notes, "the courts required proof of an overt act of preparation to kill, in addition to mere words, and this was laid down as a necessary element in 1628."[94] A writer of Defoe's evident legal acumen certainly knows this, and yet once again he insists on calling "murder" what is not murder. Once again he converts one kind of act (kissing, nursing, breastfeeding, worrying, wishing, resolving) into another, more heinous, act (homicide).

It is possible to read Roxana's indictment of Amy as a defensive projection onto someone else of what is her own bloodthirsty wish fulfillment. Roxana begins to think of Susan as murdered from the moment Amy gives her

> the History of her *Greenwich* Voyage, when she spoke of drowning and killing the Girl in so serious a manner, and with such an apparent Resolution of doing it, that, *as I said,* put me in a Rage with her, so that I effectually turn'd her away from me. (316)

"As for the poor Girl herself," Roxana says, "she was ever before my Eyes": "Sometimes I thought I saw her with her Throat cut; sometimes with her Head cut, and her Brains knock'd out; other-times hang'd up upon a Beam; another time drown'd in the Great Pond at *Camberwell*" (325). Susan's mutilated body "haunts [Roxana's] imagination," although she has been assured that after the trip to Greenwich, Amy "dismiss'd her, and got rid of her again; and finding an empty Hackney-Coach in the Town, came away by Land to *London:* and the Girl going down to the Water-side, came by Boat"—an account confirmed by Susan's subsequent pursuit of her mother, now in Tunbridge, where she "hunted me, as if, *like a Hound,* she had had a hot Scent" (317). It is possible, that is, to understand Roxana's calling Amy a "murderer already" as an index of her own unconscious desire for Susan's death. ("It is hard not to see Susan's killing," Castle says, "as an act that Roxana in some sense desires.")[95] But we needn't answer the (at any rate unanswerable) question of Roxana's desire to observe that the instrumentality of her thought—the way a mechanistic causality ties thoughts to ends one does not intend—is the reductio ad absurdum of a pervasive model of agency, relationship, and accountability built around accident: the accidental effects of things (money, interest, ships, storms, jewels), of persons (agents, spies, servants, children, husbands), of a type of person (master, mother) fastened to the acts and the bodies of others.

Roxana cannot, however much she might wish to, "turn Amy away from her," nor can she turn the effects of any of her instruments from her own account. If "one person makes use of another's act or of some natural occurrence to further his own ends, then the law holds him as responsible as if he had brought about these ends by his own act," observes a historian of criminal law: "The instruments which people use are not restricted to animals and inanimate objects."[96] As Castle shows, the novel obsessively canvases the identity and simultaneity of master and maid. But it equally obsessively marks Roxana's responsibility *for* Amy, and never more so than when it returns to the scene of her rape. "Tho' [Amy] had lain with her Master," Roxana reflects, "it was with her Mistress's Knowledge and consent, and which was worse, was her Mistresses own doing; *I record it to the Reproach of my own Vice*" (130). The claim that *she* has raped Amy is reinforced by the famous undressing scene, where Roxana removes Amy's "Stockings and Shoes, and all her Cloaths, Piece by Piece": "So I fairly stript her," says Roxana, "and then I threw open the Bed, and thrust her in" (46). Defoe initially highlights the limits of Roxana's agency by emphasizing the landlord's consummation of the act. "Nay, *Amy*, you see your Mistress has put you to-Bed," he says, "'tis all her doing, you must blame her; so he held her fast, and the Wench, being naked in the Bed with him, 'twas too late to look back, so she lay still, and let him do what he wou'd with her" (46–47). The landlord's "blame" of Roxana is ironized by its placement within a diegesis emphasizing his penetration of the plaint, near senseless, Amy. Yet what begins as a joke becomes in earnest Roxana's—and the novel's—analysis of the act: "Tho' he had, indeed, debauch'd the Wench," Roxana says, "I knew that I was the principal Occasion of it" (47).

The doctrine of agency governing principals and agents—one that ultimately makes Roxana responsible for crimes committed *by* Amy—is here invoked to tie her to crimes committed *on* Amy. Roxana's claim that she has "occasioned," or is causally responsible for, acts performed by another asks us to think of responsibility as something that can be disseminated across bodies, space, and time. It asks us to think of responsible persons as causes rather than agents. And it asks us to think of causality in terms of remoteness rather than proximity.[97] When Castle describes Roxana as characterized by a "willingness to skirt responsibility, to evade direct action and conscious choice," therefore, the sentence syntactically performs an alignment of "responsibility," "direct action," and "conscious choice" that contradicts the novel's normative model of responsibility.[98] Because Castle thinks responsibility is agential and intentional, she doesn't register its presence in a writer for whom—and in a *form* for which—responsibility is profoundly accidental.[99] In the epigraph to this chapter Cavell describes "Shakespeare's mode of tragedy" as "an enactment not of fate but of responsibility, including the responsibility for fate."[100] It is a mode, he says, that "disappears" with the emergence of empiricist epistemology and its commitment to the idea that "we can save our lives by knowing them."[101] As I have said, I do not believe empiricism is as sanguine as Cavell imagines about the possibility of preventing accidents, but this is a discussion for another, different, book. Here I want merely to suggest (or rather to insist) that Defoe's novels reveal the persistence of a tragic model of responsibility—responsibility understood *as* responsibility for lives we have not chosen—in a form intimately, obsessively, linked with empiricism. "There was no retreat; no shifting-anything off" (278), Roxana observes on encountering the embodied, instrumental effect that is her daughter Susan. Not being able to shift anything off: Williams calls this "recognition" (anagnorisis); Cavell calls it "acknowledgment"; I have been calling it what the law calls it, "liability." Roxana, for her part, calls it something else. "What a Glorious Testimony it is to the Justice of Providence . . . that the most secret Crimes are, by the most unforeseen Accidents, brought to light, and discover'd" (297).

CHAPTER TWO

The Encroachments of Others

Without accusation we have no causes to plead.

Bruno Latour, *We Have Never Been Modern*

"I am afraid there will be murder," Clarissa tells Anna Howe early in their correspondence, and "to avoid that, if there were no other way," she says, "I would most willingly be buried alive."[1] Days before Lovelace abducts her from her home, she wakes in terror from a dream which she proceeds to transcribe for her friend:

> Methought my brother, my uncle Anthony, and Mr Solmes had formed a plot to destroy Mr Lovelace; who discovering it turned all his rage against me, believing I had a hand in it. I thought he made them all fly into foreign parts upon it; and afterwards seizing upon me, carried me into a churchyard; and there, notwithstanding all my prayers and tears, and protestations of innocence, stabbed me to the heart, and then tumbled me into a deep grave ready dug, among two or three half-dissolved carcases; throwing in the dirt and earth upon me with his hands, and trampling it down with his feet. (342–43)

Although she has been "stabbed to the heart," the third-person point of view creates the chilling impression that Clarissa has been buried alive—that she perceives the state of decay of the (other) corpses and feels the earth close in on her. It is tempting to read the sequence as a dream of penetration, presaging the rape that occupies the center of Clarissa's story and stories about *Clarissa*. But Clarissa's fear as she describes it is fixed on the threat of a different harm: murder.

Critical preoccupation with the rape of Clarissa has meant that the novel's obsessive return to the specter of murder has been almost entirely overlooked. The emphasis makes sense: rape seems not so much the central as the sole action of *Clarissa*, its special status reinforced by the fact that as a crime, rape raises hermeneutic and political questions—questions, in other words, of representation—that other criminal actions do not. "It is remarkable," Frances Ferguson has argued, "for focusing attention on mental states and their apprehension."[2] Murder, in contrast, is a crime predicated on a disambiguation of questions of thought and action. As we saw in chapter 1, from the sixteenth century onward the category of murder was understood to turn on the combined presence of actus reus and mens rea: murder marked a clearly determinate (guilty) act accompanied by an equally transparent (guilty) motive.[3] We also saw, however, that deaths occasioned by acts and motives lacking the requisite malignity were a more perplexing legal and conceptual problem, and I have argued that this problem—how to conceive of an agent's responsibility for *accidental,* fatal harms to others—is the organizing concern of Defoe's novels and of the form those novels bring into being. Richardson's novel, revolving as it does around an elaborately premeditated harm, would appear to fall outside this genealogy. And yet rape only becomes the major action of *Clarissa* as an effect of the interruption of another action that sets both story and plot in motion.

Anna's opening letter to Clarissa begins in the middle of this action. "I long to have the particulars from yourself," she writes, "of the usage I am told you receive upon an accident you could not help and in which, as far I can learn, the sufferer was the aggressor" (39). The accident to which Anna refers is the abortive duel between Lovelace and Clarissa's brother James Harlowe. The imperative to prevent this action from completing itself occasions Clarissa's correspondence with Lovelace—the first step, as she comes to understand it, in a causal sequence leading inexorably to her ruin. "I saw plainly that to have denied myself his visits," she tells Anna, "was to bring forward some desperate issue between the two, since the offence so readily given on one side was only brooked by the other out of consideration to me. And thus did my brother's rashness lay me under an obligation where I would least have owned it" (51). Lovelace ruthlessly exploits both the menace of the duel and Clarissa's sense that she is obliged to prevent it: "Fly, my dearest life!" he urges at her garden gate as Joseph Leman counterfeits the sounds of armed resistance; "if you would not see two or three murders committed at your feet, fly, fly, I beseech you!" (380). "I ran as fast as he," she recalls of her abduction, "yet knew not that I ran; my fears at the same time that they took all power of thinking from me adding wings to my feet" (380).

In what follows I want to take seriously the formal and conceptual implications of *Clarissa*'s beginning in medias res, and in the middle of a very specific kind of act (dueling). Ian Watt has argued that Richardson's formal innovation was "remarkably simple": "He avoided an episodic plot," Watt says, "by basing his novels on a single action."[4] This insight is itself remarkably simple—so deceptively simple that we have failed to confront its profundity. (It is an example, Nietzsche might say, of Watt's "gift for being superficial out of profundity.")[5] Watt calls this action "courtship," an uncomfortable though, as Ferguson has shown, not wholly improbable term for what happens in *Clarissa*. Yet if *Clarissa* comes closest of any novel to representing a single action, that action, as I have come to conceive of it, is the action of action itself: *plot*. *Clarissa* opens in the middle of the middle of an action, literalizing what it means to begin in the middle of things. In doing so the novel reveals something about this formal practice: namely, that what sounds plural ("things" as a plurality of actions) is in fact singular ("things" as the unified action of plot). For the duel is not interrupted at all: in one of the great ironies in the history of the novel, the suspension of this act culminates not only in the murder its suspension was designed to prevent but in the killing prefigured in Clarissa's dream and relentlessly enforced by the novel's tragic plot.

In *Clarissa*, actions once begun do not come to rest. The profound inertia of actions and agents is an important and underexamined feature of the novel's plot, one that comes into view only when, with a legal precision as acute as Richardson's, one thinks through the question of responsibility. Minutes before her feet send her flying into his arms, Lovelace makes an unsuccessful appeal to what Clarissa calls her "precaution"—the conviction that she is responsible "for the safety of others" (428). "My happiness, madam, both here and hereafter, and the safety of all your implacable family, depend upon this moment," Lovelace asserts, to which Clarissa replies: "To Providence, Mr Lovelace, and to the Law will I leave the safety of my friends" (376). It is common, given Clarissa's scrupulous refusal of litigation, for critics to read "Law" as a moral law synonymous with providential fiat (this despite the conjunction that would seem to distinguish "law" from "providence"). Although Anna might "blame" Clarissa for her "resolution not to litigate for your right, if occasion were to be given you" (210), Richardson, it is assumed, does not. "Richardson's constant theme is the law's inadequacy," argues Joan Schwarz, "the inability of the law to rectify the moral wrongs done to innocents like Clarissa."[6] It bears noting, however, that Lovelace too resists litigation and does so in order to perpetuate the threat of the duel and thus Clarissa's obligation to him. "His relations, the ladies particularly, advise him to have recourse to a legal remedy" against James, Clarissa informs Anna. "But how," she recounts him saying, "can a man of honour go to law for verbal abuses, given by people entitled to wear swords?" (126). As we shall see in chapter 3, Fielding is among the first to register as "Richardsonian" an interest in the kind of "legal remedy" Lovelace cynically rejects. Like Fielding himself, Lovelace sees fighting as a specifically masculine technology of remediation, one he opposes to a womanish investment in blame. "She began with me like a true woman," he recounts of one of Clarissa's few encounters with him after the rape: "*She* in the fault, *I* to be blamed" (908). He laments a similar tendency on the part of his aunt and cousins and the emasculate Lord M. "They are fond of occasions to find fault with me" (783), he observes, occasions that escalate in the months following the rape. He tells Belford that

> Charlotte and her sister could not help weeping at the base aspersion. . . . And thus
> am I blamed for everyone's faults!—When her brutal father curses her, it is I. I
> upbraid her with her severe mother. Her stupid uncles' implacableness is all mine.
> Her brother's virulence, and her sister's spite and envy, are entirely owing to me.
> . . . Oh Jack, what a wretch is thy Lovelace! (1291)

What makes Lovelace wretched is the notion that he might be responsible for the acts of others. "Mr Lovelace, you are a very unaccountable man" (527), Clarissa raves when, after the abduction, she is deposited at the home of the sinister Mrs. Sinclair. And her instinctive alignment of the problem of Lovelace's (un)accountability with the obscure threat represented by Sinclair is an important moment for understanding how Richardson confronts the question of harm and legal remedy. Although Lovelace insists it is the "privilege of a principal . . . to lay all his own faults upon his underlings, and never be to blame himself" (741), he increasingly finds himself tied to the remote and unintended consequences of his own actions and the actions of those, like Sinclair, in his employ. The doctrine of agency that was so central to Defoe's project in *Roxana* acquires formal and conceptual prominence as the plot of *Clarissa* unfolds—a plot within which characters explicitly and with some sophistication debate the liability of principals and agents, a plot *through which* Lovelace and his instruments are rigorously punished. That Lovelace, unlike Roxana, wants to imagine himself indemnified against the acts of his agents is one of the many signs of his archaism. But the novel also takes seriously the problem Sinclair in her unauthorized imprisonment of Clarissa poses to Lovelace—which is to say, the problem she poses to familiar accounts of agency and responsibility. For the way Lovelace goes about clearing himself of Sinclair's "cursed job" (1046) involves the deployment of a compelling logic: the logic of the subject.

Lovelace argues throughout the novel, but especially as it becomes clear that the crime for which he might be responsible is murder rather than rape, that acts of others bear a more proximate relation to Clarissa's death than any action of his own. It is a perfectly coherent defense, one consistent with the definition of murder as a crime tied to discrete acts and discrete individuals. "I am not answerable for all the extravagant and unforeseen consequences that this affair has been attended with," Lovelace asserts when Anna Howe and his fault-finding relations threaten to indict him. "Is death the natural consequence of a rape?—Did you ever hear, my lord, or did you, my ladies, that it was?—And if not the natural consequence, and a lady will destroy herself . . . is there more than one fault the *man's*? Is not the other *hers*?" (1438–39). Lovelace seeks to limit his fault to rape and in so doing to clarify the contours of his action, mark off actions that have come to rest, discriminate acts he owns from those he can disown: "Were my life to be a forfeit to the law," he observes, "it would not be for murder" (1439). Lovelace's insistence that Clarissa's death is her act rather than his replicates earlier attempts on his part to distinguish actions encompassed by his "plot" (understood as motive) from actions, like Sinclair's, that fall outside it and thus belong to someone else: "May damnation seize quick the accursed woman who could set death upon taking that *large stride,* as the dear creature calls it!—I had no hand in it" (1340); "that accident was an accident," we are enjoined to understand, "and no plot or contrivance of a wretch too full of them" (1050). One interesting thing about Lovelace's defense is that it is true: he had no hand in Clarissa's devastating imprisonment; technically, he has had no hand in her death. "I hold myself, of consequence, acquitted of the death" (1050), he concludes. Another interesting thing is that the defense is unsuccessful: "Not so," Lovelace recounts his uncle as responding. "For if by committing an unlawful act, a capital crime is the consequence, you are answerable to both" (1438).

Lord M.'s indictment of Lovelace explicitly invokes a category of criminal liability that was coming into focus as a legal principal in the decades surrounding the publication of *Clarissa*. The doctrine of felony murder, as it came to be called, is central not only to the debate between Lovelace and those who would blame him but to the novel's (and the Novel's) larger formal and conceptual project. Felony murder emerges as a way to address the kinds of accidental killings that preoccupy Defoe, for whom "murder" is less a legal than a literary category of indictment. In *Conjugal Lewdness*, for example, "murder" marks the dangerousness of the rake's trademark commitment to mendacity, exploitation, seduction and rape. Defoe describes *Conjugal Lewdness* as a "satire"; and indeed, his tendency to call acts that have unintentionally caused death "murder" can be seen as a thought experiment, *in the mode of invective*, about the possibilities of strict liability.[7] By the time Richardson is calling *his* rapist a "murderer," however, changes in the law in the middle decades of the seventeenth century had been such that what he is doing is very different from what Defoe had done.

Until 1846, Baker observes, "death barred an action for damages."[8] Defoe turns to carrier liability and vicarious liability for a logic of blame that he imaginatively extends to accidental fatality but that in practice was applicable only to accidental *harm*. Death was the province of criminal law, but because of the mens rea requirement, no one quite knew what to do about deaths that occurred *per infortunium*. Deodand was one way of responding to the unintentional taking of a life—a response, as we saw in chapter 1 (and as we shall see again in chapter 4), that avoided the question of mens rea by attaching responsibility to the mindless instrument of death and only thereby to its owner. In criminal law it was theoretically possible to apply a principle of automatic liability "to the man whose conduct killed another, even if he had no guilty mind," but this did not tend to happen. The grant of a pardon in the case of accidental or excusable killings was a matter of course, and beginning in the late fourteenth century, says Baker, many who killed by accident "were probably not arraigned at all."[9] By the early seventeenth century, however, Edward Coke came to think that there *was* a way for the criminal law to deal with accidental deaths—or at least with deaths that were an unintended consequence of acts not entirely innocent. In his account of a sixteenth-century precedent, *Lord Dacre's Case* (1535), Coke argued: "If the act be unlawful it is murder. As if A. meaning to steale a deere in the park of B., shooteth at the deer, and by the glance of the arrow killeth a boy that is hidden in a bush: this is murder, for that the act was unlawfull, although A. had no intent to hurt the boy, nor knew not of him."[10] Legal historians see Coke's account of *Lord Dacre's Case* as the basis for a new form of strict liability, one that receives its fullest expression in the legal reporting of the first half of the eighteenth century.

A number of things are crucial about felony murder for our purposes. Like the models of civil liability canvassed in chapter 1, felony murder sees responsibility as causal rather than intentional and is a mechanism for holding persons accountable for things they did not mean to do. Tied to the doctrine of agency, felony murder is also a way of blaming persons for things they did *not* do. Felony murder affirms the liability of principals for the unsolicited acts of their agents, and it recursively maps strict liability back onto those agents, comprising under the heading of a single action more than one act and more than one person. "In order to justify a verdict of murder, it was not necessary to prove that any one of the accused actually did any act that produced death; but that if he were engaged in an unlawful enterprise that was likely to end in some one being killed, and did so end, any one of the accused men, though he had never anticipated such a catastrophe, might nevertheless be held guilty of murder," Justice Michael Foster argues in one of the cases collected in the six-volume edition of *State Trials* printed by Richardson in 1749.[11] "The Person Actually giving the Stoke," Foster explains elsewhere, "is no more than the Hand or Instrument by which the Others strike": "Malice *Egreditur Personam*."[12]

Malice exceeds the person. In felony murder, as in *Clarissa*, neither persons nor actions come to rest. The reproducibility of persons in the novel has seemed to many readers an epistemological problem (indeterminacy); and indeed, epistemology has been the governing rubric for most secondary criticism on *Clarissa*, from Watt to the deconstructive turn and beyond. One exception to this is Ferguson's stunning revision of deconstructive formalism in "Rape and the Rise of the Novel," which argues that "Richardson's achievement in *Clarissa* is to insist on a fundamental mistake in the idea of equating epistemology and psychology."[13] For Ferguson, epistemological indeterminacy is not a scandal for the subject (as it is in William Warner's *Reading "Clarissa,"* where Clarissa cannot be sure she does not desire her own violation). It is instead the way subjectivity works. "Psychological complexity," Ferguson says, "pits the stipulated mental state against one's actual mental state"; "psychology [is] the ongoing possibility of the contradiction between what one must mean and what one wants to mean."[14] Form (legal formalism, social convention, linguistic convention) is an "affront" to and a "trivialization" of the psychology it emblazons; but the tension between depth and form is necessary to personhood and occasions a "mimesis of distinction" that finally insists on "the inability of form to carry mental states in anything but excessively capacious (that is, ambiguous) or potentially self-contradictory stipulated forms."[15] "A system that eliminates ambiguity," Ferguson concludes, is a system that "eliminates persons."[16]

If the elimination of persons is what a certain kind of bad formalism seeks, in Ferguson's formalism persons persist in their capacity to experience themselves as distinct from the way they are represented by others. Personhood is a thin hermeneutics of the self that answers a skepticism too easily "assimilable

to distrust of women" by breaking the "link between the self and the representation of it." Persons are those things—the only things—that might be "opposite" of what they appear.[17] Ontology remains here epistemology. This notion of
personhood is in marked contrast with the model of legal personhood at work
in the doctrine of felony murder, however, which leaves no room for "distinction," which does not allow persons to explain or excuse themselves (even to
themselves), and which thus, on Ferguson's account, does not allow them to *be*
persons. Felony murder is where Richardson consistently turns to answer questions of responsibility, and its centrality to *Clarissa* asks us to rethink the importance of even a thin hermeneutics to this novel and the form it occasions. In the
legal logic Richardson invokes to think through the question of who has caused
and who is to blame for Clarissa's death, persons *are* causes, and personhood is
a question of action rather than understanding—of plot rather than character.
Emplotment—a formalist account of action indifferent to questions of motive
and practices of interiority—emerges not as a challenge to the possibility of
responsibility, as it is, for example, in the deconstructive account of *Clarissa*, nor
as a challenge to the possibility of personhood, as it is for Ferguson.[18] Emplotment is the form responsibility and personhood take.

☙

If murder is a logic of the subject, felony murder is a logic of plot. This is not
simply to say that murder requires mens rea and felony murder does not, for
there is vigorous debate among legal theorists and historians on precisely this
point. In *Lord Dacre's Case*, the defendant and his accomplices entered a park
without permission to hunt, vowing to kill anyone who might resist them; when
one of the members of the group *did* kill a gamekeeper, all were found guilty of
murder and hanged. The case and the doctrine continue to be of interest to legal
scholars because although English law abolished the category of felony murder in 1957, the crime persists in American jurisprudence (as any number of
episodes of *Law and Order* attest). Many commentators see the doctrine as concerned with what is variously called "implied," "constructive," or "transferred"
malice. "The felon's intent in committing the felony attaches, fictitiously, to the
killing," speculates one historian, "and somehow becomes transformed into the
malice aforethought required for murder."[19] Another suggests that the case was
really about the doctrine of agency: "Those not present physically at the killing
were held liable as principals on the theory of constructive *presence*" rather than
constructive malice, he says: "Because *Lord Dacres*' [sic] case involved express
malice, no doctrine finding malice from the intention to commit an unlawful

act was necessary or in fact utilized."[20] Others argue that if felony murder *is* based on a notion of transferred malice, then the idea of felony murder is at best incoherent and at worst unconstitutional. Culpability, they insist, is "nontransferable": because homicide law requires "proof of particular acts and thoughts," felony murder cannot be justified as a "mens rea–imposing mechanism" but only as a rule "justifying a conviction for murder simply on the basis that the defendant committed a felony and a killing occurred."[21] Felony murder is thus more properly thought of as a crime in which "premeditation or malice aforethought is simply not an element": the rule "eliminates a mens rea element in convicting a felon for a killing during the commission of a felony, and results in the rule operating as a strict liability crime: the occurrence of a killing is punished as murder regardless of the defendant's culpability."[22]

The more felony murder moves away from constructive presumptions of malice and toward strict liability—the more it disregards culpability—the more noxious it is to lawyers and legal historians. The test of felony murder, argues George Fletcher, is formal: "The jury does not inquire whether in fact the defendant took an excessive risk of killing another; the inquiry falls rather on whether the defendant committed the underlying felony." "Formal tests of liability," he concludes, are "intrinsic[ally] unjust."[23] Like Oliver Wendell Holmes, Fletcher wants blameworthiness to require negligence ("excessive risk"), which is to say he wants responsibility grounded in an agentive rather than a formal account of the act (for this reason he strenuously objects to the liability of coconspirators "for the substantive crimes, even the unexpected crimes, of [their] partners.")[24] But felony murder instead works on the principal that a "felon must answer for a human death for no reason other than that he or his accomplices *caused* it"; a principal Fletcher ties to other "primitive" modes of expiation—deodand, strict liability, conspiracy and vicarious liability—and that he claims receives its fullest expression in the eighteenth century. "The earlier commentators, Coke and Hale, stressed the role of the unlawful act as a rejoinder to a defense of *per infortunium*," he observes. "It was only with the eighteenth-century commentators, Hawkins and Foster, that the argument shifted to the positive thesis that a felonious intent renders an incidental killing murder."[25] "The felony murder rule arose from obscure historical origins and has developed haphazardly into a harsh and unjust legal doctrine," argues another of its critics. "The contention that an injury can amount to a crime only when inflicted by intention is no provincial or transient notion. It is as universal and persistent in mature systems of law as belief in freedom of the human will and a consequent ability and duty of the normal individual to choose between good and evil."[26]

Two consensus positions emerge from the contemporary literature on felony murder: that there is something deeply wrong with the doctrine and that the excrescence can be traced to eighteenth century jurisprudence.[27] Indeed, the two positions are linked, for what is wrong with the eighteenth century is what is wrong with felony murder: both fail to commit themselves to "modern" principals of responsibility based on intention, volition, and assent. For Fletcher, the problem is the way felony murder transposes the intentionality of one act onto a separate and unintentional act; for other of its critics, the problem is the rule's indifference to intentionality—the way its emphasis on the substantive fact of harm brackets questions about how and why that harm came to be. For some, in other words, felony murder involves a formalist construction of intentionality while for others it involves an equally formalist indifference to intentionality; but in each case, modernity, "maturity," and "justice" emerge only when and if we cease to blame persons for things they did not consciously intend. Yet if, as Fletcher admits, felony murder receives new justification in the eighteenth century, that is because the oscillation between constructive and causal accounts of agency and liability transforms felony murder from the procedural issue it is in Coke (a way of responding to the plea of *per infortunium*) into a theory of responsibility and (legal) subjectivity. It is a theory, it is true, that fails to conform to the model of modernity that emphasizes volition and intention. But perhaps there is more than one way of being modern.[28]

William Hawkins's discussion of felony murder in his 1716 *Treatise of the Pleas of the Crown* begins by opposing accidental killings that are excusable because they occur *per infortunium*—"where one lawfully using a innocent Diversion, as shooting at Butts, or at a bird, &c. by the glancing of an Arrow, or such like Accident, kills another"—with those that are similarly unfortunate but are not thereby excusable.[29] As one reads closely the list of actions that make up the category of inexcusable homicide, however, it is increasingly difficult to discriminate excusable from inexcusable harms and less egregious inexcusable harms, such as manslaughter, from murder. "If a Person kill another by shooting at a Deer, &c. in a third Person's Park, in the doing whereof he is a Trespasser," says Hawkins,

> or by shooting off a gun, or throwing Stones in a City or Highway, or other Place where Men usually resort; or by throwing Stones at another wantonly in Play, which is a dangerous Sport, and has not the least Appearance of any good Intent; or by doing any other such idle Action as cannot but indanger the bodily Hurt of some one or other; or by tilting or playing at Hand-sword without the King's

command; or by parrying with naked Swords covered with Buttons at the Points, or with Swords in the Scabbards, or such like rash Sports, which cannot be used without the manifest Hazard of Life, He is guilty of Manslaughter. And if a Man happen to kill another in the Execution of a malicious and deliberate Purpose to do him a personal Hurt, by wounding or beating him; or in the willful Commission of any unlawful Act, which necessarily tends to raise Tumults and Quarrels, and consequently cannot but be attended with the Danger of personal Hurt to some one or other; as by committing a Riot, robbing a Park, &c. he shall be adjudged guilty of Murder.[30]

Under the category of "homicide" Hawkins includes not only the examples one finds in Coke (shooting at deer in another's park; shooting at fowl with an intent to steal them), but trespasses similar in kind to the "innocent diversions" from which they are nonetheless distinguished. Yet if any "idle action" that "indanger[s] the bodily Hurt of some one or other" is inexcusable—shooting off a gun, throwing stones at play, playing at hand swords—it's hard to see what would indemnify harms caused by playfully shooting at butts or birds.

In calling the killing that occurs as a result of trespassing on another's park "manslaughter," Hawkins follows Sir Matthew Hale's analysis of *Lord Dacre's Case* rather than Coke's, and his doing so signals his desire—one the logic of felony murder continually frustrates—to hang onto the category of the merely accidental (which is to say the excusable) act. Eighteenth-century commentators are often anxious about what it would mean to call accidents "murder," and some, like Hale, refuse to do so. "If A. in his own park shoot at a deer, and the arrow glancing against a tree hits and kills B. this is homicide *per infortunium*, because it was lawful for him to shoot in his own park," says Hale. "But if A. without the license of B. hunt in the park of B. and his arrow glancing from a tree killeth a by-stander, to whom he intended no hurt, this is manslaughter, because the act was unlawful."[31] In *Rex v. Plummer* (1702)—a case in which an accessory to a theft was killed in the course of the felony—Chief Justice Holt ruminates at some length on the difference between Coke and Hale: "Shooting a Deer in another's Park is an unlawful Act: If the Arrow glanceth and kills a Man, this is but Manslaughter, which is contrary to 3 *Inst.* 56 that holds it to be Murder: But Lord *Hale* 31 saith it is but Manslaughter."[32] Holt happens to agree with Coke: "The Design of doing any Act makes it deliberate," he argues, "and if the Fact be deliberate, though no hurt to any Person can be foreseen, yet if the Intent be felonious, and the Fact designed, if committed, would be Felony, and in pursuit thereof a Person is killed by Accident, it will be Murder in him and all his Accomplices." Yet he also sees himself as clarifying something about felony murder that Coke had left unclear: "So if two Men have a Design to steal a Hen," Holt explains, "and one shoots at the Hen for that Purpose, and a Man be killed, it is Murder in both, *because the Design was felonious.* So is Lord *Coke* 56 surely to be understood."[33]

For Holt, an accident can rise to the level of murder only if one retains some commitment to the definition of felony as a crime of intention: "The unlawful Act ought to be deliberate to make the killing Murder," he insists.[34] But Foster notices something about the difference between Coke and Hale that Holt does not: "If [an act] be done in Prosecution of a Felonious Intent it will be Murder, but if the Intent went no further than to commit a bare Trespass, Manslaughter. Though I confess, Lord *Coke* seemeth to think otherwise."[35] Foster sees that intention doesn't solve the problem of whether to call an accidental killing manslaughter or murder, because at issue is not the state of an agent's mind but the form of her action—what Holt calls "design." Certain actions are murderous whether one intends to kill another or not: dueling, rioting, robbery, shooting off guns or throwing stones in a city or at play, and perhaps trespass. "Any formed Design of doing Mischief may be called Malice," Hawkins observes; "not such Killing only as proceeds from premeditated hatred or Revenge against the Person killed, but also in many other Cases, such as is accompanied with those Circumstances that shew the Heart to be perversely Wicked, is adjudged to be of Malice prepense, and consequently Murder."[36] Malice is a "formed Design," but "design" is not identical with "premeditation"; indeed, in all but the most clear-cut of cases (poisoning, stabbing), prepensed malice is extracted after the fact from circumstances or consequences that "shew the Heart": "Malice *post-pense*," Hawkins might have called it. What he does call it is "implied malice,"

> such as happens in the Execution of an unlawful Action, principally intended for some other Purpose, and not to do a personal Injury to him in particular who is slain. . . . 1. In Duelling. 2. In killing another without any Provocation, or upon a slight one. 3. In killing one whom the Person killing intended to hurt in a less Degree.[37]

"When the Law maketh use of the Term *Malice aforethought* as descriptive of the Crime of Murder," Foster agrees,

> it is not to be understood in that Narrow Restrained Sense to which the Modern Use of the Word *Malice* is apt to lead one, *a Principle of Malevolence to Particulars;* for the Law by the Malice in this Instance meaneth that the Fact hath been at-

tended with such Circumstances as are the ordinary Symptoms of a Wicked, Depraved, Malignant Spirit.[38]

Foster distinguishes between malice understood as a disposition one person has toward another and as an epiphenomenon of a subject's emplotment in a structure that exceeds her but also describes her. "Malice" thus marks a legal subject's character, but character manifested in the tendency of her action rather than the quality of her mind. "The *Malus Animus,* which is to be collected from all the Circumstances," Foster concludes, "is what bringeth the Offence within the Denomination of Wilful Malicious Murder, *whatever might be the immediate Motive to it.*"[39] "Willfulness" is distinguished from "motive" here, and Foster's murderer is in the odd position of finding that her will was directed toward something other than she intended.

If will is not motive, what is it? For Foster, "will" is less a property of an agent than of her action; it marks the directionality of an offense—those circumstances that "attended" an act and which alone make it malicious—and something like its subatomic structure, the motive force manifested in the form of a given action (form as the entelechy of an act). In both Hawkins's and Foster's histories, dueling is one of the more frequently invoked of those actions that are, as Foster puts it, *malem in se:*

> Deliberate Duelling, if Death ensueth, is in the Eye of the Law Murder; . . . and though a Person should be drawn into a duel, not upon a Motive so criminal, but merely upon the Punctilio of what the *Swordsmen falsly call Honour,* that will not Excuse. For He that Deliberately seeketh the Blood of another upon a private Quarrel acteth in Defiance of all Laws Human and Divine, whatever his Motive may be.[40]

Once again we find terms that would seem to be synonymous—deliberation, motive—distinguished from one another. Distinction is not, perhaps, contradiction: "deliberation" describes a mental operation (whether to act or forbear acting) and "motive" a rationale for the course of action that is decided on.[41] Yet there *is* something contradictory about Foster's claim that a duelist deliberately does what he means not to do; the syntax of the sentence insists that even a duelist whose express motive is *not* "to seeketh the Blood of another" deliberately seeks blood: the act is murder and the actor is a murderer even though he intended to prevent harm, even though he (and others) might see himself as engaged in an undertaking of the highest virtue. "Where-ever two Persons in cool Blood meet and fight on a precedent Quarrel, and one of them is killed, the other is guilty of Murder," explains Hawkins, "and cannot help himself by alleging that . . . he meant not to kill, but only to disarm, his Adversary: For since he deliberately engaged in an Act highly unlawful, in Defiance of the Laws, he must at his Peril abide the Consequences thereof."[42]

The man who acts at his peril, according to Holmes, is acting under the jurisdiction of the law of torts, whose overarching principle is that "a man is answerable for all the consequences of his acts, or, in other words . . . he acts at his peril always and wholly irrespective of the state of his consciousness upon the matter."[43] Although Hawkins and Foster mean for the doctrine of felony murder to be consistent with the intentionalism of the criminal law, the logic of their arguments—the way the attempt to ground liability for accidental killings in a constructive model of intent continually points to the irrelevance of an agent's state of mind—is in the end a tortious one. This is indeed how many modern commentators understand their legacy (and thus there is an interesting isomorphism between the practices Hawkins and Foster describe and their own practice, which turns out to have done one thing when it imagines itself to be doing another). "With the exception of involuntary manslaughter, which carries a significantly lighter sanction, felony murder is the only form of homicide that requires no specific mental element as to the death," argues an anonymous author in the *Harvard Law Review*. "Absence of a mens rea requirement is commonplace in tort law, and in this respect felony murder resembles a tort more than it resembles a murder."[44] Like others, this author objects to the absence of mens rea: "A crime of homicide in which the mental state is irrelevant [cannot] possibly be reconciled with the basic principles of criminal law," she insists. "It is [not] acceptable to have a strict liability homicide comparable to a strict liability tort."[45] For his part, Holmes thinks that even a strict liability tort is unacceptable. Such laws "make a defendant responsible for all damage, however remote, of which his act could be called the cause," he complains, and this emphasis on causation entails a troubling (and paradoxical) lack of emphasis on the actness of an act—entails thinking of action as motion rather than volition.[46] The law's "requirement of an act," Holmes insists, "is the requirement that the defendant should have made a choice": "A choice which entails a concealed consequence is as to that consequence no choice."[47]

The doctrine of felony murder depends on the assumption that certain acts manifest "concealed consequences," and this assumption, as Holmes understands it, does something peculiar to the relationship between agents and their actions. The peculiarity is not lost on the eighteenth-century commentators. "The Law so abhors all Duelling in cold Blood, that not only the Principal who actually kills the other, but also his Seconds are guilty of Murder, whether they fought or not," Hawkins observes, "and some have gone so far as to hold, That the Seconds of the Person killed are also equally guilty"—a position that to him "seems too severe a construction to make a Man by such Reasoning the Murderer of his Friend, to whom he was so far from intending any Mischief, that he was ready to hazard his own Life in his Quarrel."[48] Hawkins is concerned here with what has come to be called the "merger doctrine," a version of felony murder in which the constructive logic tying an agent to the unintended consequences of his own act is invoked to tie accessories to the acts of principals. According to Foster, "merger" is what *Lord Dacre's Case* is all about. The case turns on the assumption that

> every Person *present in the Sense of the Law* when the Homicide hath been Committed, hath been involved in the Guilt of Him that gave the mortal Blow. . . . The Offences [the parties] stood charged with as Principals were Committed far out of their Sight and Hearing; and yet [they] were held to be present. It was sufficient that at the Instant the Facts were committed They were of the same party and upon the same Pursuit, and under the same Engagement . . . with Those that did the Facts.[49]

The merger doctrine converts inaction into action (the seconds, in Hawkins's example, are guilty "whether they fought or not"), self-sacrificial friendship into execution, absence into presence, accessories into principals, multiple acts into one act (the "fact"), multiple persons into one person (the "principal"). Foster's description highlights the odd temporality and spatiality of the doctrine: at "the instant the Facts are committed," bodies are transported from one location to another and distinct pursuits are distilled into a moment. But this instantaneousness is also a radical form of duration, since what's being said is that the act of killing originated in the conspiracy to commit robbery—a felonious act that has not come to rest or rather that comes to rest only when it is transmuted into the killing it always already was.

As the landmark twentieth-century cases of felony murder attest, the doctrine is most controversial, and most itself, when remoteness is at issue. Two cases are particularly significant for the way they foreground the sort of questions that perplex Lovelace: how can an agent be responsible for what she could not have foreseen, and how can she be responsible for someone else's intervening act? In *People v. Stamp* (1969), robbers were convicted of murder when the victim suffered a heart attack after the robbery, the court arguing (along lines that echo the debate between Lord M. and his nephew) that felony murder is not limited to those deaths which are foreseeable. Rather, a felon is held strictly liable for all killings committed by him or his accomplices in the course of the felony. As long as the homicide is the direct causal result of the robbery the felony-murder rule applies *whether or not the death was a natural or probable consequence* of the robbery.[50]

In *Stephenson v. State* (1932), a homicide conviction was upheld when a rape victim poisoned herself in the hours following the crime and died a month later.[51] Both cases are characterized by interruptions in a strictly linear model of causation; both are cases in which the court "recognized felony murder liability in the absence of foreseeability, based solely upon cause-in-fact."[52] I want to concentrate on the rape case, however, because it has been talked about by philosophers of (legal) causation and because the way it is talked about brings into focus the ontological stakes of felony murder doctrine—for Richardson, and for us.

According to H. L. A. Hart and Tony Honoré's *Causation in the Law, Stephenson v. State* was less about "whether or not the defendant's force had continued to operate harmfully until death occurred" than about "whether it was socially advantageous to give legal effect to the relation between the defendant's acts and the death."[53] The claim, in other words, is that the case is not concerned with what I have been calling "plot" (actions that do not come to rest) but with character. The accused "raped [the] deceased," they note,

> in circumstances of great brutality, biting her all over the body. He then removed her to a hotel room where she took a large dose of bi-chloride of mercury. . . . She died a month later partly of the effects of the chloride poisoning and partly from a breast wound inflicted by defendant which resulted in an abscess.[54]

Stephenson appealed the felony murder conviction, arguing that the "taking of poison was the intervening act of a responsible actor, viz. a voluntary act," and although the appeal was not successful, Hart and Honoré argue that it should have been. "The real question," they insist, was not whether this was a defendant of "unexampled viciousness" but "whether the provision, by an unlawful act, of a reason for another voluntarily to kill himself amounts to 'killing' that person or 'causing' his death."[55] "The solution most in accordance with common-sense principles," they conclude, "is that it does not amount to 'causing' the death, considered as a physical event, because a voluntary act intervenes, nor to 'causing' the deceased to take her own life, because no compulsion is used."[56]

The naive literalism of Hart and Honoré's account of "volition" and "compulsion" is typical of critiques of strict liability. (As is the misogyny: one sees here why feminism has for the most part committed itself to a skepticism about volition, and why, as I go on to suggest, strict liability might be a feminist alternative to volitionist standards of responsibility.) The decision in *Stephenson v. State*, they argue, is predicated on a "dangerous" principle: "that a person whose conduct excites moral disapproval may be punished for doing what he has not done."[57] Because they cannot imagine action in anything but volitional terms, they cannot imagine punishing persons for accidents—and so they invoke a rationale that sits uncomfortably with the logic of strict liability: "moral disapproval."

I return to this observation below. For now I want to note that for Hart and Honoré, *Stephenson v. State* manifests the kind of "noncommonsensical" thinking about causality that *Causation in the Law* is designed to contest. The details of their critique of those (like Richard Posner) who see tort as an issue of economic policy and those (like Richard Epstein) who see tort as a form of corrective justice are not important for our purposes. What *is* important is what they take to be at stake in the two positions. The problem with Posner's "causal minimalism," for Hart and Honoré, is that a model of causation committed to determining the person best able to bear the economic burden of liability—the person whose "conduct must have been at least a sine qua non of the increased cost for which he is required to compensate"—requires the conflation of different actions and different agents.[58] Although "it will very often be the case that one man A has by his earlier action created conditions which another, B, later exploits; and that A's action is a condition sine qua non of what B brings about by his," they object, "this relationship does not lead to the conclusion that B's action is part of A's action. A's action ends where B's action begins; the latter is, despite their sine qua non connection, a 'new action,' *novus actus*."[59] The problem with Epstein's "causal maximalism," on the other hand, is that the assumption that liability is a "moral principal that those who cause harm to others should compensate them for the harm so caused" "implies a system of universal strict liability, such that no activity could be pursued except at the cost of paying for the harm . . . which it generates."[60] The problem, in other words, is that in their contrary ways causal minimalism and causal maximalism are indifferent to a value that preoccupies Hart and Honoré: the individual. "The idea that individuals are primarily responsible for the harm which their actions are sufficient to produce without the intervention of others or of extraordinary natural events is important, not merely to law and morality, but to the preservation of something else of great moment in human life," they assert. This thing of great moment in human life is nothing less than the status of the human person *as such*—"the individual's sense of himself as a separate person whose character is manifested in such actions":

> This sense of respect for ourselves and others as distinct persons would be much weakened, if not dissolved, if we could not think of ourselves as separate authors of the changes we make in the world. . . . For the allocation and apportionment of responsibility for the changes which human action brings about would in that case be inherently a matter of dispute; there would be nothing that we could unequivocally claim to be *our doing*.[61]

Hart and Honoré are right that felony murder "dissolves" the idea of "distinct persons" and *novum actum*. But if this dissolution of the category of the individual is a kind of ethical gesture—and it is—then it is a gesture that does not concern itself with the "viciousness" of one person or the "moral disapproval" of another. Richardson's understanding of the logic of strict liability is more precise on this score than theirs, for he recognizes it as a species of judgment that detaches responsibility from "viciousness" and blame from the disapprobation of character. Richardson understands that if strict liability makes it difficult for persons to think of themselves as separate from others, this does not mean there is nothing we can unequivocally claim to be "our doing." It means, on the contrary, that there is nothing we can unequivocally claim is *not* our doing. This is an insight *Clarissa* insists on and that the novel's characters—all but Clarissa herself—refuse. Clarissa strenuously condemns herself for that "unhappy rashness; which (although involuntary as to the act) from the moment it was committed carried with it its own punishment" (1372). "I know not how it comes about," she explains to Anna early in her trials, "but I am, in my own opinion, a poor lost creature: and yet cannot charge myself with one criminal or faulty inclination" (565). "Do you know, my dear, how this can be?" she asks and answers: "Yes I can tell you *how*, I believe—One devious step at setting out!" (565–66). A logic of action and accountability that is pervasive in the novel informs Clarissa's sense that "the event has justified [her family] and condemned me" (1119), that abduction, rape, and death are "remote, yet sure" (381) consequences of the proscribed communication with Lovelace, that these actions, as the use of the singular ("event") implies are in some sense *the same action*. It is a logic, like felony murder itself, that oscillates between constructive intent and causal maximalism—it does not easily give up the notion that responsibility is tied to fault (and thus to intention, volition, foresight), and yet it also ultimately imagines what Clarissa imagines: that it is possible to be responsible without being "faulty." Belford says that Clarissa is "the most unblamable lady in the world" (1296)—"No dividing of blame with her!" (1344), Lovelace agrees. But the novel *does* divide blame, distributing it between Lovelace and Clarissa and among all of those whose actions are, however accidentally, the sine qua non of the novel's tragic plot.

❦

The language of constructive intent is everywhere in *Clarissa,* never more so than when Lovelace is doing the talking. Following Clarissa's abduction, Lovelace "sit[s] down to argue with [himself]" (427) about whom to blame for the event. "Why does she blame herself!" he wonders. "Had she been capable of error? . . . The fact, the error, is not before us," he concludes (427). Lovelace invokes and quickly dismisses Clarissa's explanation for their correspondence:

> Her principal view was to prevent mischief between her brother and her other friends, and the man vilely insulted by them all.
>
> But why should she be more concerned for the safety of others than they were for their own? (428)

Unable to imagine such concern, Lovelace "suppose[s] another motive": "Let LOVE then be the motive—love of *whom? A Lovelace* is the answer" (428). The imperative voice highlights Lovelace's investment in the practice of construction, and the motive that he constructs for Clarissa is, as he anticipates, one with normative force in the world of the novel. Just before the abduction, Anna, who describes herself as one "for ever . . . endeavouring to trace effects to their causes," attributes to Clarissa the same "latent, unowned inclination" (356) as Lovelace construes for her, and after the abduction Belford asserts: "That she loves thee, wicked as thou art, and cruel as a panther, there is no reason to doubt" (502).

Clarissa is quick to recognize the pervasiveness of the logic of constructive motive and to see how intimately it is tied to the logic of heteronormative affiliation. "See you not how from step to step, he grows upon me?" she asks Anna less than a month before she is raped. "I tremble to look back upon his encroachments" (643). Since the abduction, Clarissa has taken to describing her fault as an overinvestment in her own agency and as a failure to take seriously Lovelace's "encroachments":

> Oh the vile encroacher! Thus to lead a young creature (too much indeed relying upon her own strength) from evil to evil!—This last, although the remote, yet the sure consequences of my first—my prohibited correspondence! (381)

"I thought I could proceed or stop as I pleased," she reflects; yet even before the abduction Clarissa learns that "one step brings on another with this encroaching sex!" (345). "I can see by this man that once a woman embarks with this sex," Clarissa tells Anna, "there is no receding. One concession is but the prelude to another with them (525): "How vain a thing to say what we will or what we will not do, when we have put ourselves into the power of this sex!" (528). A woman who gives a man "the least encouragement" is invariably "carried beyond her intentions, and out of her own power!" (345):

> Well are we instructed to keep this sex at a distance. An undesigning open heart, where it is loath to disoblige, is easily drawn in, I see, to oblige more than ever it designed. (269–70)

The abduction scene literalizes the logic of constructive consent outlined by Clarissa—how men "lead," "carry," and "draw" women from small to larger forms of assent. Clarissa describes Lovelace as "drawing me after him" (374), "putting his arm round me and again drawing me with a gentle force" (375), "again drawing me after him" (376), "drawing me swiftly after him" (380): "My fears . . . would not have suffered me to know what course to take," she says, "had I not had him to urge and draw me after him" (380).

Clarissa's alignment of the temporality of assent with the temporality of seduction is affirmed by Lovelace, who makes it clear why motive—and "love" as the most universally comprehensible of motives—is necessary to the rake. "Love is an encroacher," he says. "Love never goes backward. Love is always aspiring. Always must aspire" (704). Love's aspiration is in large part an effect of the inertia of male desire: "*The woman who resents no initiatory freedoms must be lost*," Lovelace asserts, for "nothing but the highest act of love can satisfy an indulged love" (704). Desire once set in motion will not—cannot—be stopped, and Clarissa's cousin Morden confirms that this resistless instrumental causality characterizes the rake's plots as well as his body: "How do you know, if you once give way, where you shall be suffered, where you shall be *able*, to stop?" (563), he asks her. "A libertine, my dear cousin, a plotting, an intriguing libertine, must be generally remorseless—*unjust* he must always be" (563). What the libertine is particularly remorseless about is fulfilling the (seduction) plot he has initiated: "He is always plotting to extend the mischiefs he delights in" (563).

If the libertine is "a plotting, an intriguing" being, however, the repetition of the word "must" calls into question any simple association of plot with volitional action (or motive). Initially, and especially following the abduction,

Lovelace describes himself not only as the agent of his own intricate contrivance but of the acts of those caught in its web. "I knew that the whole stupid family were in a combination to do my business for me," he confides to Belford:

> I told thee that they were all working for me, like so many underground moles; and still more blind than the moles are said to be, unknowing that they did so. I myself, the director of their principal motions; which falling in with the malice of their little hearts, they took to be all their own. (387)

Earlier he explains to Belford how he uses James Harlowe's servant, Joseph Leman, to

> play [Harlowe] off as I please; . . . permitting so much to be revealed of my life and actions, and intentions, as may give him such a confidence in his double-faced agent, as shall enable me to dance his employer upon my own wires. . . . By this engine, whose springs I am continually oiling, I play them all off. (144–145)

James, Joseph, and the entire Harlowe clan are automata moved by Lovelace's plot; and Joseph—who unlike the Harlowes knows he is being moved—describes Lovelace's encroachment on him in ways that echo Clarissa: "How have I been led from littel stepps to grate stepps!" he complains (385).

But as the *novel*'s plot unfolds—a plot that begins to diverge in significant ways from Lovelace's—the rake finds that he is more encroached on than encroaching. Belford is among the first to challenge Lovelace's sovereign motivity, and the form this challenge takes turns explicitly on the question of plotting and emplotment. "At the time thou art forming schemes to ruin [Clarissa]," he observes, "is she not labouring under a father's curse laid upon her by thy means, and for thy sake? And wouldst thou give operation and completion to this curse?" (604). Belford's account of Lovelace's agency is quite delicate. Lovelace is somehow at once the source of and a mere vehicle for the sentence imposed on Clarissa; his schemes fulfill an action against her that is no longer, perhaps never was, his own:

> Thou that vainly imaginest that the whole family of the Harlowe's, and that of the Howes too, are but thy machines, unknown to themselves, to bring about thy purposes and thy revenge, what art thou more or better than the instrument even of her implacable brother and envious sister, to perpetuate the disgrace of the most excellent of sisters, which they are moved to by vilely low and sordid motives?— Canst thou bear, Lovelace, to be thought the machine of thy inveterate enemy James Harlowe? (604)

Belford means to chasten Lovelace by suggesting that the Harlowes control a plot he only helps to implement; yet it is a notion Lovelace himself has put in circulation to serve his own interests: "But don't think me the *cause* neither of her family's malice and resentment," he has cautioned Belford. "I work but with their materials. . . . I only guide the effects: the cause is in their malignant hearts" (464). Lovelace accedes to his instrumentality here not because he thinks himself a machine ("I guide the effects") but because he knows that if others think him a machine they will assume he is not responsible for what he is moved to do.

Once he begins to contemplate the necessity of Clarissa's rape, however, Lovelace begins to speak more seriously of his mechanism: "So now, Belford, as thou hast said, I am a machine at last, and no free agent" (848), he asserts in the days leading up to the crime. Indeed, after the fire scene—the scene of attempted rape that briefly sends Clarissa out of Lovelace's clutches and confirms him in his resolve against her—there is a perceptible shift from talk of his "encroaching" mastery of "the world's construction" (575) to talk of his compulsion by the constructions (of plots and persons) he has set in motion. That the shift happens around an event Lovelace calls "*truly* accidental" (827) but that simulates accident in a complex, and final, effort to construe Clarissa's consent is significant. Lovelace assures Clarissa that both the fire that sent her into his arms in a state of undress and the uncontrollable effusion of passion that this unexpected intimacy produced were accidental. "Mrs Sinclair and the nymphs are all of opinion that I am now so much of a favourite," he explains to Belford, "that I may do what I will, and plead violence of *passion;* which, they will have it, makes violence of *action* pardonable with their sex; as well as an allowed extenuation with the unconcerned of both sexes" (702). Lovelace admits to exploiting a normative social logic that conceives of passion as a form of compulsion that turns agents into (sex) machines, a logic tying passion to accident and accident, necessarily, to "extenuation." He assumes Clarissa will be persuaded by such a logic, but she is not: "*If* a sudden impulse, the effects of an unthought-of accident, cannot be forgiven—" (729), he fumes, angered by Clarissa's perverse tendency to blame rather than excuse accident. The anger is bluster of course: he knows, and she does too, that neither the room's heat nor his own was accidental. And yet if he is not acting accidentally, he is not quite acting on his own terms. Lovelace's confession to Belford that the "nymphs" provoked this last plot that can plausibly be called his own reveals a dependency on others that escalates as the tragic plot unfolds. "Yet already have I not gone too far?" he asks Belford as he decides whether to marry or to rape. "Shall Tomlinson, shall these women, be engaged?" he reflects. "Shall so many engines be set at work, at an immense expense, with infinite contrivance; and all to no purpose?" (878).

Lovelace's claim that he *must* rape Clarissa because the engines in his employ and the engine of his plot have been "set at work" has not, for the most part, been taken seriously by critics of the novel. The notion that he might not bear sole responsibility for the calamities visited on Clarissa has been anathema to feminists in particular (including myself in an earlier incarnation).[62] There is good reason for this: deconstructive critics, self-consciously modeling themselves on Lovelace's own strategies of inculpation, deflected attention away from the rake, making "language," or Clarissa herself, the agent of violation. (Close reading was a hermeneutics of suspicion culminating in a hackneyed misogyny: she wanted it, she asked for it.) Thus, Ferguson, for example, criticizes Lovelace for wanting responsibility "always to be dispersed, diffused among a number of persons other than himself," a strategy evident in his "desperate effort to multiply himself retroactively to make it look as though there was anyone at the rape except himself."[63] She discounts, as I once did, the possibility that the agency of and responsibility for the rape might truly *be* "diffused." But it is precisely this possibility that Clarissa repeatedly invokes. "What you, or Mrs. Sinclair, or somebody I cannot tell who, have done to my poor head, you best know," she writes in her first letter to Lovelace following the rape. "Alas! You have killed my head among you—I don't say who did it—God forgive you all!" (894–95). "I was so senseless that I dare not aver that the horrid creatures of the house were personally aiding and abetting," she tells Anna, "but some visionary remembrances I have of female figures flitting, as I may say, before my sight; the wretched woman's particularly" (1011). Clarissa's suggestion that Sinclair and her myrmidons "aided and abetted" Lovelace in his crime is consistent with Lovelace's own account of the event: "Thou wilt guess," he admits to Belford, "that some *little* art has been made use of. . . . A contrivance I never had occasion for before, and had not thought of now if Mrs. Sinclair had not proposed it to me: to whom I left the management of it" (887). "Mrs. Sinclair is a true heroine," he continues in a subsequent letter

> and, I think, shames us all. And she is a woman too! Thou'lt say the best things corrupted become the worst. But this is certain, that whatever the sex set their hearts upon, they make thorough work of it. And hence it is that a mischief which would end in simple robbery among men-rogues, becomes murder if a woman be in it. (896)

Judith Wilt is alone among critics in suggesting that Clarissa's rape "was carried out by the man's female 'accomplices.' "[64] Ferguson complains that Wilt "argues that the rape may well not have occurred"; but Wilt seems to me less interested in the metaphysical question of whether the act occurred or the epistemological question of whether the act was rape than in what it would mean to imagine that whatever was done, Lovelace wasn't the one (or the only one) to do it. "In the rhetoric of the book as a whole," she observes,

> we are not really invited to consider Lovelace merely a cowardly egoist for trying to palm off responsibility for his nature or his "art" on the women in his life. . . . The rhetoric of the book somehow proposes both that he is a coward and egoist for using this excuse and that it is not an excuse but the truth. They did it, and Lovelace was their tool.[65]

Wilt assumes that to imagine that Lovelace does not act is to imagine that he is not to blame, and she indicts Richardson for this apparent deflection of blame away from Lovelace and onto Sinclair, which is to say away from man and onto woman. The "intuition that governs [Richardson's] imagination," she concludes, is "the intuition that Sin and Death are woman."[66] Yet the claim that instrumentality (being someone's tool) precludes responsibility is a position Lovelace himself articulates through the course of the novel, one that it would be a mistake to align with Richardson. Wilt raises questions about Lovelace's agency and his guilt, she says, "not so that they may be answered as in a court of law." But Richardson's imagination is nothing if not legal, and the way he goes about thinking through the problem of Lovelace's accomplices requires a reformulation of Wilt's own intuition: he did it, the novel insists, and he was their tool.

That the novel complicates the question of Lovelace's agency but not the question of his responsibility can be difficult to see given how strenuously Clarissa and her champions tie (his) responsibility to premeditation and (her) innocence to accident. Nowhere is the claim that accidental acts are "unblamable" more powerfully deployed than in Clarissa's defense. "She is quite blameless," Anna tells Clarissa's governess Mrs. Norton after the abduction; "she had no intention to go off with this man" (583). After the rape Clarissa commits herself to uncovering evidence of Lovelace's complex perfidy and her corresponding ignorance—evidence proving that "I have been not accidentally but premeditatively, and of set purpose, drawn in after him" (985), that "all his guilt was premeditated" (1077), that hers was "an accidental, not a premeditated error" (987). Despite her early education in the constructive logic of Lovelace's encroachments, Clarissa's investment in the integrity of her intentions dies hard. She escapes from Mrs. Sinclair after the fire because she correctly perceives that seduction is the final encroachment toward which Lovelace's constructions have been leading. And yet her response to her liberation is to forget the lesson of her imprisonment and to return to a language of agency, intention, and consent that had reached its apogee in the struggle over Solmes—"I will say nothing but No, as long as I shall be able to speak. And who will presume to look upon such an act of violence as a marriage?" (365)—but that the experience of abduction had persuaded her to abandon: the experience, as Clarissa describes it, of "my voice . . . contradicting my action; crying, No, no, no" (380) all the while Lovelace draws her after him.

Clarissa reads her escape from Mrs. Sinclair's house, that is, as an escape from an aberrant lair of constructive assent to a realm of freedom marked by the possibility of authentic agency and agreement. "I will transact for myself what relates to myself" (777), she informs Lovelace; "I will, now that I have escaped from you, and that I am out of the reach of your mysterious desires, wrap myself up in my own innocence (and then she passionately folded her arms about herself)" (797). This self-embrace reinforces the disastrous conflations at work in Clarissa's declaration of independence: the naive conflation of one's own assessment with that of others, the conflation of innocence with an innocence of intention. She fails to remember that the problem with intention and consent is not that they are deformed by the constructions of others: "To say you did not intend it when you met him," Anna observes after the abduction, "who will believe it?" (407), and Clarissa knows that she is right, that intentions are always, as Justice Foster reminds us, extracted ex post facto from acts that they are retroactively invoked to explain. "A dear silly soul!" reflects Lovelace, "to depend upon the goodness of her own heart, when the heart cannot be seen into but by its actions; and she, to appearance, a runaway, an eloper, from a tender, a most indulgent husband!" (789). Intention *is* a constructive logic, and Lovelace's constructions do not mark any special depravity on his part but his thoroughgoing conventionality. This is what Ferguson makes us see in "Rape and the Rise of the Novel": that Lovelace, like everyone else, thinks "the forms of actions . . . carry mental states like intention and consent within them."[67] Clarissa's "achievement," she says, is to refuse to allow Lovelace to construe consent from nonconsent, which she accomplishes by answering his insistent representationalism (the equation of a self with its representation) with a mimesis of distinction that while it does not solve the problem of intention makes it possible, as I've noted, to imagine that intentions, and selves, might be "opposite" of what they appear.[68] I want us to see something else: that such an argument continues to tie questions of responsibility and personhood to practices of interiority that it is *Richardson*'s achievement to have moved beyond.[69]

Richardson detaches responsibility from individuals and their interiors in the course of—and as a consequence of—a complex meditation on the liability of principals and accessories. "It is good," Lovelace explains to Joseph Leman in the letter laying out the plan for Clarissa's abduction, "to provide against every accident in such an important case as this" (384–85). Lovelace often describes the use of accessories as an index of his own agency and foresight—his capacity to provide, as he puts it, against accident. But accessories also function *as* accidents, signs that the principal has not acted. *"Always be careful of back doors* is a maxim with me in all my exploits," Lovelace tells Belford; "I can talk as familiarly to servants as to principals, when I have a mind to make it worth their while to oblige me in anything—Then servants are but as the common soldiers in an army: they do all the mischief; frequently without malice, and merely, good souls! for mischief sake" (448). Lovelace cynically inverts the language of vicarious liability here, acknowledging that servants engage in undertakings whose motives lie elsewhere and yet insisting that the mischief that ensues is done by and belongs to them. Such a claim goes against late seventeenth-century developments in the doctrine of agency discussed in chapter 1, which established that a master who was previously liable for a servant's acts only if he had commanded them "could be made vicariously liable for acts which he did not command, provided that they were for his benefit and in the course of employment."[70] Lovelace's rejection of vicarious liability is explicitly contravened by his own servants, who are quite conscious that it is *not*, in fact, "the privilege of a principal to lay all his own faults upon his underlings, and never be to blame himself" (741). "Joseph is plaguy squeamish again" (465), Lovelace tells Belford after the boy writes to express concern that his "dearest young lady should come to harm" and that he should be held accountable for "all bad mischiefs, and all bad ends." "But *natheless* I am in hope of repentance hereafter, being but a young man, if I do wrong through ignorance," Joseph gently threatens, "your honour being a great man and great wit; and I a poor creature not worthy notice; and your honour able to answer for all" (495).

Joseph's letter arrives in the context of another threat—the threat of legal action against Lovelace for the rape and subsequent death of a Miss Betterton of Nottingham. This minor subplot hasn't much interested critics of the novel, but it interests me for the way a story about the metamorphosis of action (rape into death) emerges in the context of a meditation on the metamorphosis of persons (servants into masters). Joseph informs Lovelace that the Harlowes are "plotting to revive the resentments of that family against [him]" (465), and Anna tells Clarissa that "they talk of a prosecution which will be set up against him for some crime or other that they have got a notion of" (475). The crime remains ambiguous until the editor, summarizing Joseph's letter, confirms that the charge is "for a rape upon Miss Betterton, whom by a stratagem [Lovelace] had got into his hands; and who afterwards died in child-bed" (494). That the crime is designated a rape does not dispel the sense that there is another crime at stake in the story, for Miss Betterton's pregnancy and death is a familiar apotheosis of the encroaching logic of heterosexuality, and, it turns out, a familiar end to Lovelace's predations. Anna tells Clarissa that "had he a dozen lives, if all I have heard be true, he might have forfeited them all, and been dead *twenty crimes* ago": "Ask him after Miss Betterton and what became of her" she enjoins Clarissa, "and if he shuffle and prevaricate, question him about Miss Lockyear—Oh my dear, the man's a villain!" (576). Since he has boasted of seducing countless women (he has "served twenty and twenty women as bad or worse," Mowbray later avers [1360]), what ties Miss Lockyear to Miss Betterton must be the fatal consequences of the seduction rather than the seduction itself.

Lovelace confirms that his plots have a tendency to move in this macabre direction, recounting for Belford the "seduction" of a French woman whose lack of consent he doesn't even bother to conceal. "I took my advantage of the lady herself, who durst not for her life cry out: drew her after me to the next apartment," he says. "We had contrivances afterwards equally ingenious, in which the lady, the ice once broken (*once subdued, always subdued*), co-operated." After being thrown out of doors by her husband, he explains, she "was obliged to throw herself into my protection—nor thought herself unhappy in it, till childbed pangs seized her: then penitence, and death, overtook her in the same hour!" (675). When he intercepts a letter from Anna to Clarissa referring to "new stories" about him, he adds more fatalities to the list: "Can this particular story, which this girl hints at, be Lucy Villars?—Or can she have heard of my intrigue with the pretty gipsy, who met me in Norwood, and of the trap I caught her cruel husband in?" "But he was not quite drowned. The man is alive at this day" (863), Lovelace objects, and in the objection establishes that the kind of story one might have heard about him is a story in which rape repeatedly metastasizes into death.

If Lovelace is an avowed serial rapist, then, he is also a serial *killer*. But he is an odd sort of killer, for with the exception of the not-quite-drowned husband, each of these deaths occurs at a temporal distance from the initial crime and in the absence of any proximate act of his own. For Lovelace, action at a distance is no action, and if one has not acted one is not to blame. This presumption accounts for his confidence in assuring Joseph that in the affair of Miss Betterton "there is no room to fear for either his head or his neck" (495). The ambiguous pronominal reference produced by the editor's second person reportage implies that the indemnity he extends to himself extends as well to his servant: "The law was not made for such a man as me" (569), Lovelace elsewhere proclaims. When Tomlinson too begins to worry that "if anything should happen amiss to this admirable lady, through my means, I shall have more cause for self-reproach than for all the bad actions of my life put together," Lovelace assures him that he employs agents in order to avoid harm by procuring (or at least construing) consent: "What, thinkest thou, have I taken all the pains I have taken, and engaged so many persons in my cause, but to avoid the necessity of violent compulsion?" (837). Again Lovelace insists that action at a distance is a kind of inaction: the consent secured by Tomlinson deflects responsibility away from him and his employer, making sex the woman's own deed and thus making it impossible to imagine that she has been harmed. This thought momentarily placates Tomlinson: "I am dough in your hands, to be moulded into what shape you please," he acquiesces. But he soon returns to the question of Clarissa's harm and his own liability and is interrupted by Lovelace who accuses him of "washing thine own hands (don't I know thee?), that thou mayst have something to silence thy conscience with by loading me." "We have gone too far to recede," Lovelace asserts; "Are not all our engines in readiness?" The plural possessive registers Lovelace's attempt to escape responsibility by sharing it, attributing to Tomlinson an action he only pretends to answer for: "If thou *art* dough, *be* dough; and I slapped himself on the shoulder," he recounts himself saying. "Resume but thy former shape—and I'll be answerable for the event" (838).

What Lovelace means, of course, is that he will answer for the event of animating his engines but not for any event occasioned by such alchemy. On the one hand he turns the persons in his employ into machines. But what looks like dehumanization is more properly a kind of personification, as the creatures thus set in motion are imagined to act under their own power and on their own behalf rather than their maker's. Lovelace's commitment to limiting his liability turns on a value that is often aligned with Clarissa (and with *Clarissa*) but that the novel repudiates as ruthlessly as it withholds Lovelace's indemnity: the individual. Lovelace wants his agents to be individuals so that they cannot be mistaken for anyone else, most essentially for himself. This is what he wants for his victims as well, whose (construed) consent ensures that sex acts appear as *their* acts, things they own as surely, and as solely, as they own the pregnant bodies that kill them. Given that he aligns responsibility with clearly individuated acts and agents, it makes sense that Lovelace disavows responsibility for the crowded rape scene described by Clarissa. As I've said, I want to think of this as something other than cynicism, to take seriously Lovelace's claim that he is *"compelled to be the wretch my choice has made me!"*—that the rape is an unwanted outcome of a plot he no longer controls. "Yet already have I not gone too far?" he asks. "Like a repentant thief, afraid of his gang and obliged to go on in fear of hanging till he comes to be hanged, I am afraid of the gang of my cursed contrivances" (848). But if Lovelace's claim that he is haplessly moved along by others is meant to exculpate him, the legal metaphor he invokes—the law of accomplices, the merger doctrine—ironically forecloses the exculpation it seems to ensure.

Once again, Lovelace's agents understand this more clearly than he. When, following the rape, Clarissa begins to describe Sinclair and her women as aiding and abetting the crime, Lovelace objects: "Nor let even *honest* people, so *called,* blame poor Dorcas for her fidelity in a bad cause" (920). As we've seen, Lovelace likes to extend the indemnity he grants to himself to others. After the rape he assures Belford that because Clarissa was *"insensible* in the moments of trial," she has "no *accomplice*-inclination" (943; emphasis mine), redeploying the logic of his earlier self-exoneration to insist that if a person acts without the accompaniment of inclination—if she is *merely* an accomplice—she is not to blame. But Clarissa repudiates the blamelessness of the mere accomplice: "No order of another ought to make them detain a free person," she warns Sinclair and the others; "let *them* look to the consequence" (965). Polly perceives this as a threat of legal action and

> gave it as her opinion (with apprehension for their own safety) that, having so good a handle to punish them all, [Clarissa] would not go away if she might. And what, inferred Polly, is the indemnity of a man who has committed the vilest of rapes on a person of condition; and must himself, if prosecuted for it, either fly, or be hanged? (965)

Polly correctly infers that if Lovelace is not indemnified, neither are they. And "upon this representation of Polly," Sinclair foresees *"the ruin of her poor house* in the issue of this *strange* business, as she called it; and Sally and Dorcas bore their parts in the apprehension" (965).

Lovelace, however, continues to insist on his indemnity by continuing to reject, even self-consciously to pervert, the logic of strict liability. Invoking what he calls a "volant metaphor," he likens the rake's serial seduction of women to the business of the carnival operator, reminding Belford of how they

pursued from pretty girl to pretty girl, as fast as we had set one down, taking another up—just as the fellows do with their flying coaches and flying-horses at a
country fair—with a *Who rides next! Who rides next!* (970)

Suppose, he asks Belford, that one of these pretty girls is "taken with the invi-
tation of the *laced-hat* orator, and seeing several pretty little bib-wearers stuck
together in the flying-coaches, cutting safely the yielding air in the one-go-up,
the other-go-down picture-of-the-world vehicle, and all with as little fear as wit,
is tempted to ride next." If, he demands,

> after two or three ups and down, her pretty little head turns giddy, and she throws
> herself out of the coach when at its elevation, and so dashes out her pretty little
> brains, who can help it!—And would you hang the poor fellow, whose *professed
> trade* it was to set the pretty little creatures a-flying? (971)

According to the laws governing common carriers discussed in chapter 1, the
poor coachman *would* be accountable for any accidents occurring in the commission of his profession. At a historical moment in which there is no legal action for accidental fatalities, Defoe turns to carrier liability in order to imagine
what such an action might look like. But for Lovelace, it's not just the idea that
one could be responsible for a *fatal* accident that is absurd; it's also the idea that
one could be held accountable for accidents of any kind. The volant metaphor
emerges in the context of a letter to Belford informing him that Clarissa has
escaped from Mrs. Sinclair: "I cannot forbear to own it, that I am stung to the
very soul with this unhappy—*accident*, must I call it?" Lovelace reflects. "Have I
nobody, whose throat, either for carelessness or treachery, I ought to cut in order
to pacify my vengeance!" (971).

Lovelace describes the metaphor as a game designed to mollify himself over
the accident of Clarissa's escape, but it is a serious game dedicated ultimately to
mollifying Belford: "All this is but a copy of my countenance, drawn to evade thy
malice" (971). Not surprisingly, Lovelace attempts to manage Belford's censure
by redescribing what looks intentional as accidental: "When I reflect upon my
last iniquitous intention, the first outrage so nobly resented, as well as so far as
she was able, so nobly *resisted,* I cannot but conclude that I was under the power
of fascination from these accursed Circes, who pretending to know their own
sex, would have it that there is in every woman a yielding, or a weak-resisting
moment to be met with" (971). The content of the volant metaphor is thus isomorphic with the content of the surrounding diegesis: both deflect responsibility away from Lovelace by insisting that the rape was from his perspective

an unforeseeable accident, one occasioned by the carelessness of others—the victim who "throws herself out of the coach," the Circes who wrongly assume that Clarissa will acquiesce in her seduction.

But the metaphor is even more complicated than this, for there are *two* accidents for which Lovelace seeks indemnification, two tenors and two vehicles to his vehicular metaphor—the flying coach whose tenor is rape and the rape, which is a vehicle (as it so inevitably is in this novel) for death. The metaphor conflates rape and murder, but it does so ironically and in an attempt to *delimit* action—to distinguish acts that can plausibly be charged to the coachman (setting creatures flying) from those that cannot (killing them). This helps to explain why the metaphor is deployed in the midst of and as a way of resisting the "apprehensions" of Sinclair and her gang that like their principal they live under the threat of indictment. Such a threat is explicitly invoked by Anna in a letter intercepted by Lovelace and that follows quickly on the heels of the news of Clarissa's escape. "I must call upon you, my dear," she enjoins her friend, "to resolve upon taking legal vengeance of the infernal wretch" (1014), explaining that her mother thinks "and so do I, that the vile creatures, his accomplices, ought by all means to be brought to condign punishment, as they must and will be, upon bringing him to his trial" (1017). It's not that Lovelace rejects the idea of being a principal as such. Elsewhere he criticizes Lord M. for his "sneaking" sinfulness, for "never daring to rise to the joy of an enterprise at first hand, which could bring him within view of a tilting, or of the honour of being considered as the principal man in a court of justice" (1023). If the volant metaphor reveals Lovelace's own resistance to being considered a principal man in a court of justice, the resistance seems to stem from some ambiguity about the status of the act for which he is being asked to account. The metaphor's complex tenor marks Lovelace's sense that the act of rape is less than agentive, that it is not "an enterprise at first hand." But it also marks his sense that the act has not yet come to rest—that we do not know for certain what the act *is*. "Who the devil could have expected such strange effects from a cause so common, and so slight?" he wonders, worried already that Clarissa is "irreparably hurt" (888–89).

The cause whose strange effects no one could have expected, and thus that Lovelace insists he can't be expected to own, is of course the rape; but more immediately, and more literally, it is the medicinal "contrivance" forced on him by the enterprising Sinclair. It is around the question of Sinclair's responsibility that the language of accident escalates, as Lovelace begins to suffer from the same sort of constructive logic that he had used against Clarissa. "Clear me of this cursed job," he asks Belford when he hears that Sinclair has had Clarissa thrown in debtor's prison: "It will be thought done by my contrivance," he complains, "and if I am absent from this place, that will confirm the suspicion" (1046). As they had with Clarissa, a number of characters engage in a campaign to exonerate him by clarifying his motives. "Vile wretch as he is," Charlotte writes to Anna, "he is however innocent of this new evil" (1047), and her sisters confirm that they too are "convinced that the accident was an accident" (1050). Belford's mission to Clarissa is explicitly motivated by the need to "clear [Love-lace's] intentions of this brutal, this sordid-looking, villainy" (1068): "Indeed, madam," he tells her, "guilty, abominably guilty as he is in all the rest, he is innocent of this last wicked outrage" (1105). Anna informs Clarissa that after receiving the earnest pleadings of Lovelace's family, "I really believe him innocent of the arrest." And Clarissa too declares herself

> willing to believe, not only from your own opinion, but from the assurances of one of Mr Lovelace's friends, Mr Belford, a good-natured and humane man, who spares not to censure the author of my calamities (I *think*, with undissembled and undesigning sincerity), that that man is innocent of the disgraceful arrest. (1115)

At the same time as Lovelace's innocence (which is to say his ignorance) is invoked to limit his responsibility, however, Clarissa's tendency to blame herself for outcomes she has not intended and could not have foreseen dramatically increases, and one begins to see that if the belief that accidents are things for which no one is responsible is a normative position within the novel, it is not normative *for* the novel. After the rape, Anna writes to caution Clarissa against what she calls her "dejection": "Comfort yourself," she tells her, "in the triumphs of a virtue unsullied; a will wholly faultless" (1020). Like Lovelace, Anna aligns the question of fault with the status of the will, insisting that faultlessness—not acting badly, not acting at all—vitiates responsibility: "Many happy days may you yet see; and much good may you still do," she assures Clarissa, "if you will not heighten unavoidable accidents into guilty despondency" (1020). But in the days leading up to her death Clarissa accounts for herself precisely by detaching fault from volition: "Let your poor penitent implore your forgiveness of all her faults and follies," she writes to her father, reminding him, "you know, sir, that I have never been faulty in my will" (1371). She writes to thank her uncles "for your kind indulgence to me, and to beg your forgiveness of my last, my *only* great fault to you and to my family," describing that fault as a "terrible misfortune" and reminding them too that "my fault was not that of a culpable will" (1375). Clarissa's commitment to holding herself accountable for "unavoidable accidents" is something many of the novel's critics follow Anna in describing as a kind of pathology—"despondency," Anna calls it, but lately we have been calling it "masochism."[71] At stake in the vocabulary of masochism and the argument aligning Clarissa's abjection with Richardson's sadistic subjection of her are two related assumptions: that Clarissa blames herself in order to harm herself and that to ally innocence and culpability is at best mad, at worst perversely inhumane. To think so, however, is to think like Lovelace—to cultivate the obverse idea that blamable persons are not innocent, and if they are not innocent they have not been harmed. "Clarissa was not drawn absolutely perfect, but as having something to blame herself for, tho' not in Intention," Richardson once said.[72] And if detaching blameworthiness from intent seems a barbarous chastisement of the paragon, it is also a way around the more invidious—and antifeminist—cruelties of constructive intent.It is a way, the *only* way, for Richardson to mark the obdurate materiality of Clarissa's harm and Lovelace's causal connection to it, to insist on victimization even in the absence of incontrovertible evidence of the victim's faultlessness, to prevent questions about Clarissa's motives from converting harm into a benefit to which she has assented.

It is a way of thinking of responsibility that Lovelace rejects until the bitter end. "Who dare call me to account?" (1382), he demands in the aftermath of Clarissa's death, continuing to refuse to be yoked to actions that are not unambiguously his own. When Clarissa admits that Sinclair's imprisonment of her was "a large DEATH-STRIDE upon me—I should have *suffered longer else!*" Lovelace seizes on this. "I had no hand in it!" he asserts and turns quickly from blaming Sinclair to blaming the Harlowes: "But her relations, her implacable relations, have done the business" (1340). It is significant that the mock trial scene in which Lovelace is accused of felony murder emerges within the context of—and as if in response to—the latest and most egregious of his repudiations of the acts of his accessories. Belford has written to inform him of the terrible deaths of two of his instruments: "Providence, which has already given you the fates of your agents Sinclair and Tomlinson to take warning by, will not let the principal offender escape, if he slight the warning" (1436), he tells him. Anna responds to a similar letter by reflecting, "It may be presumed, from the exits you mention of two of the infernal man's accomplices, that the thunderbolt will not stop short of the principal" (1453). But Lovelace's reply is once again to deflect blame away from himself and onto his accomplices, this time by making explicit what has been implicit all along: that he conceives of them and not himself as agents. "Wilt thou give me the particulars of *their* distress, who were my *auxiliaries* in bringing on the event that affects me?" he complains. "Nay, *principals* rather: since, say what thou wilt, what did I do worth a woman's breaking her heart for?" (1437).

When Lovelace first raises the possibility of Sinclair's responsibility for the rape, he does so by claiming that "a mischief which would end in simple robbery among men-rogues, becomes murder if a woman be in it" (896). He frequently figures rape as a robbery gone unaccountably, catastrophically bad. "LORD, Jack, what shall I do now!" he writes to Belford in the days leading up to the rape: "How one evil brings on another!—Dreadful news to tell thee!—While I was meditating a simple robbery, here have I (in my own defence indeed) been guilty of murder! A bloody murder!" (847). The "murder" to which he refers is the obliteration of his conscience: "At her last gasp!—Poor impertinent opposer! Eternally resisting!—Eternally contradicting! There she lies, weltering in her blood! Her death's wound have I given her!" (848). But the scene clearly foreshadows both the imminent rape and the death that is its final effect, and the semantic similarities between this passage and the exchange between Lovelace and Lord M. (some six hundred pages later) are too striking to ignore. In her "madness" after the rape Clarissa imagines disappearing "never more to be seen, or to be produced to anybody, except in your own vindication, if you should be charged with the murder of my person" (896). Once Lovelace *is* charged with the murder of her person, he responds by returning to the question of robbery. Characterizing himself as "a poor, single, harmless prowler" who "in order to satisfy my hunger, steal but one poor lamb" (1437), he deploys an extended series of legal exempla designed to prove that he "can be only a *thief*" and "ought to be acquitted of everything but a common theft, a private larceny" (1438). Imagine a miser, he says (moving from poaching to burglary), who, "on waking and searching for, and finding his treasure gone, takes it so much to heart, that he starves himself." "Who but himself is to blame for that?" he asks, anticipating Hart and Honoré's volitionist analysis of *Stephenson v. State:* "Would either equity, law, or conscience, hang B for a murder?" (1438).

Lovelace wants to insist that he and his act are "single": that he ought not to be conflated with Sinclair or with the victim and her perverse self-immolation, that rape ought not to be conflated with murder. The maneuvers he makes to prevent this conflation (or, as he sees it, *in*flation) are rather ingenious and involve some compensatory *de*flation. By calling rape "larceny" Lovelace means to trivialize even the crime of which he acknowledges himself guilty. Under the common law, larceny was a capital offense only if the purloined object were worth more than twelve shillings; the vocabulary of "common" taking implies a less-than-capital offense, suggesting that if he should not hang for murder, perhaps he should not hang at all.[73] A similar thing happens by designating the object in question a lamb: on the one hand, poaching is a more serious offense than larceny, but it too is capital only under specific conditions (blacking the face, killing someone by accident in the course of a trespass).[74] The turn from poaching to felony burglary, on the other hand, is a more perplexing move, since this unambiguously capital offense would seem to ratchet up the stakes of Lovelace's actions just as he was ratcheting them down. What he gains from the example is the emphasis on the miser's intervening act. But his strategy begins to get away from him here (though not from Richardson), since the miser's death, tied explicitly to the burglary and implicitly to the trespass, raises the specter of a new legal remedy concerned precisely with situations in which felonious acts culminate in unintended fatalities. As we recall, and as Richardson surely knows, poaching in the course of which death ensues is the paradigmatic instance of a category of strict liability predicated on the conflating logic Lovelace wishes to escape—a logic that draws together one act (robbery/rape) and another (murder), one person (accessory) and another (principal). The answer Lord M gives, the answer the *novel* gives to the question of whether Lovelace is to blame, therefore, is yes: "If by committing an unlawful act, a capital crime is the consequence, you are answerable to both" (1438).

Lovelace's encroachments on Clarissa are thus answered by a more intense form of encroachment: by a legal logic according to which self and other are merged so thoroughly as to be indistinguishable—indistinguishable one from another, indistinguishable from the plot that yokes them together. Once again Richardson marks this by way of a meditation on the liability of principals and accessories. Although Belford has been assigned the task of clarifying Lovelace's motives with respect to Sinclair's unilateral imprisonment of Clarissa—of detaching that act *from* Lovelace—and although he like everyone else registers Lovelace's innocence on this score, he nonetheless persists in describing that act "however unintended by thee, yet a consequence of thy general orders" (1051). "What pains thou takest to persuade thyself that the lady's ill health is owing to the vile arrest, and to her friends' implacableness! Both, primarily (if they were), to be laid at thy door," Belford insists. "What fools must he suppose the rest of the world to be," he complains of Lovelace's self-serving perversion of the doctrine of agency, "if he imagines them as easily to be imposed upon as he can impose upon himself?" (1123): "But if that happens to her which is likely to happen, wilt thou not tremble for what may befall the principal?" (1378).

The novel famously punishes the principal and his accessories and alike, subjecting Lovelace, Sinclair, Tomlinson, Joseph, Polly, and Sally to a most ruthless judgment.[75] We have tended to call this "poetic justice," by which we mean that the novel imagines just remedies that the law cannot or will not perform. This is a familiar way to think about literature and the law, to assume that the former produces equitable judgments sensitive to the contingencies and particularities of individuals—judgments whose humaneness is marked by a rejection of the rigid formalism of the law.[76] I hope to have shown that the poetry of Richardson's justice is one and the same as the formalism of the law and that both are ultimately indifferent to the claims of the person and her exculpating idiosyncrasies. Watt begins his chapter on *Clarissa* in the *Rise of the Novel* by affirming Anna Laetitia Barbauld's distinction between Defoe and Richardson: "The minuteness of Defoe was more employed about things," she is quoted as saying, "and that of Richardson about persons and sentiments."[77] In chapter 1, we saw how Defoe's interest in things *is* an interest in persons: what Watt calls his "blind and almost purposeless concentration on the actions of his heroes and heroines" (rather than on their minds) is not a failure of literary method but a statement of literary method, a way of understanding what characters and persons *are*.[78] In this chapter we have seen that Richardson's interest in persons is an interest in things—that despite the novel's minute discriminations of feeling and motive, Richardson's persons, like Defoe's, move with the inertia of matter. The formalism that Ferguson observes in *Clarissa*—which produces psychology as a response to the pathos of abstraction—is therefore also a kind of hypermaterialization. Or rather there are two formalisms at work in the novel, one that is committed to representing states of mind and one that sees the commitment to interiority as the ground of Lovelace's predation of women and his relentless self-absolution. If it is true that Richardson's characters are "rounder" than Defoe's, this roundness only serves to bring into sharper relief the tragic ethos of the novel form—an ethos (as Hart and Honoré fear) in which individuation and individualism are made casualties of responsibility.

It is an ethos to which none of the characters, Clarissa included, accedes. On her deathbed Sinclair turns the words Lovelace had used to indict her against him: "Oh that cursed man! Had it not been for him! I had never had this, the most crying of all my sins, to answer for!" (1389). For her part, Clarissa writes to Morden to beg "that the author of my calamities may not be vindictively sought after": "He could not have been the author of them but for a strange concurrence of unhappy causes," she asserts. "As the law will not be able to reach him when I am gone, any other sort of vengeance terrifies me but to think of it"

(1301). Although Clarissa calls Lovelace an "author," she in fact distinguishes between what it means to be an author and what it means to be a cause: Lovelace's responsibility for her injuries is called into question by the complex causal environment of his actions. It is a distinction no doubt suggested to her by the way her own intentions constantly go awry. "What a deep error is mine!" she elsewhere reflects. "What evils have I been the occasion of?" (1328). The language of causality and the language of blame coincide here: Clarissa describes herself as occasioning events that if she does not author them she nonetheless owns. But in the letter to Morden Clarissa suggests that in not authoring calamities Lovelace is indemnified against them. "As to myself, you have only robbed me of what once were my favourite expectations in the transient life I shall have quitted when you receive this," she writes to Lovelace. "You have only been the cause that I have been cut off in the bloom of youth." (1426).

Even Lovelace is baffled by Clarissa's generous acquittal of him: "What a frame must thou be in," he responds, "to be able to use the word ONLY in mentioning these important deprivations!" (1429). Lovelace misreads the grammar of Clarissa's sentence: he imagines that "only" modifies the cutting off of Clarissa's youth—that it attaches to the *content* of her harm. But "only" works to modify (by diminishing the importance of) the word "cause," and though he doesn't quite understand it, *this* is what is baffling about what Clarissa has said, for she has repudiated a position that she has staked out throughout the novel and that the novel stakes out in Lord M's indictment of Lovelace—the position, that is, that to be a cause of harm *is* to be responsible for it.

That its characters universally fail to recognize how the novel thinks about blame—refusing for themselves and others the strictures of strict liability—begins to suggest what is wrong with a model of responsibility grounded in the practice of interiority and the individualist ethics this practice sanctions and enables. "Don't you see, my dear, that we seem all to be *impelled*, as it were, by a perverse fate which none of us are able to resist?—and yet all arising . . . from ourselves?" (333), Clarissa writes to Anna in the early stages of her calamity. Clarissa comes close here to an account of emplotted personhood; to understanding accident not only as something that happens to persons and from which they might therefore be distinguished but also as something that comes from them—something they own. And yet she misunderstands the implications of this insight, asserting that although she resigns herself to the will of Providence, she wants nonetheless to be "*justly* acquitted of willful and premeditated faults" (333). Even she can't let go of the assumption that not knowing the complexities of the plot in which one is embedded mitigates one's responsibility for it. To think so, however, is to fail to confront what it means for Clarissa—and for *Clarissa*—to be tragic. As I noted in the introduction, Terry Eagleton considers neither properly tragic: although Clarissa is "one of the great tragic figures of English writing," he says, "Aristotle would not have found her so. She is too innocent."[79] *Clarissa* is thus, he argues, "another case of the strange discrepancy between tragic theory and tragic practice," further evidence that the novel is not a tragic form. For Eagleton, Clarissa's innocence is ensured by the profundity of her ignorance: she does not know what is coming; she cannot prevent but only endure the tragic course of events. On the face of it this would seem to make her the paradigmatic tragic hero, whose predicament, Aristotle tells us, is attributable "not to depravity but to a serious error" that is "performed in ignorance."[80] But Eagleton, like many readers of the *Poetics*, conceives of the tragic hero's ignorance *as* error—a negligent failure of foresight, hamartia as a flaw incompatible with innocence.

In *Clarissa*, however, hamartia retains its lexical meaning as a missed marked, an action against design, an accident—not negligence but mistake.[81] Ignorance is so thoroughly a feature of agency, indeed of personhood, that it makes no sense to think of it as something that a person might fix about herself. "What a fine subject for a tragedy would the injuries of this lady, and her behaviour under them, both with regard to her implacable friends and to her persecutor, make!" (1205) Belford reflects at one point, aligning, like Eagleton, Clarissa's exemplarity with the flawlessness of her behavior. Clarissa is an "unblameable lady" because she acts well, and while for Eagleton this disqualifies her from being a tragic hero (who is tragic because he is responsible and responsible because he has acted badly), for Belford the tragic hero suffers but does not produce harm. Clarissa is a "subject for tragedy," a tragic subject, only insofar as she is subjected *to* injury. But both of these configurations of the tragic seem to me to miss the mark. Clarissa is a tragic subject precisely because she is *not* what we recognize as a subject at all: like each of the characters, flat and round alike, who populate this novel she is a cause—and a cause, moreover, of injury.[82] No more than Lovelace is she to be distinguished from those effects to which her blameless actions might be tied: she is the person who did those things.

To conceive of persons as causes is paradoxically to cease to think of them in terms of what Nietzsche calls the "thread of causality."[83] This paradox is one of the more significant effects of shifting attention, as *Harm's Way* does, from an account of modernity focused on the interleaved histories of science and political philosophy to one focused on the history of law. In *We Have Never Been Modern*, a virtuosic account of Enlightenment dualism, its presumptive separation of humans from nonhumans, Bruno Latour observes: "Without accusation we have no causes to plead, and we cannot assign causes to phenomena." The observation occurs in the midst of Latour's remystification of empiricism's demystification of causality. Although the English experimentalists and other moderns think they dispassionately trace effects to causes, he says, "we have no idea of the aspect things would have outside the tribunal, beyond our civil wars, and outside our trials and our courtrooms." Modern society imagines itself to have been liberated from "the hell of social relationships, from the obscurantism of religion, from the tyranny of politics," but "just like all the others, it is redistributing the accusations that replace a cause—judiciary, collective, social—by a cause—scientific, nonsocial, matter-of-factual." Accusation, or what Latour describes as "prescientific," "anthropological," "mythological" investments, underwrites the science of causation. And because of this, he concludes, "nowhere can one observe an object and a subject, one society that would be primitive and another that would be modern."[84]

For Latour, as for Nietzsche, modernity is characterized by a commitment to the practice of causal thinking, and causal thinking is predicated on a distinction between the subject who thinks and the object she thinks about. Causality is thus isomorphic with liberal sovereigntism—sign and symptom of a desire (one Latour rightly calls "humanist") "to attribute action to a small number of powers, leaving the rest of the world with nothing but simple mute forces."[85] Nietzsche, we recall, saw the novel as the paradigmatically causal, modern form. Yet *Clarissa* asks us to refine, perhaps to abandon, these influential accounts of the modern constitution with its habits of explanation and (self-) control, its putative opposition between persons and things. Without cause, Richardson insists, we have no accusation. Like Latour, Richardson is sensitive to the way accusation registers the "hell of social relationships"; but the hellishness of relationship—its inescapability, its inevitable harmfulness—is not for him a sign that "we are still in the Dark Ages."[86] The encroachment of others marks an ethical and ontological possibility more radical than Latour's reenchantment—his *repersonification*—of the world. A possibility not that persons might be constituted by their relation to objects conceived as "quasi subjects" and invested with "action, will, meaning, even speech" ("Nothing is sufficiently inhuman to dissolve human beings in it and announce their death. Their will, their actions, their words are too abundant"), not that objects might attain the fecund meaningfulness of subjects, but that subjects might *be* objects in all their mute and forceful simplicity.[87]

CHAPTER THREE

Fighting Men

No guilt at heart, no wrongdoing to turn us pale.

—Horace, *Epistles 1.1.61*

In a Fielding novel, there is no harm and there are no accidents. There are, however, fights, and that these frequent and bloody mêlées do not register as harmful is one of the most distinctive characteristics of Fielding's fiction. R. S. Crane long ago suggested that the form of *Tom Jones* is "rather special" for how a plot that contains all the ingredients for tragedy—or at least a "tragicomedy of common life"—continually resolves into the "security that no genuine harm has been done."[1] Noting that "we have been prepared to expect much unmerited calamity and distress for [Tom], and at the same time to view the prospect without much alarm," Crane offers a number of explanations for the reader's equanimity, each resting "on the principle that we fear less or not at all when the agents of harm to a hero are more or less laughable persons": for who, he asks, "can really fear that the persecutions directed against the determined and resourceful Sophia by such a blundering pair of tyrants [as Squire Western and his sister] can ever issue in serious harm?"[2] Ian Watt is less sanguine than Crane about Sophia's safety, invoking with evident discomfort the scene in which Squire Western breaks from his daughter "with such Violence, that her Face dashed against the Floor," "leaving poor *Sophia* prostrate on the Ground," "with the Tears trickling from her Eyes, and the Blood running from her Lips."[3]

Yet Watt likewise observes that it is "an essential condition for the realisation of Fielding's comic aim that the scene should not be rendered in all its physical and psychological detail"—should not be rendered, that is, as though a blow to the face were harmful:

Fielding must temper our alarm for Sophia's fate by assuring us that we are witnessing, not real anguish, but that conventional kind of comic perplexity which serves to heighten our eventual pleasure at the happy ending, without in the meantime involving any unnecessary expenditure of tears on our part.[4]

The claim that the reader of a Fielding novel is not alarmed by the physical violence that permeates his fiction is something of a critical commonplace, even among feminist critics wary of what Susan Staves calls the "comedy of attempted rape."[5] In her introduction to the Penguin edition of *Joseph Andrews,* for example, Judith Hawley describes as "perverse" Fielding's willingness to "torture his heroine" but goes on to say that "just as the violence is always treated as slapstick, his victims are always rescued, disaster is always averted." The threat of harm, she concludes, is "fit . . . into a comic frame."[6] "In the world of comic romance," Staves agrees, "female chastity is always safe from violation": "*Joseph Andrews* and *Tom Jones* establish comic universes in which we can neither doubt the chastity of the heroines nor suppose that—however often their chastity might be attacked—rapists could ever ruin them."[7] Here comedy marks the *avoidance* of harm, in particular the harm of rape. But elsewhere Staves describes as comic the retroactive *recuperation* of the harm of rape into the benefit of marriage. Invoking a case overseen by Fielding, in which charges against the defendant were dropped after the complainant admitted she had been "over persuaded" to marry her attacker, Staves observes: "Surely such cases appealed to the comic sensibility of the novelist and to the very human wish to believe that—despite lover's quarrels—no real harm has been done."[8] The tone of this observation is difficult to parse. According to Staves, eighteenth-century rape trials confirm Clarissa's worry about the

contest of stories . . . that would occur should she accuse Lovelace of rape: the woman's tragic narrative against the man's comic one, with the comic story of the ambivalent woman who first consents and then falsely cries rape frequently prevailing.[9]

Staves's own tale ends on a "tragic" note, with the gruesome testimony of an eighteenth-century rape victim whose "story was not believed."[10] Yet she also seems to endorse the suggestion that "no real harm has been done" to the woman who marries her seducer: marriage is a species of comedy in its conversion of sexual injury into "a lover's quarrel." And comedy, like marriage, is what human beings want.

Staves's way of distinguishing quarreling from injuring, her alignment of comedy *with* this distinction and with the human as such, is replicated in the countless encomia on the "humanity" of Fielding's fiction. Mark Spilka, for example, describes Parson Adams as "harmless" even though—even *when*—he delivers Mrs. Slipslop "an almost fatal beating" and goes on to make this noninjurious beating homologous with Fielding's novelistic enterprise, which is to say with the comic epic in prose: "If Fielding deals [Slipslop] a sound drubbing in the night scenes at Booby Hall," he asserts, "he also 'deals' her a last warm laugh."[11] A version of such a homology is reiterated, and carefully historicized, in Christopher Johnson's " 'British Championism': Early Pugilism and the Works of Fielding." Arguing that "Fielding regards boxing as more than comic light relief," Johnson observes: "It is comic also in the sense that it is a vital weapon in the attempt to achieve the order of comedy—reasonable, humane, and loving—in his portrait of a world which is dangerous and corrupt."[12] Like Staves, Johnson stands at some distance from the idea—pervasive, as he shows, in the literature of sports and politeness in the period—that "the weapon which embodies the best values of society is the fist."[13] But also like her he appears to find this distance difficult to maintain, as though only the most cheerless of readers could fail to understand a "sound drubbing" as an index of "warmth" and "love":

> Boxing is depicted as violence at its most therapeutic—requiring courage and strength, but inflicting no injury. . . . In fact, boxing seems wholly integrated into a comic vision of the world, never at any point in [Fielding's] novels threatening even the possibility of tragedy.

"There is nothing unsettling in the thrashing given to the Reverend Mr Thwackum," Johnson avers.[14]

I *am* unsettled by this and other thrashings and admit to being a cheerless—or, in other words, a feminist—reader of Fielding. Yet while I do not share other critics' equanimity on the subject of Fielding's fighting men, I do share their sense that tragedy is a genre in which fighting hurts and comedy a genre in which it does not. The self-evidence of this claim threatens to obscure its profundity. Particularly striking is Staves's insight that the difference between the kind of story Clarissa tells and the kind of story Lovelace tells is the difference between a tragic narrative in which harm registers *as* harm and a comic narrative in which harm is obscured or ameliorated by the operations of consent.[15] In chapter 2, I showed how ruthlessly *Clarissa* rejects a model of relationship and responsibility grounded in consent, and Staves helps one to see what was only inchoate in that chapter: that *consent theory is a comic genre*. Her own, ambivalent, investment in the comedy of consent helps us to see something else. Objecting to another feminist historian's "severity" about Fielding's judicial record on rape, Staves emphasizes the magistrate's sympathy "for those [he] was convinced were real victims," and insists:

> A few of the allegations certainly did not appear well- founded. Simpson has discovered that not only did a number of real victims of rape and attempted rape negotiate for monetary damages but also that marriage, even from strangers, was sometimes offered as recompense, and that "working-class women sometimes accepted marriage as suitable recompense for sexual attack."[16]

Implicit in Staves's defense of Fielding is the assumption that the pursuit of monetary damages or other forms of compensation—in particular the compensation that is marriage—calls into question the severity, perhaps the facticity, of a complainant's injury. Compensation comes to look like complicity, which is to say like implied consent, and skepticism about compensation leads inevitably to a skepticism about harm. It is not surprising that such skepticism—call it anti-Pamelism—should emerge in the context of an essay on Fielding. For as I will show, Fielding's comic revision of the novel form is one and the same as an attack on realism's tragic—its *feminist*—logic of strict liability.

❧

Fielding is the first critic to register the novel form's characteristic preoccupation with injury and responsibility. Nowhere is this clearer than in book 2, chapter 5, of *Joseph Andrews,* framed at one end by a debate about the hero's harm and at the other by an elaborate, and poorly understood, debate about liability. Joseph has by this point emerged *as* the novel's hero precisely because of a propensity for bodily injury, one that marks him as Pamela's kin as thoroughly as it seems to distinguish him from the impregnable Parson Adams. The parson cannot be injured, not even by the horse whose sole "Intention" it is to throw his riders:

> This Foible . . . was of no great Inconvenience to the Parson, who . . . threw himself forward on such Occasions with so much dexterity, that he never received any Mischief; the Horse and he frequently rolling many Paces distance, and afterwards both getting up and meeting as good Friends as ever.

Poor *Joseph* did not so happily disengage himself: but falling with his Leg under the Beast, received a violent Contusion.[17]

A tussle over the status of Joseph's contusion morphs seamlessly into the first of
the novel's epic brawls—the hostess worrying that the "poor young Man's Leg
is very much bruised," her husband asserting that "he did not believe the young
Fellow's Leg was so bad as he pretended," Parson Adams chastising the host's
"inhumanity" with a fist to the face, all culminating in the "horrible Spectacle"
of Adams covered in blood that is only mistakenly "concluded to be his own"
(119–20).

Jill Campbell has argued that at stake in scenes that foreground Joseph's vulnerability to harm is the question of masculinity: Fielding, she says, hints "at
a metonymic association of Joseph's leg with his genitals, his injury signifying
as a figurative castration that keeps him out of the masculine physical struggle
even after the hostess and Slipslop have joined in."[18] For Campbell, Joseph's
feminization points to Fielding's skepticism about "the very notion of the masculine hero," whose "reliance on force—whether a public official's reliance on
institutional authority or a poor man's reliance on physical strength—turns
him into a kind of solidified puppet."[19] She distinguishes between two versions
of masculinity in *Joseph Andrews:* between the hypermasculinity of the "roasting" squire, whose "crude physical abuse" is linked with the aggressions of sat
ire, and the feminized masculinity of Joseph, whose fists and cudgel serve the
gentler justice of comedy.[20] It is a beautifully rendered, compelling argument.
Yet it takes for granted something I'm not finally persuaded by: that what looks
like injury in a Fielding novel *is* injury; that men *can* be harmed.

Joseph recovers. After the battery in book 1, chapter 12, that fulfills Lady
Booby's repeated threats to "strip" Joseph of his livery—and where woman's
ineffectual sexual predation is succeeded (that is, followed and fulfilled) by the
highwaymen who order him to "*strip and be d—n'd to you*" and who then fall
to "be-labouring poor *Joseph* with their Sticks" (51–52)—the hero, we're told,
"found himself very sore from the Bruises, but had no reason to think any of
his Bones injured, or that he had received any Harm in his Inside" (68). "*Joseph*
passed that day and three following with his Friend *Adams,*" we learn a few
chapters later, "in which nothing so remarkable happened as the swift Progress of his Recovery" (78). And after convalescing for a mere day and a half
following his fall from the horse, Joseph once again finds himself "surprisingly
recovered" (161). Indeed, the episode of Joseph's leg is an extended joke about
"recovery," one that turns on a distinction between recovering *from* injury—

what men do—and recovering *for* injury—what lawyers do. One of these latter personages, learning from the host the particulars of his fight with the pugnacious parson,

> and being assured by him that *Adams* had struck the first Blow, whispered in his Ear: "he'd warrant he would *recover.*" "Recover! Master," said the Host, smiling: "Yes, yes, I am not afraid of dying with a Blow or two neither; I am not such a Chicken as that." "Pugh!" said the Gentleman, "I mean you will recover Damages, in that Action which undoubtedly you intend to bring, as soon as a Writ can be returned from *London;* for you look like a Man of too much Spirit and Courage to suffer any one to beat you without bringing your Action against him: He must be a scandalous Fellow indeed, who would put up a Drubbing whilst the Law is open to revenge it; besides, he hath drawn Blood from you and spoiled your Coat, and the Jury will give Damages for that too."

"You may take your own Opinion," concludes the gentleman, "but was I in your Circumstances, every Drop of my Blood should convey an Ounce of Gold into my Pocket" (121). That the host "has no stomach to Law" (122) confirms at once his good nature and his masculinity: "spirit" and "courage" are aligned with an imperviousness to harm; the man who pursues legal redress for injury, the passage insists, is at best mercenary and worst "a chicken."

It is therefore inevitable that the supremely durable Adams will reject the consolations of civil liability, and the terms in which he does so brings into focus the ethico-juridical logic of comic epic. "Whilst one of the above-mentioned Gentlemen was employed, as we have seen him, on the behalf of the Landlord," the narrator continues,

> the other was no less hearty on the side of Mr *Adams,* whom he advised to bring his Action immediately. . . . "How, Sir," says *Adams,* "do you take me for a Villain, who would prosecute Revenge in cold Blood, and use unjustifiable Means to obtain it?" (122)

Adams's claim that the law of damages is a species of vengeance rather than justice is at once a historical and a polemical observation, one that reveals Fielding's intimate knowledge of English legal history. "Personal injury is in the first place a cause of feud, of private war between the kindreds of the wrong-doer and of the person wronged," observe legal historians Frederick Pollock and Frederic Maitland in the chapter on Anglo Saxon law in their monumental *History of English Law.* "The next stage is a scale of compensation fixed by custom or enactment for death or minor injuries."[21]

On the eve of the Norman Conquest what we may call the criminal law of England (but it was also the law of "torts" or civil wrongs) contained four elements which deserve attention; its past history had in the main consisted of the varying relations between them. We have to speak of outlawry, of the bloodfeud, of the tariffs of *wer* and *bót* and *wíte,* of punishment in life and limb.[22]

Arguing that a "ready recourse to outlawry is, we are told, one of the tests by which the relative barbarousness of various bodies of ancient law may be measured," they conclude that "gradually law learns how to inflict punishment with a discriminating hand" and that "gradually more and more offences become emendable; outlawry remained for those who would not or could not pay."[23]

For Pollock and Maitland, as for most legal historians, the move toward monetary compensation for injury is a move away from the primitive literalism of talion law—from Babylonian, Old Testament, early Roman, and Anglo-Saxon conventions demanding that wrongdoers receive precisely those injuries they had inflicted on others. "Hence it will be evident," opines Blackstone,

> that what some have so highly extolled for its equity, the *lex talionis* or law of retaliation, can never be in all cases an adequate or permanent rule of punishment. In some cases indeed it seems to be dictated by natural reason. . . . But, in general, the difference of persons, place, time, provocation, or other circumstances, may enhance or mitigate the offence; and in such cases retaliation can never be a proper measure of justice. . . . Theft cannot be punished by theft, defamation by defamation, forgery by forgery, adultery by adultery, and the like.[24]

The blunt instrument of retaliation progressively gives way to more mediated, and nuanced, forms of compensation. Among the rights protected by the common law, says Blackstone, is the English subject's "right to some damages or other, the instant he receives [an] injury." "By the general system of our law," explains Theodore Sedgwick in his *Treatise on the Measure of Damages* (1847), one of the earliest histories of the common law of damages, "for every invasion of right there is a remedy, and that remedy is compensation. This compensation is furnished in the damages, which are awarded according to established rules; and these rules form what is called the Measure of Damages."[25] According to Sedgwick, compensation is initially itself rather barbaric. "It is a curious fact, that the laws of remote and barbarous periods show the most minute care in fixing the amount of compensation to be recovered by way of damages," he observes, parodying the "minute classification of wrongs and remedies" found in the sixth-century Anglo-Saxon legal code, the laws of Ethelbert:

If the hair be plucked, or pulled, let fifty sceattas be paid in compensation. If the scalp be cut to the bone [of the skull] so that the latter appear, let compensation be made by payment of fifty shillings. . . . Whoever fractures the chin bone, let him forfeit twenty shillings for the offence. For each of the front teeth, six shillings. For the tooth that stands by the front teeth (on either side), four shillings.[26]

Minuteness, "on its face appears to indicate the care and watchfulness of the lawgiver," Sedgwick notes. But he goes on to insist that minuteness marks instead the arbitrariness of the law and the "barbarous and disturbed state of society."[27] That Sedgwick's own society is committed to the production of treatises *measuring* damages—rationalizing and formalizing them and paradoxically making them more flexible—is only one of many signs of its civility.[28]

For Fielding, however, the law of damages not only remains the retaliatory response it imagines itself to transcend; it also represents a debased and effeminate *form* of retaliation. The reason it does so is because it is tied to the very practice of mediation that for Blackstone and his heirs was the vehicle of modernization. In the debate between Parson Adams and the lawyer in book 2, chapter 5, Fielding implicitly contrasts the cold-blooded vengeance of tort law with the warm-blooded justice of the fistfight that has just transpired. The contrast between warmth and coldness, proximity and mediation, hinges on the lawyers' repeated invocations of the word "action," a term denoting the form in which a legal case is addressed and whose formalism registers a nonagentive agency that for Fielding isn't agency at all. The problem of action receives some extended treatment in the inset narrative the episode of Joseph's leg interrupts—the fable of Leonora the "Unfortunate Jilt," whose story, like that of book 2, chapter 5, centers on a fight. Leonora's suitor, Horatio, has surprised her with her lover, Bellarmine, to whom Horatio immediately offers "a good drubbing" (114). He is thwarted in this endeavor by Leonora and her aunt and forced to depart alone, "leaving the Lady with his Rival to consult for his Safety, which *Leonora* feared her Indiscretion might have endangered." Her aunt, we are told, "comforted her with Assurances, that *Horatio* would not venture his Person against so accomplished a Cavalier as *Bellarmine,* and that being a Lawyer, he would seek Revenge his own way, and the most they had to apprehend from him was an Action" (115).

Horatio's moral superiority over Bellarmine, which the remainder of the story confirms, is anticipated in his commitment to "drubbing," but his masculinity is potentially compromised by his status as a lawyer, which is to say as the type of man who might seek revenge through legal action rather than dueling—who might, that is, fail to act. But Leonora wakes to news "that *Bellarmine* was run through the Body by *Horatio*, that he lay languishing at an Inn, and the Surgeons had declared the Wound mortal" (115). That Horatio has not served but rather stabbed Bellarmine ensures the equivalence of his sexual and moral authority. Yet if the duel seems preferable to legal action in this context, elsewhere in Fielding duels are themselves an overly mediated form of action. After the fateful fistfight between Tom and Blifil in book 5, chapter 12, of *Tom Jones*, the narrator admits he "cannot suppress a pious Wish, that all Quarrels were to be decided by those Weapons only, with which Nature, knowing what is proper for us, hath supplied us; and that cold Iron was to be used in digging no Bowels, but those of the Earth" (265). Asking whether a battle might not "be as well decided by the greater Number of broken Heads, bloody Noses, and black Eyes, as by the greater Heaps of mangled and murdered human Bodies," the narrator pauses to reflect that "this may be thought too detrimental a Scheme to the *French* Interest, since they would thus lose the Advantage they have over other Nations, in the Superiority of their Engineers." But "when I consider the Gallantry and Generosity of that People," he concludes, "I am persuaded they would never decline putting themselves upon a Par with their Adversary; or, as the Phrase is, *making themselves his Match*" (266).

The alignment of generosity with the eschewal of instrumentalized violence is so pervasive in Fielding's fiction that Johnson's ending "'British Championism'" with a hint of nostalgia for "the pugilistic egalitarianism which enlivens *Joseph Andrews* and much of *Tom Jones*," thereby elevating fistfighting to a technique of justice—and, moreover, a form of *caritas*—perfectly reflects the ethos of those novels.[29] "D——n me if ever I love my Friend better than when I am fighting with him," declares the sergeant in book 9 of *Tom Jones*, whose sentiment stands as a benediction on the "treaty" struck between Tom and the most recent landlord to receive from the hero a "Bellyful of Drubbing" (507–8). Partridge, too, is pleased with these "Symptoms of Reconciliation" and offers *his* hand to the chambermaid who has used hers to bloody his nose and face: "Between these two," the narrator informs us, "a League was struck, and those Hands which had been the Instruments of War, became now the Mediators of Peace" (507). (Fielding's use of the word "instrument" here is ironic, an effect of the mock-heroic style of a scene whose point is to offer fistfighting as an alternative to the instrumentality of war.) According to the sergeant, reconciliation is a peculiarly English virtue: "To bear Malice is more like a *Frenchman* than an *Englishman*" (508), he observes. And the narrator agrees:

No Nation produces so many drunken Quarrels . . . as *England*. . . . [Yet] there is seldom anything ungenerous, unfair, or ill-natured exercised on these Occasions: Nay, it is common for the Combatants to express Good-will for each other, even at the Time of the Conflict; and as their drunken Mirth generally ends in Battle, so do most of their Battles end in Friendship. (253)

The claim that boxing is an English pastime is confirmed by the Italian traveler in book 2, chapter 5, of *Joseph Andrews*, who, at the conclusion of the brawl between Adams and his hosts desires one of the ladies present "not to be frightened: for here had been only a little Boxing, which he said to their *Disgracia* the *English* were *accustomata* to" (121). That the traveler dislikes the practice marks him as un-English, and, more subtly, as ungenerous, his lack of magnanimity signaled by a concern with who is to blame for the "dreadful Quarrel" (118). Telling Adams that he looks like the ghost of Othello, and bidding him "*not shake his gory Locks at him, for he could not say he did it,*" the traveler misquotes Macbeth's line to the ghost of Banquo at 3.4.49–50: "Thou canst not say I did it. Never shake / Thy gory locks at me." In Shakespeare, the line highlights the problem of responsibility that is the subject of this (as it is any) tragedy. In Fielding, however, the problem registered by the line is not responsibility but accusation, as "*Adams* very innocently answered": "*Sir, I am far from accusing you*" (121).

The "perfect Simplicity" (10) of Adams's character announced in the preface to *Joseph Andrews* is thus revealed to coincide with a resistance to blame—or more precisely, with a tendency to be blamed and a corresponding lack of interest in blaming others. If laws of recovery insist on damages (the damaged victim, the forms of compensation that that make harm visible), the law of comedy and its avatar, masculinity, insist that men are damaged by one thing only: accusation. The plot of the comic epic continually revolves around the specter of accidental responsibility, and the comic hero's exemplarity consists in his refusal to engage in what Johnnie Cochrane called the "blame game." That this is so helps to explain an otherwise peculiar feature of the diegesis in *Joseph Andrews*, the fact that we are introduced to our hero in book 1, chapter 2 ("Of Mr Joseph Andrews"), as an indifferent "*Whipper-in,*" an object of the huntsman's resentment, he always laying "every Fault the Dogs were at, to the Account of the poor Boy" (21–22).[30] In the novels of Defoe and Richardson (and as we shall see, Sheridan), animal liability—the liability of persons for the acts of animals—is a paradigmatic example of an ethos of responsibility predicated on strangeness, an ethos that ties agents to acts and to others that are not in any simple sense *theirs* (the infected cats and dogs of the *Journal of the Plague Year*, for example, or Clarissa's dream that Lovelace is a wild beast for whose predations she is responsible). From the opening pages of *Joseph Andrews*, Fielding makes it clear that he understands this ethos to be an important feature of the new novel form, and his revision of the form emphasizes the absurdity of making "poor boys" responsible for the actions of dogs—which is to say, of making human beings responsible for things they did not do or did not mean to do.

This formal and thematic rejection of accidental responsibility is what is at stake in the famous scene in book 1, chapter 12, which has always been read as invoking the biblical parable of the Good Samaritan and thus as centrally preoccupied with the problem of charity.[31] If, as Paul Hunter has argued, this scene marks a "shift in thematic emphasis from chastity to charity," what has not emerged clearly in the critical tradition on Fielding is how charity is explicitly configured as an alternative to liability.[32] The difference between the two models of obligation turns on the status of the will, or, in other words, on what should be by now familiar as the doctrine of agency. For book 1, chapter 12, is first and foremost a meditation on vicarious liability and on the role of vicarious liability in the emergent practice of realist characterization. That this is so is signaled by the most important change Fielding makes to the episode in Luke 10:30, the assertion in the chapter heading that Joseph's "surprising adventure"—the adventure, that is, of bodily injury—is somehow essentially tied to *stagecoaches*. (The adventure, we are told, is "scarce credible by those who have never traveled in a Stage-Coach" [51].) What has gone unnoticed in discussions of the scene emphasizing the biblical paradigm is the fact that the elaborate discussion of liability that ensues is directed at the *coachman*. A lawyer, worried that "now they might be proved to have been *last in his Company*; if he should die, they might be called to some account for his Murther" (52), asks that Joseph be taken into the coach and carried to the next inn. When the coachman refuses, the lawyer, "afraid of some Mischief happening to himself if the Wretch was left behind in that Condition," warns the coachman that

> "no Man could be too cautious in these Matters, and that he remembered very extraordinary Cases in the Books," threatened the Coachman, and bid him deny taking him up at his Peril; "for that if he died, he should be indicted for his Murther, and if he lived, and brought an Action against him, he would willingly take a Brief in it." (52)

"These Words had a sensible Effect on the Coachman," the narrator observes, and he "at length agreed" to take Joseph into the coach (52–53).

Fielding's satire in this scene is immensely subtle and crucial for understanding the work of the novel as a whole. As critics have observed, an opposition is established between the lawyer's contorted rationale for dispensing aid to Joseph and the postillion's reflexive charity. Less remarked on is the specific content of the lawyer's arguments, the way Fielding pits charity against laws of trespass governing "common carriers" such as the coachman. "Common callings" were the only contexts in which the old common-law adage that "nonfeasance was no trespass" did not hold: "To charge a man for not acting," Oliver Wendell Holmes observes, "you must show that it was his duty to act."[33] As it developed over the course of the later seventeenth century, carrier liability appropriated to itself "the general obligation of those exercising a public or 'common' business to practice their art on demand, and show skill in it."[34] In doing so, legal historians agree, carrier liability marked the emergence of "a new general principle: that a man was 'answerable for all mischief proceeding from his neglect or his actions, unless they were of unavoidable necessity.'" As Holmes puts it, under carrier liability, "a man is answerable for all the consequences of his acts, or, in other words, . . . he acts at his peril always, and wholly irrespective of the state of his consciousness upon the matter."[35]

That Fielding knows all this is evinced by the lawyer's strenuous reminder to the coachman that his failure to act might be actionable and also by the precision with which Fielding distinguishes between two ways of conceiving of the duty to act. Carrier liability, like the lawyer who invokes it, Fielding insists, is supremely narcissistic. The vicarious logic of the common calling makes obligation a coercive effect of one's status: under a legal regime in which persons are presumed to act always "at their peril," the duty of care represents not a moral or pathetic concern for others, but a structural expectation bordering on self-interest—another species of coldness. Fielding develops this line of critique around the lawyer's repeated invocations of the word "murder." We've seen in the last two chapters how the tragic model of responsibility articulated in the novels of Richardson and Defoe centers around the category of murder. Defoe applies the term "murder" to acts that lack the requisite malignity to qualify as murder in order to extend the vicarious liability of certain kinds of agents—innkeepers, masters, common carriers—to *all* agents. Mapping the vocabulary of criminal liability onto the logic of civil liability, Defoe imagines what the law has not yet imagined: a way of responding to accidental, fatal injuries. When in the 1730s the category of felony murder emerges as a mechanism for dealing with some fatal accidents, Richardson seizes on it not only to indict Lovelace for Clarissa's death but also to articulate a model of moral "subjectivity" predicated on the object likeness, the instrumentality, of persons. For Defoe and Richardson, vicarious liability is at once a gothic (that is, terrifying) and a tragic (that is, ethical) possibility. Through it, obligation is configured as fundamentally accidental: as arising out of adventitious rather than volitional relationships, as determined by an agent's professional position—sometimes literalized to include the position of her body vis-à-vis another—rather than her state of mind. Obligation on this account is something we primarily owe to strangers. And by committing his version of the novel to a distinction between charity and liability that hinges on a bathetic deflation of carrier liability with its hyperbolized rhetoric of homicide, Fielding reveals himself to be remarkably clearheaded about the vaunted differences between himself and Richardson. Despite Samuel Johnson's frequent (and frequently reiterated) assertions that Richardson "dives into the recesses of the human heart," that "there is more knowledge of the heart in one letter of Richardson's, than in all 'Tom Jones,'" it is *Fielding* who concerns himself with hearts. For the reason to prefer charity to liability (and thus Fielding to Richardson) is that charity requires compassion understood as a capacity to view strangers as friends.[36]

This helps to explain why Fielding might want to describe boxing as a form of disagreement in which assailants invariably emerge as friends and also why this trademark of the English pastime makes it an emblem of ethical—and as we shall see, sentimental—relationship. And it helps to explain what is wrong with a man, like the lawyer in book 2, chapter 5, who would insist on reading friendship as battery. I will return to the question of Fielding's sentimentality; for now I want to observe that if charity's superiority to liability involves the status of one's heart, it also involves the status of the will. Strict liability, as I've repeatedly observed, is strict because it makes persons responsible whether or not they mean or want to be responsible. The specter of strict liability is an obsessive worry of many of Fielding's more debased characters, in particular the innkeepers under whose roofs the catastrophes of plot transpire. "Here's a pretty Kettle of Fish . . . you have brought upon us!" cries Mrs. Tow-wouse when Joseph is deposited by the coachman at her inn: "We are like to have a Funeral at our own expence." "My Dear, I am not to blame: he was brought hither by the Stage-Coach," objects her "charitable" husband, attempting to shift the obligations of his calling back onto the similarly obliged coachmen (57). When by "accident" one of Joseph's attackers escapes from the inn (an event that is not, predictably, accidental but a consequence of the constable's negligence or complicity), Mr. Tow-wouse, we're told, "was in some Tribulation; the Surgeon having declared, that by Law, he was liable to be indicted for the Thief's Escape, as it was out of his House." "If he could be indicted without any harm to his Wife and Children, I should be glad of it" (72), observes his bloodthirsty spouse, her heartlessness isomorphic with the heartlessness of a law that would make a man who had done no wrong—who had not acted at all—liable. And after the captain who has abducted Fanny is "suffered to go off" by an innkeeper's servants in book 3, chapter 12, the host's wife likewise begs forgiveness for her husband's negligence, saying she hoped he would be pardoned "for the sake of his poor Family; and indeed if he could be ruined alone, she should be very willing of it, *for because as why*, his Worship very well knew he deserved it" (271).

We recall that in *Clarissa*, Lovelace suggests that women are peculiarly invested in blame—and in legal technologies of accusation—and that men, in contrast, concern themselves with retaliation rather than blame. Fielding, as we've seen, is not a fan Lovelace's preferred method of retaliation, but he likewise articulates a gendered distinction between blaming and fighting. For unlike the harridans populating the inns of Fielding's fictional universe, men are by and large "good natured," and to be good natured is to be willing to punch another person in the face but not to impugn his character.[37] "Men of true Wisdom and Goodness are contended to take Persons and Things as they are, without complaining of their Imperfections, or attempting to amend them" (107), explains the narrator of *Tom Jones:* "Upon the whole then, the Man of Candour, and of true Understanding, is never hasty to condemn" (329). This particular form of generosity is practiced by Tom as well as by Joseph, who resists understanding the "Drift" of Lady Booby's advances toward him, for example, because of "an Unwillingness in him to discover what he must condemn in her as a Fault" (46). In *Tom Jones* Fielding makes it clear that there are two problems with a reflexive commitment to blame: first, one might be wrong about whether or not a person has committed a bad act and second, blame makes the adjudication of that act an account of the person *as such*.

The only harm men suffer in a Fielding novel is the harm of being called guilty when they are innocent. When Adams—whose inability to experience harm is matched only by an inability to perceive it—is brought before a justice of the peace in book 2, chapter 11, after being falsely accused by Fanny's would-be rapist of attempted robbery and attempted murder, he expresses a rare concern with his own safety. Remarking that "he hoped he should not be condemned unheard," the justice informs him that "you will be asked what you have to say for yourself, when you come on your Trial, we are not trying you now; I shall only commit you to Gaol: if you can prove your Innocence at *Size,* you will be found *Ignoramus,* and so no Harm done." "Is it no Punishment, Sir, for an innocent Man to lie several Months in Gaol?" Adams anxiously responds, acknowledging for a moment the possibility that harm might indeed be done (147–48). This moment of anxiety is interesting given what has just transpired—the fight with the rapist in which it looks for a moment as though Adams has accidentally killed him. In the scene Adams is once again impervious to harm. Although we are told that his assailant

> threw himself upon him, and laying hold on the Ground with his left Hand, he with his right belaboured the Body of *Adams* 'till he was weary, and indeed, 'till he concluded (to use the Language of fighting) *that he had done his Business;* or, in the Language of Poetry, *that he had sent him to the Shades below;* in plain *English, that he was dead,*

Adams, "who was no Chicken, and could bear a drubbing as well as any boxing Champion in the Universe," is not in fact dead but lying still, awaiting the opportunity to retaliate. This he does by giving the man

> so dextrous a Blow just under his Chin, that the Fellow no longer retained any Motion, and *Adams* began to fear he had struck him once too often; for he often asserted, "he should be concerned to have the Blood of even the Wicked upon him." (138–39)

In the tragic fiction of Defoe or Richardson, the point of such a scene would be to highlight how actions/persons not themselves unjust produce catastrophic effects—the catastrophe of fatal harm, the catastrophe of accidental culpability. In the comic epic, of course, the man does not, cannot, die. But this is not the only or the primary difference in the way the scene plays out, for even before Adams knows that he has not unwittingly killed another, he serenely observes that " 'e wished indeed he had not deprived the wicked Wretch of Life, but G––'s Will be done;' he said, 'he hoped the Goodness of his Intention would excuse him in the next World, and he trusted in her Evidence to acquit him in this' " (139). Adams's complacency—especially his assumption that virtue will out—receives some comeuppance in the scene with the justice that follows, which ironizes his recommendation to Fanny after her escape that she "repose thy Trust in the same Providence, which hath hitherto protected thee, and never will forsake the Innocent" (141). Elsewhere his tendency to obfuscate harm by mobilizing a providential quietism is similarly ironized (his consolation of Joseph in book 3, chapter 11). And yet although it is clearly not the case that innocence never will be forsaken, what remains indisputable—subjected to no ironic reversal—is the *fact* of Adams's innocence grounded in the "Goodness of his Intention."

The harm of (false) accusation is an even more prominent engine of plot in *Tom Jones*, and here too the depredations of a culture of accusation and liability are marked by explicit invocations of the laws of trespass. When the "Hero of this great History appears with very bad Omens" in book 3, chapter 2, the universal opinion that Tom is "born to be hanged" seems confirmed by Squire Western's arrival at Paradise Hall complaining "of the Trespass on his Manor, in as high Terms, and as bitter Language, as if his House had been broken open, and the most valuable Furniture stole out of it" (118, 121). It is striking, given that Tom's dire fate is predicated on three robberies, that what is emphasized in this scene is civil rather than criminal liability. Western calls poaching a *trespass*, and this has baffled editors of the novel from Battestin to Bender. According to Battestin, "Tom and the gamekeeper would have been judged guilty of an offence only if they had trespassed on a game warren," and he wonders why Fielding neglects to designate Squire Western's estate such a haven.[38] John Allen Stevenson argues that the scene invokes instead the recent Black Act (1723) making it illegal for any person not worth £100 per anum to hunt game, but he admits that "Western does not prosecute for a violation of the game law, only for a trespass." Bender and Simon Stern agree that game law doesn't cover a case like this. "Civil law permitted property-owners to recover the value of any stolen goods," they observe, but they don't explain the observation in any detail.[39] Less interesting to me than determining the precise legal-historical point at issue (Coke is content to describe poaching as a trespass; he does, for example, in *Lord Dacre's Case*, discussed in chapter 2) is how Fielding's simile—"*as if* his house had been broken open"—deliberately conflates trespass and burglary, civil and criminal liability. Or rather, the simile registers *Western's* conflation of these things, his tendency (implicitly denounced by the narrative voice) to overestimate harm and damage by converting trespass into criminal liability. Nor is this an individual idiosyncrasy: Tom's vulnerability is not merely an effect of his illegitimacy, Fielding suggests, but of his culture's broad commitment to hyperbolic (or strict) models of responsibility.

Once again Fielding is astute in his recognition of such a commitment, which as we have seen structures the plot of *Clarissa* and the doctrine of felony murder developing out of *Lord Dacre's Case*. (That case, we recall, performs an even more extreme conversion—that of trespass into murder.) It should not be surprising, then, that the scene with Western turns on a legal question that underwrites all contemporary extensions of liability: the question of vicarious liability. In the three robberies attributed to Tom—which look more like trespass *de bonis asportatis,* from which robbery is distinguished by a specific intent to steal that Tom clearly lacks—the narrator informs us that Tom has been "what the Law calls an Accessory after the Fact": "As *Jones* alone was discovered, the poor Lad bore not only the whole Smart, but the whole Blame; both which fell again to his Lot, on the following Occasion" (119).[40] As in the episode of the partridge, Tom's coconspirator, Black George, has once again "happily concealed himself" (120), and although grammatically this is made to look like George's action, in fact the act of concealment is Tom's: "He had promised the poor Fellow to conceal him" (131), Tom tells Allworthy. Tom's concern with concealing or absorbing the culpability of others—his willingness to be considered principal when he is in fact an accessory—is a prominent and recurrent feature of his good nature. He entreats Allworthy, for example, to "have Compassion on the poor Girl [Molly Seagrim], and to consider, if there was any Guilt in the Case, it lay *principally* at his Door" (193; emphasis mine) and begs him to "have Compassion on the poor Fellow's [George Seagrim] Family, especially as *he himself only* had been guilty, and the other had been very difficultly prevailed on to do what he did" (131; emphasis mine).

This looks like vicarious liability, but it is not. The doctrine of agency that made Roxana liable for the unsanctioned and unanticipated acts of her servant Amy—or that threatens to make Fielding's innkeepers liable for the negligent behavior of those in their employ—ironically superimposes what is called "agency" on those who have not acted. As I've been arguing, the doctrine of agency understands the agent as a form of a person, an instrumental thing whose thoughts, even whose actions, are quite irrelevant to the question of her responsibility. In Tom's hands, however, vicarious liability is a choice, an expression of an agency that is entirely his own. Which is to say that in Fielding's hands, vicarious liability follows the *ideology* rather than the *doctrine* of agency. It is not, in fact, vicarious liability but charity, a way of being obliged to others that is importantly volitional. Fielding's narrator himself makes a version of this point in the episode centering on the question of Tom's responsibility for Partridge. "I must begin by telling you, sir, that you yourself have been the greatest enemy I ever had," says the barber-surgeon, ministering to Tom after his brawl with Lieutenant Northerton. When Tom expresses surprise that he could have harmed someone he has never met, Partridge explains: "You are perfectly innocent of having intended me any Wrong; for you was then an Infant" (424). Tom's immediate reply is to offer to "make you Amends for your Sufferings on

my Account" (425), an offer he admits is compromised by his impecunious-
ness (and which Partridge in any case just as promptly rejects). One might want
to argue that Tom's compensation is rejected because Partridge is after what
looks like bigger game: the reward money he imagines he'll receive when he
returns Tom to Allworthy. But there's a strong suggestion that Partridge rejects
Tom's compensation because he has not, in fact, "suffered on his account"—
because although Tom might be said to have *caused* Partridge's harm, he has
not intended it. That Tom wants to compensate harms that the novel insists
are not his ties his generosity to that of Allworthy, who, we are informed at the
close of this scene, has privately been paying Partridge an annuity that the latter
"looked upon as a kind of Smart-money, or rather by way of Atonement for In-
justice; For it is very uncommon, I believe, for Men to ascribe the Benefactions
they receive to pure Charity, when they can possibly impute them to any other
Motive" (427).

Charity, Fielding maintains, is not "smart-money" (a contemporary term for
pecuniary damages): it is not, significantly, atonement. Charity is that whose
dispensation confirms the blamelessness of the donor. The difference between
the innkeepers who worry about the possibility of being obliged and Allworthy,
Tom, or Abraham Adams who embrace their obligation to others is the comic
hero's conviction of his innocence understood as an innocence of intention: his
conviction that he is obliged *rather than* liable. Indeed, the difference between
a status being such as an innkeeper and the comic hero as Fielding conceives
him is that the comic hero *has* intentions: to be a comic hero is to be a person
rather than a type. If this claim flies in the face of conventional wisdom about
Fielding—who has long been understood to represent an "eclectic" interest in
typology amid the rise of psychological subjectivity—I want to suggest that despite Henry James's famous assertion that Fielding's hero has "so much 'life'
that it amounts . . . almost to his having a mind, that is to his having reactions and a full consciousness"—an assertion, in other words, that Tom Jones is
mind*less*—it is to Fielding's characters rather than Richardson's that one must
look for persons who are something more than forms.[41]

The nontypological quality of Fielding's characters—their "depth"—only
comes into focus when one thinks about the question of accidental responsibility. For although Fielding's heroes are responsible persons, they do not imagine
themselves to be nor are they made responsible for accidents. We have seen
how even before the logic of genre absolves Adams, he has absolved himself
of responsibility for the apparent death of his assailant in book 2, chapter 9, of
Joseph Andrews, and absolution characterizes Wilson's inset narrative in book 3

as well. At one point in his story of degradation and redemption Wilson pauses to consider the consequences of his acts for one of the women he has seduced:

> having reflected that I had been the first Aggressor, and had done her an Injury for which I could make her no Reparation, by robbing her of the Innocence of her Mind; and hearing at the same time that the poor old Woman her Mother had broke her Heart, on her Daughter's Elopement from her, I, concluding myself her Murderer ("As you very well might," cries *Adams,* with a Groan;) was pleased that God Almighty had taken this Method of punishing me, and resolved quietly to submit to the Loss. (208)

Wilson's experience has all the markings of a story of "matrimonial murder": a woman debauched with the promise of marriage, the promise broken, and ruin and death the consequence. Even Adams's fondness for exculpation fails him when confronted with these details: "How much more will your Indignation be raised when you hear the fatal Consequences of this barbarous, this villainous Action?" Wilson wonders at the outset of his tale, and by the end Adams is affirming Wilson's description of himself as a "murderer." And yet, what does it mean that Wilson is "pleased" that God has taken this method of punishing him if not that he has *not* been punished? That "murder" is a wholly rhetorical category? That neither he nor anyone else should take seriously the notion that this death is something for which he is responsible? That what might be "fatal consequences" for another is for him a piece of the greatest good fortune? When death is a consequence of another of his seductions, its fortuitousness is again emphasized. Of his affair with a married woman whose husband divorces her and who thus "came upon my hands," Wilson reflects: "At length Death delivered me of an Inconvenience, which the Consideration of my having been the Author of her Misfortunes, would never suffer me to take any other Method of discarding" (211). What in Richardson's hands might have been a story about woman's misfortune becomes here a story about man's—one in which the only harm man experiences *as* harm is the harm of accusation: "He [the husband] then prosecuted me at Law, and recovered 3000 *l.* Damages, which much distressed my Fortune to pay" (211), Wilson recounts; "strange Punishment," he later concludes, "for a little Inadvertency and Indiscretion" (220).

When in *Tom Jones* the lawyer Dowling insists that Tom has been unfairly punished by Allworthy for *his* inadvertency and indiscretion—displaying a concern with the disproportions of retributive justice that reveals Dowling "had not divested himself of Humanity by being an Attorney" (658)—Tom replies: "I know, I feel,—I feel my Innocence, my Friend; and I would not part with that Feeling for the World—For as long as I know I have never done, nor even designed an Injury to any Being whatever, *Pone me pigris ubi nulla campis / Arbor aestiva recreatur aura . . ."* (659). The quote from Horace's *Odes* 1.22 invokes the threat of harm only to insist that harm is "charmed," disarmed by the consolations of love. Horace's speaker is solaced by the love of women; but what soothes Tom is something more akin to self-love. His feeling *for* himself is a feeling *of* himself, and self-justification yields up the emolument of self-consciousness. The exchange with Dowling thus begins to explain the counterintuitive claim made a few paragraphs ago, that the normative criteria of realist characterization—self-consciousness, psychological motivation, implied personhood—are properly the stuff of comic epic. But it also foreshadows the injury Tom delivers to Mr. Fitzpatrick in book 16—an episode that puts Tom's innocence, and the exculpatory powers of comedy, most strenuously to the test.

For it is in the fight with Fitzpatrick rather than the incest plot that Fielding conjures the specter of tragedy. He marks the turn toward tragedy—and thus toward *Clarissa*—by way of an extended meditation on the logic of felony murder. The "tragical incident," as the narrator calls it, begins with a blow to the head. Or rather, it begins with blows exchanged between Tom and Fitzpatrick six books earlier (book 10, chapter 2) at Upton. When they meet again Tom expresses the hope that their "foolish Quarrel" will be forgotten "over a Bottle," and Fitzpatrick says he "will drink a Bottle with you presently; but first I will give you a great Knock over the Pate. There is for you, you Rascal. Upon my Soul, if you do not give me Satisfaction for that Blow, I will give you another" (872). It looks from his willingness to drink that Fitzpatrick will be satisfied with a fistfight—that he is the kind of man (an Englishman) for whom quarreling is but a prelude to friendship. But instead he draws his sword—"which was the only Science he understood," the narrator contemptuously explains—and although he is "a little staggered by the Blow" Tom is described as "presently recovering himself" and drawing as well: "He understood nothing of Fencing," the narrator observes approvingly, yet "prest on so boldly upon *Fitzpatrick* that he beat down his Guard, and sheathed one half of his Sword in the Body of the said Gentleman" (872). "I have Satisfaction enough; I am a dead Man," Fitzpatrick declares, and Tom replies: "I hope not . . . but whatever be the Consequence you must be sensible that you have drawn it upon yourself" (872). Tom's claim that his assailant has "drawn it upon himself" comes very close to a claim that he has "drawn upon himself"—that Fitzpatrick has sheathed Tom's sword in his own body, that Fitzpatrick has injured, perhaps murdered, himself. This position is reiterated when the

Report brought back was that the Wound was certainly mortal, and there were no Hopes of Life. Upon which the Constable informed *Jones,* that he must go before a Justice. He answered, "Wherever you please; I am indifferent as to what happens to me, for tho' I am convinced I am not guilty of Murder in the Eye of the Law, yet the Weight of Blood I find intolerable upon my Mind." (873)

In the chapters that follow the energy of the plot is directed toward unearthing witnesses to support Tom's contention that he is "not guilty of murder": what has happened, Nightingale agrees, is an

Accident, which, whatever be the Consequence, can be attended with no Danger to you, and in which your Conscience cannot accuse you of having been in the least to blame. If the Fellow should die, what have you done more than taken away the Life of a Ruffian in your own Defense? (893)

Although the novel appears to endorse the position that Tom is innocent because he has acted in self-defense—because he has not acted but *reacted*—it is not clear that such equanimity is entirely warranted. The issue centers on the distinction between murder and manslaughter, which, it turns out, is also a distinction between fighting and dueling, between retaliation in "hot" and in "cold" blood. If two men meet "accidentally," "and A. assaults B. first, and B. merely in his own defence, without any other malicious design kills A. this is not murder in B," reports Sir Matthew Hale in the *Historia placitorum coronae* (which was written around 1670 but not published until 1738). If, however, "A. and B. had met deliberately to fight, and A. strikes B. and pursues B. so closely, that B. in safeguard of his own life kills A. this is murder in B. because their meeting was a compact, and an act of deliberation."[42] Accidental meetings are distinguished from deliberate ones by questions of intimacy—whether the assailants are known to one another, whether the present quarrel is an outbreak of new or old, hot or cold, hostilities. Hale goes on to explain that

if A. and B. fall suddenly out, and they presently agree to fight in the field, and run and fetch their weapons, and go into the field and fight, and A. kills B. this is not murder but homicide, for it is but a continuance of the sudden falling out, and the blood was never cooled.[43]

From Tom's perspective, the encounter with Fitzgerald is an unexpected surprise and he is therefore guiltless of the crime with which he is threatened. But in the writings of Michael Foster and William Hawkins, in which, as we saw in chapter 2, a category of homicide is developing that includes actions such as dueling and battering that are repeatedly transformed into murder, the issue is not so clear cut. In his *Discourse of Homicide*—published in 1762 but "*written many Years ago, and the whole in a Manner completed before the Accession of his present Majesty,*" he notes in a preface—Foster repeats Hale's argument, stating that if "upon a sudden Quarrel the Parties fight upon the Spot, or if they presently fetch their Weapons and go into the Field and fight, and One of them falleth, it will be but Manslaughter; because it may be presumed the Blood never cooled."[44] By the 1740s, however, the question of the temperature of one's blood—which is to say the state of one's mind—is more ambiguous than it was for Hale. Foster observes that

> It will be Otherwise if they appoint to fight the next Day, or even upon the same Day at such an Interval as that the Passion might have subsided: or if from any Circum-stances attending the Case it may be reasonably concluded, that their Judgment had actually controuled the First Transports of Passion before they engaged.[45]

"And where-ever it appears from the whole Circumstances of the Case, That he who kills another on a sudden Quarrel, was Master of his Temper at the Time," announces Hawkins, "he is guilty of Murder."[46] In Hale, mental states are for-mally construed by temporal and spatial indices: the question of deliberation is answered by asking how far a pair of assailants might have moved from the origin of their encounter or how long ago that encounter occurred. In Hawk-ins and Foster, the appeal to "other circumstances" invokes more abstract for-mal markers of intentionality, enhancing the number and kinds of actions that count as "cool" and therefore culpable. "Where-ever two Persons in cool Blood meet and fight," says Hawkins

> and one of them is killed, the other is guilty of Murder, and cannot help himself by alleging that he was first struck by the Deceased; . . . or that he meant not to kill, but only to disarm, his Adversary: For since he deliberately engaged in an Act highly unlawful, in Defiance of the Laws, he must at his Peril abide the Conse-quences thereof.[47]

The question, then, is what happens when, after he is "staggered by the blow" from Fitzpatrick, Jones is described as "presently *recovering* himself" (872; em-phasis mine). On the face of it the term would seem to suggest deliberation—that Tom realizes what has happened and in a considered fashion takes up the sword that he wears about him, thereby in that moment transforming fighting into dueling, chance-medley into murder, accident into circumspection. But "recovery," as we have seen, plays a complicated part in Fielding's lexicon, and in *Joseph Andrews* points to something less like deliberation and more like the instrumentality of a male body reflexively primed to deliver and to sustain injury. In order to secure Tom's innocence, recovery needs to work in this way—to register an exculpatory thoughtlessness rather than an inculpatory mental competence, to signal a restoration of balance that barely distinguishes Tom from an animal. I have noted how Fielding rejects an idea central to the emerging realist novel: that animals might be guilty of harm and that persons might be guilty of harm in precisely the same way as an animal—because they have caused though not intended injury. By emphasizing Tom's animality, which is to say his sheer *animateness*, Fielding reaffirms the guiding principle of his fiction, that persons cannot be responsible for what they did not intend. The way he does this is extraordinarily complex, for if in the episode with Fitzpatrick it looks as though the man who fights is not a man but a beast, ultimately fighting comes to represent a type of interiority that distinguishes *homo pugnax* from other animated species.[48]

In *Joseph Andrews*, the pugnacious Adams—the new man—is frequently compared to an animal. Prior to his mock-epic engagement with the roasting squire's dogs, for example, Adams is compared first to a donkey and then to a hare. The episode is at once a meditation on the question of harm and the question of human ontology, questions that I have been arguing are repeatedly aligned in the early realist novel and that mark this episode as an allegory, among other things, of Fielding's formal commitments. The scene begins, however, with a different allegory—one of sexual harm, of the difference between sex and sexual harm. While Joseph and Fanny amuse themselves in what is described as a "harmless and delightful manner," they hear "a Pack of Hounds approaching in full Cry towards them, and presently afterwards saw a Hare pop forth from the Wood, and crossing the Water, land within a few Yards of them in the Meadows" (236). Fanny's pity for the endangered creature arises from a sense of her own, gendered, vulnerability to harm. And there is a way that, in his frequent attacks on huntsmen and other hypermasculine types, Fielding can be said to share her dismay at gendered violence and at the "Barbarity of worrying a poor innocent defenceless Animal out of its Life, and putting it to the extremest Torture for Diversion" (236). Yet the formal features of mock-epic make the question of harm difficult to parse. It is true that when the captain carries Fanny away in book 3, chapter 9, his depravity is underscored by the way he departs "without any more Consideration of her Cries than a Butcher hath of those of a Lamb" (259). But does mock-epic take seriously the idea of harm to animals? Or does it burlesque the conflation of hunting and rape, harm to animate things and harm to persons? Does it invoke animal harm as an indictment of epic masculinity? Or is harm to animals—and harm to women—perfectly consistent with masculine propriety, as it is for Joseph, who will not "attempt anything contrary to the Laws of Hunting, in favour of the Hare, which he said was killed fairly" (237).

The answers to some of these questions are clearer than others. As Campbell has shown, animal baiting, woman baiting, and parson baiting are practices aligned by Fielding with debased forms of masculinity and satire.[49] Yet the way debasement is represented not only as an ethical but an *ontic* inhumanity— as the failure to *be* human (the roasting squire's men are "two-leg'd Curs on horseback" [238], more bestial than the beasts who serve them)—means the preeminence of the human remains secure. But given this, how are we to understand the animal similes that characterize descriptions of Adams, that most humane of persons? When in book 2, chapter 13, Adams is described as knowing no more of the narrator's philosophical digression on class (articulated, significantly, in the language of species) "than the Cat which sat on the Table" (158), his animal likeness designates a thoughtlessness allied with his pugnacity. Adams is a cat because he does not understand Mrs. Slipslop's contempt for Fanny—contempt predicated on a logic of metamorphosis similar in kind to that underwriting the simile the narrator has just deployed: persons of different classes, we're told, "seem scarce to regard each other as of the same Species. This the Terms *strange Persons, People one does not know, the Creature, Wretches, Beasts, Brutes,* and many other Appellations evidently demonstrate" (157). He *is* a cat, but he lacks the capacity to conceive of other persons as cats (a point to which I will return). Adams's bestiality is reinforced in the next paragraph by his recapitulation of the bout with Fanny's rapist—an event whose initial description, one is meant to recall, foregrounds the reflexivity of Adams's response to Fanny's harm. Hearing her shrieks, Adams "made no Answer, but snapt his Fingers, and brandishing his Crabstick, made directly to the Place whence the Voice issued." The narrator reflects that

> the great Abilities of Mr *Adams* were not necessary to have formed a right Judgment of this Affair, on the first sight. He did not therefore want the Entreaties of the poor Wretch to assist her, but lifting up his Crabstick, he immediately levelled a Blow at . . . the Ravisher's Head. (137)

Slipslop, when she hears the tale, is less impressed than Fielding's narrator by Adams's instinctive heroism: "She said, 'she thought him properer for the Army than the Clergy: that it did not become a Clergyman to lay violent Hands on any one'" (159).

Adams acts without mobilizing the "abilities" peculiar to his species; he acts without thinking. Yet rather than marking the absence of a mental state, such action is depicted *as* a mental state: "right Judgment." If Adams looks like an animal because he is continually impelled toward acts of violence, the peculiar form this violence takes—fistfighting—is that which finally distinguishes human persons from other animated things: "Nothing could provoke *Adams* to strike," we're told, "but an absolute Assault on himself or his Friend" (168). This account of the act of fighting as at once automatic and ethical—as a compulsion to defend oneself and others from harm—helps to explain what is at stake in Tom's fight with Fitzpatrick in the concluding chapters of *Tom Jones*. And this episode, in turn, helps to explain what it can possibly mean to distinguish humans from animals on the basis of what would seem to be a shared aversion to harm. In Tom's encounter with Fitzpatrick one begins to see more clearly what has been glimpsed before: that human persons suffer a specific kind of harm experienced by no other species—the harm of accusation. When Nightingale tracks down witnesses he hopes will support Tom's contention that he acted against Fitzpatrick in self-defense, they say "that they were at too great a Distance to overhear any Words that passed between you; but they both agree that the first Blow was given by you." "They injure me," answers the outraged Tom. "He not only struck me first, but struck me without the least Provocation. What should induce those Villains to accuse me falsely?" (908).

The novel never answers the legal question of Tom's responsibility for Fitzpatrick's injury. Instead it shifts attention to *Tom's* injury, the latest and most egregious harm perpetrated on him by a debased and effeminate culture of blame. Tom's response to this fresh wound, as in the conversation with Dowling, is to invoke self-consciousness about his innocence as compensation for the harm of false accusation. Offering "many solemn and vehement Protestations of the Truth of what he had at first asserted," Tom ends by expressing hope that "the Divine Goodness will one Day suffer my Honour to be cleared, and that the Words of a dying Man, at least, will be believed, so far as to justify his Character" (908–9). When it comes, the agency of Tom's exculpation is not divine, however: rather it takes the form of the goodness of genre; it is enabled by the felicity of that preeminent vehicle of felicity, comedy. Fitzpatrick does not die, and his not dying at once puts in abeyance the question of Tom's innocence and serves to confirm it, as comedy, like self-consciousness itself, emerges as a weapon in the novel's epic battle against blame. "Most novels are comedies, in which prosecution may be one more mishap for heroes and heroines to outlive," observes Alexander Welsh: *Tom Jones* is a "triumphant showing for the defense."[50]

In his analysis of Fielding's fiction in *Strong Representations*, Welsh notes of Tom that he "never intends any wrong, hence cannot be criminally guilty."[51] For Welsh, Tom's relentless goodness confirms the critical consensus that he lacks psychology: James's claim that Tom has life but no consciousness, he says, registers the way Fielding derives intentions from circumstantial evidence, "reconstructing the mind from the outside in, from 'the Fact' in evidence to the motive."[52] As Welsh demonstrates, this is the way the law invariably represents intention, and he goes on to claim that Fielding's investment in a circumstantial account of states of mind signals the juridical quality of his narrative practice and the practice of narration *tout court*. John Loftis is less persuaded of Fielding's commitment to a juridical account of the person. For him *Tom Jones* repeatedly highlights the failure of legal discourse to "adequately represent human characters and situations."[53] If Tom is "born to be hanged," he asks, is this "a true judgment of Tom's character or an indictment of a society and a legal system that is incapable of finding discourses, modes of inquiry and representation, adequate to a true judgment of character?"[54] The law is too "mono-vocal" to capture the complexities of persons, Loftis insists, concluding that Fielding "opts for the novel, this new form of multi-vocal aesthetic discourse, over the mono-vocal trial, as the most accurate way to judge character."[55]

According to Frances Ferguson, the tension between Welsh's formalist account of character and Loftis's antiformalist one is precisely what is at stake in the psychological novel—indeed that tension is precisely the way psychology, and character, works. For her, the novel's representation of psychological complexity

> does not at all directly express mental states but rather relies on the contradiction built into the formal stipulation of them. Psychological complexity, that is, pits the stipulated mental state against one's actual mental state. . . . [P]sychology [is] the ongoing possibility of the contradiction between what one must mean and what one wants to mean.[56]

Ferguson goes on to describe this contradiction as a "mimesis of distinction," a "new aesthetic" invented by Richardson that insists on "the inability of form to carry mental states in anything but excessively capacious (that is, ambiguous) or potentially self-contradictory stipulated forms."[57] In chapter 2, I disagreed with Ferguson that this new aesthetic could be laid at Richardson's door. In its sense that even as form defines persons, it flattens their indwelling complexity—in its preoccupation with persons *as such*—the mimesis of distinction does not seem to me to fully capture Richardson's formal commitments. It does, however, capture *Fielding*'s. For what makes a man a man in Fielding is what makes him Man: the capacity to register the harm of misrepresentation as the only harm that truly matters and a corresponding capacity to give an account of oneself that differs from the (necessarily distorted and distorting) accounts of others. To be a man in Fielding is to be able to say, with Tom, "I know, I feel,—I feel my Innocence" (659).

This is finally where—and how—the question of ontology and the question of blame converge. "A single bad Act no more constitutes a Villain in Life, than a single bad Part on the Stage" (328), insists the narrator of *Tom Jones;* the good-natured man is he who "can censure the Action, without conceiving any absolute Detestation of the Person, whom perhaps Nature may not have designed to act an ill Part in all her Dramas" (327). Blame inappropriately yokes doing to being, making actions representative of the individual in toto: it is a metonymic logic, Fielding suggests, perhaps a kind of *personification* for the way it assembles a "person" out of foreign elements—the alien and incomprehensible fragments of her acts. Put this way one begins to recognize the formal and conceptual significance of the extended satire on prosopoeia in *Joseph Andrews* and to understand the role species plays in the formal practice of comic epic. In his apostrophe to Love in book 1, chapter 7, the narrator says:

> Not the Great *Rich,* who turns Men into Monkeys, Wheelbarrows, and whatever else best humours his Fancy, hath so strangely metamorphosed the human Shape . . . as thou dost metamorphose and distort the human Senses. . . . Thou can'st make Cowardice brave, Avarice generous, Pride humble, and Cruelty tender-hearted. In short, thou turnest the Heart of Man inside-out, as a Juggler doth a Petticoat, and bringest whatsoever pleaseth thee out from it. (36–37)

This account of the alchemy of love is also an account of the alchemy of writing, as signaled by the allegory that swiftly follows in chapter 8, and that is not the befuddled Rich's but Fielding's own: "Now the Rake *Hesperus* had called for his Breeches, and having well rubbed his drowsy Eyes, prepared to dress himself for all Night; . . . In vulgar Language, it was in the Evening when *Joseph* attended his Lady's Orders" (37–38). The problem with Rich's pantomimes—which his use of metamorphosis underscores—is their indiscriminate oscillation between tragic and comic scenes.[58] Fielding's superiority is to have chosen *one* genre in which to work: a genre that might appear devoted to metamorphosis but is above all clear about the difference between men and monkeys.

The virtue of comedy is Adams's virtue: his unwillingness to mistake human persons for creatures of a different species, his tendency to treat all people as *his* people—as family rather than strangers. When in book 2, chapter 16, Adams is commended for the "Familiarity with which he conversed with *Joseph* and *Fanny*, whom he often called his Children, a Term, he explained to mean no more than his Parishioners; saying, he looked on all those whom God had entrusted to his Cure, to stand to him in that Relation," his behavior is distinguished from that of his wife, who, when we meet her in book 4, chapter 8, is described as "one of those prudent People who never do any thing to injure their Families" (306) and who considers "a pack of Nonsense" her husband's sense "that the whole Parish are is children" (321). Most emphatically his behavior is distinguished from that of Parson Trulliber, who "instead of esteeming his poor Parishioners as part of his Family, seems rather to consider them as not of the same Species with himself" (172). It's not immediately clear what species Parson Trulliber *is*, since here he is described as a "Turky-Cock" and elsewhere as a pig and a goose (162). When signs of his humanity emerge, however, they do so from a familiar source: concurring with Trulliber's claim that he is "as good a Man as [Adams]," the narrator observes: "Indeed, tho' he was now rather too corpulent for athletic Exercises, he had in his Youth been one of the best Boxers and Cudgel-players in the County" (168). If Parson Trulliber is at present too epicene to be fully a man, it is because he has fallen away from a condition of masculinity—which is to say a condition of human ontology—that is identical with an ability to fight. And when he threatens to try to reclaim this condition, his wife's response reminds us of that to which fighting, and the human, is opposed: "His Wife seeing him clench his Fist, interposed, and begged him not to fight, but to shew himself a true Christian, and take the Law of him" (168).

In Fielding, a commitment to the humanity of persons is one and the same as a commitment to fighting as an alternative to legal remediation. The fist-fight, as we see here and again in the episode of the roasting squire, whose fondness for interspecies violence (man against bear, dog against man, man against woman-as-hare) compromises his own ontology, is crucially *intraspe-cies*—a way of resolving differences between men that insists there *is* no difference between men, that everyone is a part of one (human) family, that human beings are "above the reach of any Simile" (244). Despite Fielding's vaunted conservatism, this is a profoundly liberal—and, as we shall see, sentimental—

idea. It is also a profoundly masculinist one: for the human person in Fielding is presumptively male.

It is women, after all, who, like Mrs. Trulliber (or the effeminate Pounce and Didapper), display an enthusiasm for "taking the law" of men, while the manly among men and women alike are "sufficiently contented with . . . Drubbing" (271). And it is women who are conditioned to make Rich's mistake and confound men with animals. Indeed, woman's investments in invective and anthropomorphosis are linked, since the sex's genealogical encounter with man's injuriousness leads her to (mis-)construe him as a beast. Fielding's narrator explains:

> At the Age of seven or something earlier, Miss is instructed by her Mother, that Master is a very monstrous kind of Animal, who will, if she suffers him to come too near her, infallibly eat her up and grind her to pieces. . . . [B]y the Age of Ten they have contracted such a Dread and Abhorrence of the above named Monster, that whenever they see him, they fly from him as the innocent Hare doth from the Greyhound. (299–300)

As a biological adaptation, women "endeavour by all the Methods they can invent to render themselves so amiable in [man's] Eyes, that he may have no Inclination to hurt them" (300). And so well do they succeed at this adaptive practice that man's fearsomeness is revealed as something projected onto them by women, who in a kind of mass hysteria, a neurosis at once cultural and genetic,

> still pretend the same Aversion to the Monster: And the more they love him, the more ardently they counterfeit the Antipathy. By the continual and constant Practice of which Deceit on others, they at length impose on themselves, and really believe they hate what they love. (300–301)

The idea of woman's creaturely vulnerability and man's bestial injuriousness emerges here as a misandrous fiction, one necessary to the complex erotics and intricate sportsmanship of heterosexual conjugation.

Not only are men not harmed in Fielding's fiction, but women are not harmed either. What looks like hate is in fact love; what looks like harm is love once again. Fanny might fret about the "poor reeling, staggering Prey, which fainting almost at every Step" crawls toward her only to be "instantly tore to pieces before [her] Face" (237), and Fielding might agree with her that hunting is but torture masquerading as diversion. But the logic of comic epic demands that when her own fanny is torn to pieces—when the wedding night approaches in which Joseph is "all Desire," while Fanny "had her Wishes tempered with Fears"—defloration will be experienced as a "Reward" at once "great and sweet" (343). The opening gambit of *Joseph Andrews* replaces the female body with the male body, substituting Joseph's "excellent Habit of Body" (78)—a body that "cannot be ravished against [its] Will" (87), a body whose wounds heal quickly and entirely—for a body vulnerable to a wound that never heals. And it proceeds to insist that men cannot be responsible for that injury because it is not an injury but a benefit—that women too "recover" by receiving the compensations of conjugal felicity.

It is a staple of feminist criticism on Fielding to object to the way marriage comedy confirms the hero in his sense that he has "never done, nor even designed an Injury to any Being whatever." "Fielding's amiable women . . . are incapable of seeing any fault in the men they love," complains Katherine Rogers. "Their good nature expresses itself in a love for their men which is not free but submissive" and that makes pardoning them " 'not only easy, but . . . delightful.' "[59] At stake in feminist skepticism about comedy's salubriousness is a muted formal insight, one it is the purpose of *Harm's Way* to move to the center of historiography on the novel: *comedy is a masculinist genre*—a genre that renders (women's) harm and (men's) responsibility as incoherent as when Mrs. Waters calls out "Rape! which last, some perhaps, may wonder she should mention, who do not consider that these Words of Exclamation are used by Ladies in a Fright, as Fa, la, la, ra, da, & c. are in Music, only as the Vehicles of Sound, and without any fixed Ideas" (529–30).

In its repudiation of a tragic realism that takes for granted we will hurt the ones we love and that when we do so we will be responsible for that harm, comic epic is also rigorously, *technically* sentimental. "We cannot at all sympathize with the resentment of one man against another, merely because this other has been the cause of his misfortune, unless he has been the cause of it from motives which we cannot enter into," observes Adam Smith in the *Theory of Moral Sentiments*.[60] We cannot sympathize, Smith says, but what he means is that we *ought not* to sympathize with such resentment. Smith's preoccupation with liability has rarely been noted, but he spends a great deal of time thinking about what he describes as our understandable yet unjust desire to censure persons for harms they have accidentally occasioned.[61]

Invoking ancient Aquilian laws in which "the man, who not being able to manage a horse that had accidentally taken fright, should happen to ride down his neighbor's slave, is obliged to compensate the damage," Smith notes that "to make no apology, to offer no atonement, is regarded as the highest brutality." Yet "Why should he make an apology more than any other person?" he asks. "Why should he, since he was equally innocent with any other by-stander, be thus singled out from among all mankind, to make up for the bad fortune of another?"[62] To impose liability and extract damages for accidents, especially for having "accidentally killed a man," is in some accordance with our "natural sentiments," Smith admits, but precisely because they are natural such sentiments are base and inhumane, "excessively severe," an "irregularity of human nature," an "unjust resentment," an *animal* resentment."[63] "A man of humanity, who accidentally, and without the smallest degree of blamable negligence, has been the cause of the death of another man, feels himself piacular, though not guilty," he complains:

> The distress which an innocent person feels, who, by some accident, has been led to do something which, if it had been done with knowledge and design, would have justly exposed him to the deepest reproach, has given occasion to some of the finest and most interesting scenes both of the ancient and of the modern drama. It is this fallacious sense of guilt, if I may call it so, which constitutes the whole distress of Oedipus and Jocasta upon the Greek, of Monimia and Isabella upon the English, theatre. They are all of them in the highest degree piacular, though not one of them is in the smallest degree guilty.[64]

Smith's rejection of Oedipus's guilt is an explicit rejection of the notion of "tragic responsibility," one that reveals an exquisite self-consciousness of the historical and conceptual relationship between laws of strict liability and the genre of tragedy. His insistence that the "more candid and humane part of mankind" will "exert their whole generosity and greatness of mind" to exonerate the accidental wrongdoer reveals something else that sentimentalism is a *comic* form.

⚮

In the line from Horace's *Epistles* that supplies the epigraph to this chapter, Horace tells Maecenas: "Be this our wall of bronze, to have no guilt at heart, no wrongdoing to turn us pale."[65] In the *Epistles*, the line emerges in the context of a discussion of the virtuous life; it is conditional, a recommendation about how virtue ought to feel. When it is reinvoked in *Shamela*, in a letter from Parson Williams to Mr. Booby disclaiming liability for whatever has prompted the squire to initiate an action of debt against him, the line is shortened and made declarative—it becomes an account not of virtue but of responsibility.[66] The citation has often been understood as part of Fielding's Pelagian attack on the parson's Calvinist self-righteousness, his emphasis on faith rather than works, his claim that what he knows to be true about himself is more important than what he has done or failed to do. It has been seen as registering Fielding's contrary emphasis on action and on a moral philosophy concerned with what people do rather than with what they believe.[67] Yet the claim that the man with a guiltless heart can have done no wrong ironically functions as an epigrammatic statement of Fielding's own ethics, an ethics wholly invested in self-righteousness, which is to say in the notion that we ought not to be blamed for what we have not meant to do, that we are not wrong if our heart is good. "To the intention or affection of the heart," agrees Smith (who must surely have known his Fielding), "to the beneficence or hurtfulness of the design, all praise or blame, all approbation or disapprobation of any kind, which can justly be bestowed upon any action, must ultimately belong."[68]

This investment in self-righteousness—that is, in an intentionalist and sentimental model of responsibility—is necessarily an investment in the category of the self. We have never really questioned the standard account of Fielding's aesthetic captured by Watt's exasperated response to Coleridge's famous dictum that *Tom Jones* is among the most perfect of plots. "Perfect for what?" Watt asks. "Not, certainly, for the exploration of character and of personal relations."[69] Arguing that "Fielding allotted characterization a much less important place in his total literary structure," Watt insists that there is

> an absolute connection in *Tom Jones* between the treatment of plot and of character. Plot has priority, and it is therefore plot which must contain the elements of complication and development. . . . *Tom Jones*, then, would seem to exemplify a principle of considerable significance for the novel form in general: namely, that the importance of the plot is in inverse proportion to that of character.[70]

The story of the novel—not only for Watt but also for most of his critics—is a story in which

> the Aristotelian priority of plot over character has been wholly reversed, and a new type of formal structure has been evolved in which the plot attempts only to embody the ordinary processes of life and in so doing becomes wholly dependent on the characters and the developments of their relationships. It is Defoe and above all Richardson who provide this tradition with its archetypes, just as it is Fielding who provides that for the opposite tradition.[71]

But if, as Ferguson suggests, character (that is, depth psychology) is produced through a person's capacity to given an account of her self and her motives that differs from the account that indicts her, then it is to *Fielding* and his host of unjustly accused heroes that one must look for an aesthetic committed to the depiction of character.

It is also where we must look for what is not found elsewhere in this study: a strong investment in the notion that characters are and ought to be human persons. In a wonderful recent essay on Fielding, Campbell argues that

> Fielding's prose style does not aim to empty out or transcend human personhood, in all its physical and socially determined specificity. Instead it uses the medium of its temporal and aural unfolding to activate one person's voice through another's, in the separate acts of reading that occur across historical time.[72]

Campbell's alignment of "voice" with the human as such, her moving emphasis on writing and reading as ethical, communitarian acts goes a long way toward explaining why we tend to want novels to have characters and why we tend to want characters to be human persons. Voice is how we explain ourselves to others; for her, as for Fielding, our desire and our ability to explain ourselves distinguishes us from inarticulate others—from animals, from things. At one point in "Rape and the Rise of the Novel," Ferguson observes that "a system that eliminates ambiguity . . . eliminates persons."[73] The system I have been describing in this book, the novel of tragic responsibility against which Fielding pits the project of comic epic, doesn't allow persons to explain and excuse themselves; it doesn't allow them to *be* persons. Put this way the novel of tragic responsibility is indistinguishable from a certain kind of criticism on the novel as described by Ferguson in a more recent essay, is indistinguishable from a formalist criticism in which

> agency became such a capacious and formally empty notion that one no longer needed human actors or characters to achieve it; animals and pots and kettles could carry the narrative action as well as a human could. Action, in other words, displaced character, and any sense of characterological depth looked misplaced in an analysis in which both animals and inanimate objects might play active roles.[74]

Ferguson's project in "Jane Austen, *Emma,* and the Impact of Form" is to rescue formalism from its disregard of human persons. This can be said to be Campbell's project too, directed as it is against D. A. Miller's alignment of form with *im*personality. For Ferguson, it is a mistake to think of form as antithetical to personhood, as Miller does in an earlier (Foucauldian) incarnation, rendering the novel's formal techniques for representing consciousness, and the consciousnesses so represented, "the pots and kettles of Proppian analysis."[75] On

her account, free indirect discourse makes persons through form: consciousness ceases to be an "individual project" and becomes a "communal" one; the
individual is seen as an individual "only through a chorus."[76] "Free indirect style,
like any external or logical representation," she says—like the law in "Rape and
the Rise of the Novel," like the law in *Tom Jones* or *Joseph Andrews*—"does not
provide the basis for any individual and individualized point of view."[77] That it
does not poses a challenge to individuation, but it is precisely this challenge
that sets in motion the process she once again calls "distinction," a process now
described as the capacity to give an account of one's *beloved* that differs from
others' accounts of her. "Intimacy" is what Ferguson designates this form of
distinction, that is, "dispensing with the forms of address that might be used in
public, by just anyone."[78] In Watt the proper name is a primary vehicle of characterization and individuation. In Ferguson the proper name is not proprietary
enough: intimacy requires an "exclusion of the proper name" that alone allows
a person to be distinguished from the chorus that engenders her—that allows
a person to be experienced, and to experience herself, as something more irre-
placeable than a kettle.[79]

"O my Child," cries Allworthy in the final moments of *Tom Jones;* "how have
I been to blame! How have I injured you! What Amends can I ever make you
for those unkind, those unjust Suspicions which I have entertained; and for all
the Sufferings they have occasioned to you?" "Am I not now made Amends?"
Tom replies: "Would not my Sufferings, if they had been ten Times greater,
have been now richly repaid? O my dear Uncle! this Goodness, this Tenderness
overpowers, unmans, destroys me" (959). It is common to read the resolution
of *Tom Jones* as a romance of the proper name and of the "possessive culture"
that underwrites it, but Ferguson's essay allows us to notice that what is fore-
grounded in this encounter is a more intense form of possession: "*my* child,"
"*my* uncle," forms of relation that cannot be occupied by just anyone.[80] I hope
the argument of this chapter has allowed us to notice something else: that the
practice of distinction and all that it entails—character, interiority, personhood,
voice, intimacy—is a practice of *exoneration*. To have injured someone unwittingly, Fielding insists one last time, is not to have injured them at all, and "for
Injuria sine damno there is no compensation."[81] The distinction of affection is
the only compensation a person needs, and Tom, like all fighting men, is made
a man by what only seems to him to unman him: his passionate attachment to
others.

It might seem an obvious benefit that Tom has ceased to be perceived as a
"noxious Animal" (44)—that the dehumanization entailed on him by his bas-

tardy has been answered by a salvific filiation. This is certainly the narrator's sense of things as he reflects at the beginning (and *of* the beginning) of Tom's tale:

> Miss *Bridget* had always exprest so great a regard for what the Ladies are pleased to call Virtue, and had herself maintained such a Severity of Character, that it was expected . . . that she would have vented much Bitterness on this Occasion, and would have voted for sending the Child, as a kind of noxious Animal, immediately out of the House. (44)

On the contrary, we're told, "she rather took the good-natur'd side of the question, intimated some Compassion for the helpless little Creature, and commended her Brother's Charity in what he had done" (44). It is not only that, prompted by filial tenderness, Bridget looks on Tom as a benign *form* of animal—a human animal, kin and kind. The word "noxious" puts us in more precise territory, for animals are noxious only when they have caused harm and are forfeited under an ancient form of strict liability—the law of deodand or *noxae deditio*. Even in the earliest pages of this very long book, Fielding establishes an opposition between good-natured charity and the "severity" of strict liability, between a humanist ethic predicated on fellow feeling, and an ethic that ties creatures to those who are not their fellows. It is this tragic ethic—this tragic, realist aesthetic—to which the comedy of *bildung* addresses itself. And if, as I've said, it seems churlish to fault Fielding for the robust sentimentalism of his comic aesthetic, in the chapter that follows we shall see what is gained from a (legal) formalism that erodes distinctions between human persons and animated and inanimate things: not intimacy, admittedly, but what intimacy conceals: responsibility.

CHAPTER FOUR

The Rape of the Cock

She is very pretty, very gentle, soft & insinuating. . . . A
Man must not be a Man but an It to resist such Artillery.
                          —Hester Thrale, *Thraliana*

Allegory is the armature of the modern.
                          —Walter Benjamin, *"Central Park"*

Frances Sheridan's *Memoirs of Miss Sidney Bidulph* is an odd sort of sentimental novel, despite its dedication to the "author of *Clarissa*." In R. F. Brissenden's influential account of the genre, a novel is sentimental if and when its female heroine is "in distress"—raped, or about to be raped, by men.[1] A number of studies have emerged in recent years complicating Brissenden's account of masculinity in particular, but while the sentimental hero has come to be seen as a victim of many things—gendered social norms, the norms of genre—he has not been seen as a victim of rape.[2] In the *Memoirs of Miss Sidney Bidulph,* however, it is men and not women who are in distress. The plot of *Sidney Bidulph* hinges on an abortive marriage contract between the eponymous heroine and her suitor—and beloved—Orlando Faulkland. Their wedding is called off when a Miss Burchell emerges claiming that Faulkland seduced and abandoned her and that she is pregnant with his child. Faulkland defends himself against these charges not by saying "I did not have sexual relations with that woman" but by admitting that he *did* have sex with her yet continuing to insist that he is "not a seducer."[3] He describes himself, as Clarissa frequently does, as having been "surprized into the commission of a fault for which I have paid so dear a price" (58), and this rhetorical identification with the period's most famous victim is a gesture each of the male characters repeats. When it emerges that Sidney's brother George has also had sex with Miss Burchell, he claims she took advantage of him—as Lovelace does Clarissa—while he was in a state of "vacancy" (384). When Mr. Arnold, the man Sidney eventually marries, has an affair with Mrs. Gerrarde, Miss Burchell's aunt, he is said to have been "seduced into the commission of . . . crimes which he abhorred" (297). And Faulkland gives the following account of his own seduction. "When we had done tea," he tells George in a letter,

> [Miss Burchell's] aunt looked at her watch, started off her chair, said . . . I hope, Sir, you will have the *Charity* to stay with my niece; and then hurried out of the room. I begged leave to hand her to her chair . . . but the determined gipsey was prepared for this motion, and insisting that I should not stir, thrust me back from the door, which she shut, and flew down the stairs. What was to become of me now, George? My situation was dangerous, and really critical. . . . [L]ove, foolish love did all, and led a willing victim to his altar. (338)

The love that does in our hero is in one sense Miss Burchell's desire for him. Faulkland explains that he was "upon the point of flying to avoid [this] soft contagion, when an accident happened that totally overthrew all my good resolutions" (337). The accident is presumably Mrs. Gerrarde's hurling him back into her niece's rooms and into her septic, irresistible arms. But this seduction scenario is nothing if not elaborately conceived (Mrs. Gerrarde is a "determined" gipsy), and so "accident" would seem more properly to describe Faulkland's response to being seduced—to mark *his* "foolish," easily manipulated "love." What leads this victim to the altar, it turns out, is the reflexive willingness of his own desiring body, and Faulkland persists in claiming that "love"—and the erection the sentimental vocabulary euphemistically conceals—is not assent. When Mrs. Gerrarde first invites Faulkland to tea she mocks his hesitation: "What is the pretty creature afraid of (patting my cheek) I'll stay by it all the while" (338). Faulkland bristles at this apparent insult to his manhood: "There was no withstanding this; I promised to wait on her," he recalls, imagining that the neuter pronoun impugns his manhood by aligning resistance with a frigid and impassive effeminacy. What Mrs. Gerrarde offers here, however, is less emasculation than a *theory* of masculinity, one widely shared by more respectable characters than she. For she and Faulkland assume the same thing about men: that when confronted with desire—another's or one's own—the male body is an automaton. *The Memoirs of Miss Sidney Bidulph* revises, ever so slightly, Mrs. Thrale's insight about the irrepressibility of masculine desire: it is not when a man resists but when he succumbs to desire that he is a thing.

Faulkland's gender and status make the charge of rape look somewhat implausible, and another rape scene—from an eighteenth-century novel indebted this time to the author of *Pamela*—brings this implausibility into sharp relief. *Justine's* eponymous heroine recounts watching as the pedagogue Rodin punishes a fifteen-year-old boy for a forbidden erection. Rodin seduces the boy with "threats, caresses, kisses, curses"; and when the boy responds first with an erection and then by ejaculating into Rodin's face, "the whips are picked up, Rodin flogs; . . . the child bursts into tears."[4] It seems clear that the child's erection does not register consent. But the scene is disturbing for how the presence of an erection raises the specter of desire—and therefore of complicity. Sade means for us to see the boy as an unwilling victim: it is such nonconsent on which the titillations of sadistic pornography depend. But his position as victim requires that we accept Faulkland's claim that erections are, or might be, accidental. There are no whips, no threats, no curses, no dependency in Sheridan's rape scene, yet Faulkland is understood to have been violated as surely as this boy has been, and for the same reason: because his body's mechanistic teleology is capable of being ruthlessly exploited.

The Memoirs of Miss Sidney Bidulph thus transforms the iconology of sentimental fiction, replacing the violated female body with the violated male body. This is an inversion Fielding only seems to perform in *Joseph Andrews;* as we saw in chapter 3, what makes that novel "comic" is also what makes it "epic"— an investment in the improbability of men's harm, perhaps of harm as such. Sheridan's inversion is performed with earnest seriousness, however, and clarifies a set of questions about agency and responsibility that preoccupies the realist novel from its inception but that receives a precise kind of attention in this novel of male rape. For Sheridan, raped cocks raise concerns that raped locks (or hymen) do not—or at least that they raise rather differently. Is an erection an emblem of an intentional or mental state? Is it, like the lock, a synecdoche of the human person it represents and for whom it stands? Or is the penis a different creature altogether, an alien machine whose action is an instrumental effect of the way the thing is made? Is it possible in a culture in which victimization is aligned with penetration to claim that one has been sexually violated if one has penetrated the body of another? Or is it important that penises penetrate only intransitively, that they are, as pornographers never tire of pointing out, "wielded"? But wielded by whom? Do men move their cocks or do their cocks move them?

If such questions bring Sheridan's revisionism closer to Sade's than Fielding's, this tells us something about the differences in these authors' brand of anti-Pamelism. Fielding's anti-Pamelism is considerably less skeptical than we are used to thinking. It's true that he questions Pamela's motives, attributing to her a mercenary desire that makes resistance a technique of the deepest strategy. And it's true that he questions Richardson's motives, insisting that he shares the amatory novelist's preoccupation with readerly desire and the exploitation of the distressed female body on which such desire depends. But Fielding also refuses to believe that harm happens, and this refusal makes him more sanguine than Richardson about the reparative power of marriage, more invested in a clear distinction between love and rape. Fielding imagines that it is Richardson who wants to discriminate a formal project committed to the amelioration of harm from one committed to its perpetuation. But Sade sees that his own interest in erotic inanimateness, in brutalized bodies and ruined lives, in the harms endured and the harms *caused* by the sentimental protagonist, is not something he demystifies about a Richardsonian aesthetic but something within that aesthetic that he exploits. Although Sade's novels have been called the "most devastating" of anti-Pamelas, there is an important sense in which they are not anti-Pamelist at all, absent as they are of Fielding's skepticism about the fact of harm, which is to say his sentimental faith in the healing power of companionate romance.[5]

Sheridan's preoccupation with the mechanism—the sheer motivity—of responsive bodies is therefore a striking example of what it means to be dedicated to Richardson rather than Fielding. And if we would want to call this dedication "pornographic," this is because the pornographic imagination, as Susan Sontag brilliantly suggests, conceives "of the person as a 'thing' or an 'object,' of the body as a machine[,] . . . makes one person interchangeable with another and all people interchangeable with things," and refuses to understand the person "in terms of a certain state of her will."[6] There is an "old saying" that recurs so often in *Sidney Bidulph* as to constitute a kind of slogan: "Many things . . . fall out between the cup and the lip" (30, 32, 95). The phrase captures the waywardness of action in this novel, the way, as Sidney complains, "My best purposes are perverted from their ends" (391). It is a perversion that is utterly normative, characterizing all and not only male persons' agency in the text, and the neuter pronoun Mrs. Gerrarde assigns to Faulkland comes to mark a metaphysics that exceeds (even as it describes) gendered being. The problem the male rape victim so graphically embodies—especially the male rape victim who has penetrated and impregnated his seducer—is that although he may look like the progenitor of an action, he is not an agent at all. As Faulkland puts it, reflecting on the harms his behavior has occasioned, "*I*, though innocently, the accursed cause" (171).

It is not rape law to which we must look to decipher Faulkland's paradoxes, to understand what it can possibly mean to be an innocent cause of harm or a willing victim. The rape of the cock—the unambiguous coexistence of signs of consent with the experience of harm—does something interesting to the misogynistic cultural logic of rape, with its invidious assumption that the victim must have wanted it and that she is not, therefore, a victim at all. Rape law cannot conceive of a willing victim: harm *is* the harm of nonconsent. Without it, "Volenti non fit inuria": "To one who is willing, no harm is done." In chapter 2, we saw how Richardson turns to a law that refuses to understand persons in terms of the state of their wills as a way around the malignant antifeminism of legal, intimate, and generic regimes centering on consent (rape law, marriage law, marriage comedy). Like Richardson, Sheridan derives a metaphysics of human objecthood from a legal logic that "makes people interchangeable with things," but her interest in the physiology of consent moves her to literalize what it means for persons to be (like) things. I have been arguing that the realist novel continually looks to strict liability to understand the less-than-agentive culpability of its tragic cast of characters: Defoe turns to carrier liability and the doctrine of agency to explain Roxana's improbable sense of guilt; Richardson turns to felony murder to prevent Lovelace's equally improbable self-absolution. Fielding falls outside this genealogy for the way the comedy of *bildung* transforms Tom Jones *from* a "noxious animal" into a man. But for Sheridan, there is only one context in which it makes sense to think of Faulkland as at once innocent and an "accursed cause": deodand—the law of *noxae deditio* or "accursed things."[7]

"Any moveable thing inanimate, or beast animate" becomes a deodand, according to Coke in his third *Institutes*, when it "doe move to, or cause, the intimely death of any reasonable creature by mischance in any country of the realm . . . without the will, offence, or fault of himself, or of any person."[8] The standard culprits in cases of deodand are carts, wheels, horses—the object paraphernalia of trade and agriculture. As Coke's definition suggests, deodand depends on a distinction between persons and nonpersons: thing liability evolves to take account of injuries to the former by the latter. But deodand is also a way

of making persons responsible *for* the actions of things, a mechanism for establishing liability where the criteria for blameworthiness—intentionality, malice,
forethought, foresight—are rendered superfluous or incoherent because of a
decision about the mental lives of things and animals (that they don't have a
mental life).[9] When liability is transferred from nonhumans to humans, so too
is the superfluity of the mental life; the legal person is responsible in precisely
the way an object is responsible, because "without will, offence, or fault" she has
"caused" death.

Four accidents propel the plot of *The Memoirs of Miss Sidney Bidulph,* three
of which involve horses and hackney coaches. These animate and inanimate
things come to emblematize human agency and accountability in a novel in
which sentimental protagonists are themselves "moving" vehicles.[10] Sheridan
conflates persons and things so that deodand might function as an alternative
to rape law with its anti-Pamelist and consensualist skepticism about harm. By
making states of mind irrelevant to the question of harm and responsibility,
deodand ceases to demand from victims moral exemplarity—ceases to make
injury and accountability questions of character. I've been arguing throughout
this book that the eighteenth-century novel's indifference to psychological criteria of blameworthiness represents an indifference to character, and that this
asks us to rethink the history and theory of literary characterization. Literary
historians—in particular historians of the novel—have tended to align an indifference to psychological models of character with outmoded and atavistic literary forms: allegory, typology, personification. More than this, we have tended to
equate the abstraction of inhuman figures with their *de*humanization, making
flatness ethically and politically unconscionable, making objecthood—being
the mere form of a person—a problem for persons. As we shall see, however,
in the genealogy of realism indebted, like *Sidney Bidulph,* to *Clarissa* and its
author, objecthood is the form that persons, and ethics, take.

❧

The legal history of object liability is difficult to summarize. It is unusually
polemical, perhaps because accounts of object liability tend to occur in historical or theoretical sources rather than in case law. In an influential essay entitled "On Thing-Liability (*Sachhaftung*) in Early Law," Geoffrey MacCormack
describes the debate over thing liability as centering on the question of whose
liability—the animal or object's, on the one hand, or the owner's, on the other—
is at issue. One theory, he says, "assumes that primitive man's instincts led him

to seek revenge on an animal or object which had harmed him or his property or killed a member of his family"; as man became less "primitive," he

> ceased to see the animal or object which had caused harm as itself a wrongdoer exposed to revenge; instead he looked at the owner of the animal or object and placed upon him an obligation to pay compensation for the harm caused, an obligation that might be avoided through the surrender of the animal or object.

The other theory assumes in contrast "that the starting point of legal development was the strict liability placed on the owner of the animal or object that had done harm."[11]

What interests me about MacCormack's history of the history of thing liability is the way he explains and periodizes the two theories he outlines. In the first, thing liability is seen as an animistic way of thinking that ascribes responsibility to phenomena that cannot properly be thought of as responsible because they cannot properly be seen as agents. Over time, as man becomes "more rational," this mistake is rectified and liability is placed where it belongs—on human, and therefore agentive, beings. The compensation thus imposed, on this account, is not a sign of the owner's guilt: if it is a mistake to see the animal as a wrongdoer because his act is unintentional, it is by the same token a mistake to see the owner as a wrongdoer because he has not acted at all. In the second theory, the question of animal agency is not at issue. What is meant by thing liability in this instance "is that the animal is guilty in an objective not a subjective sense. It has infringed a rule prohibiting the killing or injuring of persons or the inflicting of damage on their property and is guilty because it has caused death, injury or damage, not because it has exhibited a particular mental attitude."[12] Although MacCormack doesn't put it in these terms, it might be said that the irrelevance of the animal's mental attitude is here transferred to the owner, who is liable "either because he is deemed to have been at fault in the control exercised over the animal or object, or because he is made strictly liable in order to encourage him to exercise proper care and control."[13] The first theory MacCormack associates with Oliver Wendell Holmes and the nineteenth century, the second with William Blackstone and the eighteenth century.

This confirms Holmes's own sense of the history and theory of thing liability. In the opening chapter, "Early Forms of Liability," in *The Common Law*, Holmes develops his thesis that thing liability originates in the desire for vengeance and that liability law moves—and ought to move—away from vengeance toward policy-based standards of responsibility. Liability for things, he says, "had its

roots in the passion of revenge" and in "the personification of inanimate nature common to savages and children": "Without such personification, anger towards lifeless things would have been transitory, at most."[14] "The liability seems
to have been regarded as attached to the body doing the damage, in an almost
physical sense," he reflects, and this attribution of blame to material bodies is
what happens when an "untrained intelligence only imperfectly performs the
analysis by which jurists carry responsibility back to the beginning of a chain
of causation." "The hatred for anything giving us pain, which wreaks itself on
the manifest cause, and which leads even civilized man to kick a door when it
pinches his finger," he says, "is embodied in the *noxae deditio* and other kindred
doctrines of early Roman law" (13).

As he goes on to describe these kindred doctrines, Holmes merges the two
theories of liability outlined by MacCormack; or rather, in his account of the
history of thing liability those two theories converge. *When* they converge, and
how, helps to explain the story I am telling. *The Common Law* is an extended,
explicit attack on the logic of thing liability as it played itself out in eighteenth-
century jurisprudence—in a way of thinking about liability that in Holmes's era
(and much to his chagrin) made it possible to hold railway companies strictly
liable for harms to customers and employees caused by "noxious" steam engines. (As we shall see in the conclusion, Holmes's magisterial elaboration of
the theory of negligence in *The Common Law* is directed toward limiting the
liability of railway and other corporations.) Throughout "Early Forms of Liability," Holmes frets about the way the materialism of thing liability results on the
one hand in a personification of objects and on the other in a depersonification
of human persons. The need to wreck vengeance on an inanimate or animate
thing, he insists, involves ascribing to that thing something like intentionality:

> Vengeance imports a feeling of blame, and an opinion, however distorted by pas-
> sion, that a wrong has been done. It can hardly go very far beyond the case of a
> harm intentionally inflicted: even a dog distinguishes between being stumbled
> over and being kicked. (7)

Over time, the personifying logic of "the old noxal action, as it was called, gave
way to an action under the new law to enforce a general personal liability" (16).
Paradoxically, an old way of thinking that ascribed intentionality to things ushered in a new way of thinking that made the intentionality of human persons
irrelevant: "Still later, ship-owners and innkeepers were made liable *as if* they
were wrong-doers for wrongs committed by those in their employ on board ship

or in the tavern, although of course committed without their knowledge" (16). "The law as to ship-owners and innkeepers, Holmes editorializes,

> introduced another and more startling innovation. It made them responsible when those whom they employed were free, as well as when they were slaves. . . . [T]he principle introduced on special grounds in a special case, when servants were slaves, is now the general law of this country and England, and under it men daily have to pay large sums for other people's acts, in which they had no part and for which they are in no sense to blame. (17)

Holmes's specific target in his opening chapter is how the "barbarian" law of deodand has come to underwrite "the whole modern doctrine of master and servant, and principal and agent" (17). What worries Holmes about the "doctrine of agency"—the liability of one person for the acts of another such as one finds in the doctrine of felony murder—is its ironic *indifference* to agency understood as a capacity for willed action. Agency as a legal doctrine looks at the person in formal or status terms: that one is a certain kind of person (a master, servant, principal, or agent) is more important than the kind of person one is—more important, that is, than the quality of one's action, than the question of whether one has acted at all. Holmes explains how the animation of things becomes the deanimation of persons by focusing on a "most remarkable transformation of [deodand]" that takes place in eighteenth-century Admiralty law. In deodand, he says (citing, among other sources, the entry under "deodand" in Giles Jacob's *New Law Dictionary* [1729]), "the fact of *motion* is adverted to as of much importance": "So it was said [in Anthony Fitzherbert's *Abridgement* (1577)] that 'omne illud quod movet cum eo quod occidit homines deodandum domino Regi erit, vel feodo clerici.' The reader sees how motion gives life to the object forfeited" (24). Motion is the animating principal of deodand and its personifications, and the "most striking example" of a moving, personable thing, says Holmes, is a ship. "It is only by supposing the ship to have been treated as if endowed with personality"—and personality understood entirely as an effect of the object's extraordinary vitality—"that the arbitrary seeming peculiarities of the maritime law can be made intelligible" (25).

Holmes goes on to quote an extended passage from Judge Story (who is himself quoting Chief Justice Marshall):

> This is not a proceeding against the owner; it is a proceeding against the vessel for an offence committed by the vessel; which is not the less an offence, and does not

the less subject her to forfeiture, because it was committed without the authority and against the will of the owner. It is true that inanimate matter can commit no offence. But this body is animated and put in action by the crew, who are guided by the master. The vessel acts and speaks by the master. She reports herself by the master. It is, therefore, not unreasonable that the vessel should be affected by this report.

"The thing is here primarily considered as the offender," Story says elsewhere, "or rather the offence is primarily attached to the thing" (27). These "great judges," Holmes notes with dismay, "although of course aware that a ship is no more alive than a mill-wheel, thought that not only the law did in fact deal with it as if it were alive, but that it was reasonable that the law should do so" (27). According to him, such thinking involves a "metaphysical confusion" (30)—between animated beings that are life forms (persons) and those that are not (things). What disturbs Holmes about the way objects are personified in thing liability is that "person" comes to mark nothing more, and nothing less, than moving matter. There's a way in which Holmes's own conception of legal personhood in *The Common Law* is itself materialist, or at least non-, even antipsychological. But when materialism leads, as it does in thing liability, to the absolute liability of such persons as ship owners or railway magnates, Holmes is forced to develop a competing form of personification that retains an interest if not in the psychology, at least in the ontology of *human* beings.

Holmes's materialism is most striking in his chapter on criminal law, which calls into question the intuitive and historical emphasis on mens rea in adjudicating criminal liability. "The *mens rea,* or actual wickedness of the party, is wholly unnecessary" for determining responsibility in criminal cases, Holmes asserts. "All reference to the state of his consciousness is misleading if it means anything more than that the circumstances in connection with which the tendency of his act is judged are the circumstances known to him" (61). This is a claim Holmes develops in two subsequent chapters on the theory of torts; for the irrelevance of "consciousness" to criminal liability is merely a surprising effect of Holmes's larger argument—his attack on inappropriately *moral* standards of blameworthiness in the law. Holmes's account of "blameworthiness" is immensely complicated and deserves more careful treatment than I can give it here. The key thing, for our purposes, is that Holmes's critique of the theory of absolute liability in "Early Forms of Liability" and "Torts: Trespass and Negligence" rests on the assumption that there is, or ought to be, no such thing as a faultless wrongdoer. On the one hand, he wants to do away with a model of blameworthiness that sees wrongdoers as morally, rather than merely legally, wrong (as bad rather than liable). On the other hand, he wants liability law to retain some commitment to blameworthiness so as to prevent persons being held accountable for accidental—as opposed to negligent—acts. Holmes seeks "reconciliation of the doctrine that liability is founded on blameworthiness with the existence of liability where the party is not to blame":

> It is found in the conception of the average man, the man of ordinary intelligence and reasonable prudence. Liability is said to arise out of such conduct as would be blameworthy in him. But he is an ideal being, represented by the jury when they are appealed to, and his conduct is an external or objective standard when applied to any given individual. (43)

In a note to himself he clarifies this point: "At the bottom of liability there is a notion of blameworthiness but yet that the deft's blameworthiness is not material" (86 n. c). "The rule that the law does, in general, determine liability by blameworthiness," he concludes, "is subject to the limitation that minute differences of character are not allowed for" (87).

Like the ships and mill wheels of deodand, Holmes's artificial person—"the average man, the man of ordinary intelligence and prudence" (87)—is not a being replete with interiority. Although she might exhibit states of mind such as "conscience," "motive," or "intent," there is a sense in which this person, as a particular and particularized subject, does not exist. She is not blamed for who she is, not even for what she has done: the law considers "not the actual condition of the particular defendant, but whether his conduct would have been wrong in the fair average member of the community, whom he is expected to equal at his peril" (128). That said, as a being endowed with "intelligence" and capable of "prudence"—as a being presumed to belong to a community—such a person is also, and emphatically, not a thing. She is protected from objecthood not only by the logic of species resemblance but also, more importantly, by the logic of negligence or limited liability: the humanity of human beings, Holmes repeatedly insists, requires that they be indemnified against responsibility for accidents.

For Holmes, the theory of torts rests on two important principles: that "the general purpose of the law of torts is to secure a man indemnity against certain forms of harms to person, reputation, and or estate, at the hands of his neighbors, not because they are wrong, but because they are harms" (115) and that "a man is answerable for all the consequences of his acts, or, in other words, that he acts at his peril always, and wholly irrespective of the state of his consciousness upon the matter" (65). These principles are, to his mind, in some tension with one another. Holmes wants to claim that the "aim of liability is simply to prevent or indemnify from harm *so far as is consistent with avoiding the extreme of making a man answer for accident*" (115; emphasis mine). But if one accepts the principle that a man acts always at his peril, then one is obliged to accept the possibility that he might be held responsible for accidents if and when they cause harm. In the story Holmes tells, this possibility is borne out in eighteenth-century cases where the idea that "a man is answerable for all the consequences of his acts" reaches its fullest, most "extreme" elaboration.

As I noted in chapter 1, Holmes argues that from the 1680s through the early 1800s, influential jurists derived a powerful new doctrine of absolute liability from precedents in the law of trespass. Holmes's litany of cases—*Mitchell v. Allestry* (1676), *Dickenson v. Watson* (1682), *Scott v. Shepherd* (1773)—is virtually identical with the legal genealogy outlined in *Harm's Way*, and although I arrived at the genealogy independently, from a reading of contemporary casebooks and reports, I take this similarity as confirmation that the eighteenth century's peculiar investment in the principle of absolute liability is indisputable. Holmes begins his rehearsal of these origins by citing Sir Thomas Raymond in *Bessey v. Olliot* (1682) quoting from the contemporaneous *Dickenson v. Watson:* "In all civil acts the law doth not so much regard the intent of the actor, as the loss and damage of the party suffering." "In the famous squib case [*Scott v. Shepherd*]," Holmes continues,

> Sir William Blackstone also adopts a phrase from *Dickenson v. Watson*, just cited: "Nothing but inevitable necessity" is a justification. So Lord Ellenborough, in *Leame v. Bray* (1803): "If the injury were received from the personal act of another, it was deemed sufficient to make it trespass"; or according to the more frequently quoted language of Grose, J., in the same case: "Looking into all the cases from the Year Book in the 21 H. VII. down to the latest decision on the subject, I find the principle to be, that if the injury be done by the act of the party himself at the time, or he be the immediate cause of it, though it happen accidentally or by misfortune, yet he is answerable in trespass." (71–72)

"Further citations are deemed unnecessary," Holmes tersely concludes.

He does not like these arguments, and although he is not right to dislike them, he is right to see that something crucial is at stake in the way they conceive of human agency and accountability. He complains that

> the same reasoning would make a defendant responsible for all damage, however remote, of which his act could be called the cause. . . . [But] [a]n act is always a vol-

untary muscular contraction, and nothing else. The chain of physical sequences which it sets in motion or directs to the plaintiff's harm is no part of it, and very generally a long train of such sequences intervenes. (73–74)

"Why is a man not responsible for the consequences of an act innocent in its direct and obvious effects, when those consequences would not have followed but for the intervention of a series of extraordinary, although natural, events?" (74–75), he asks. "Nay, why need the defendant have acted at all, and why is it not enough that his existence has been at the expense of the plaintiff?" (77). He concludes, quoting Chief Justice Samuel Nelson:

> "An injury arising from inevitable accident, or, which in law or reason is the same thing, from an act that ordinary human care and foresight are unable to guard against, is but the misfortune of the sufferer, and lays no foundation for legal responsibility." If this were not so, any act would be sufficient, however remote, which set in motion or opened the door for a series of physical sequences ending in damage; such as riding the horse, in the case of the runaway, or even coming to a place where one is seized with a fit and strikes the plaintiff in an unconscious spasm. (76–77)

The "rule of absolute responsibility," he insists, "is inconsistent with admitted doctrines and sound policy," and moreover, "the common law has never known such a rule, unless in that period of dry precedent which is so often to be found midway between a creative epoch and a period of solvent philosophical reaction." Given the history he is laying down, it is quite clear that the creative epoch is that of Coke and Littleton, the philosophical epoch his own, and the "period of dry precedent"—of absolute, tragic liability for accidents of fate and the unconscious, spasmodic body—that of Raymond and Blackstone, Samuel Richardson and Frances Sheridan.

☙

Sheridan's *Memoirs of Miss Sidney Bidulph* is not conventionally described as a novel about rape, let alone male rape. The distinguished few who have written about the book (Margaret Doody, Eve Tavor Bannet) tend to focus on a different harm: the difficulty of achieving companionate affiliation in a culture dedicated to formalist marriage laws and conventions.[15] When Samuel Johnson faults Sheridan for making her readers "suffer so much," it is *Sidney*'s suffering that concerns him: what is at issue for him as for later critics is Sheridan's violation of the conventions of marriage comedy, her perverse refusal to yoke her deserving heroine to the man she loves. The fatal material harms surrounding the pathos of sentimental affiliation—the deaths of Faulkland, Miss Burchell, Mr. Arnold, and countless minor characters—have been a matter of relative indifference, collateral damage of an *affaire du coeur* whose central victim is a broken heart. Yet to say that the *Memoirs of Miss Sidney Bidulph* is about rape to the exclusion of marriage would not be accurate either: the terms are inextricable, differentiated only as the question of consent is asked and answered. That answer is supposed to distinguish harm from benefit. And while I don't mean to suggest (as Andrea Dworkin might) that marriage is always rape, there is a way the novel's feminist critics are more committed monogamists than Sheridan— more invested in the notion that marriage is what happens when harm is avoided or overcome. If Sheridan makes male rape one of her subjects, however, it is because male rape allows her to dispense with such sanguine distinctions, allows her to uncouple harm from nonconsent and marriage from reparation, broadening the injuries—and also the responsibilities—of desire and conjugation.

That *Sidney Bidulph* is interested in more than shattered vows and grieving hearts is marked by an obsessive concern with accidental harms and an equally obsessive vocabulary of fault and blame. ("Fault" occurs twenty-eight times in *Sidney Bidulph*, "blame" [along with "blameable"] twenty-one times. Compare this with a novel like *Evelina*, where "fault" and "blame" occur half as often [fourteen and nine times respectively], this despite the fact that the novels share an interest in accidents, a term that occurs twenty-one times in *Sidney Bidulph* and twenty-eight times in *Evelina*.) The first mention of "fault" occurs during Sidney's initial meeting with Faulkland, and throughout the novel "Faulkland" and "fault" are frequently conjoined. "My brother loves even [Faulkland's] faults," Sidney tells her correspondent Cecilia, "though he will not allow me to call them by that name" (27). George is consistent in resisting the novel's conceptual and formal alignment (the sly, slant homophone) of "Faulkland" and "fault," a point to which I return. For the moment, I want to linger over a seemingly minor moment in the plot—Sidney's account of the first of Faulkland's faults to which she is witness.

"[George] knows of no fault Mr Faulkland has," she continues in her letter to Cecilia, "but a violence of temper when provoked. I saw an instance of it to-day, which I was sorry for, and the more so, as I was in some measure accessory to it" (33). The tale she goes on to recount is strikingly similar in its contours to *Mitchell v. Allestry* (1676), the landmark case on the culpability of a defendant for bodily injuries produced by an out-of-control and uncontrollable horse that is central to Defoe's understanding of agency, liability, and the novel form. As

Sidney tells it, she, George, Mr. Faulkland, and a female relation of Mr. Faulkland's, having just taken a morning's ride in Hyde Park,

> rode into the stable-yard of [the lady's] house, in order to alight. My horse, which happened to be a young one that Sir George had newly bought, saw some object that made him shy of advancing, and he turned suddenly about. A footman of Mr Faulkland's, who chanced to stand just behind me, very imprudently, though I am sure without design of harm, gave him a stroke with his whip, which made the animal plunge and throw me, as I had not time to recover my seat from the first short turn he made. I luckily received not the least hurt, and was on my feet in an instant. But Mr Faulkland, who had leaped off his horse even before I fell, was so enraged at the fellow, that he gave him two or three sound lashes with his whip across the shoulders, which fell on him as quick as lightening. (34)

It is a subtle scene that traverses multiple sites of responsibility—the owner of the horse, the owner of the stable contaminated with distressing objects, the overly pusillanimous horse herself—before settling on the footman. Sidney recoils at Faulkland's violence toward the boy (if not at the boy's toward the horse) and, reminding her suitor that she has not been hurt, begs him to "forgive the footman, who had undesignedly caused the accident" (34). Her vocabulary is self-consciously legalistic: the footman has acted "imprudently though without design of harm"; he has "undesignedly caused," but has not intended, the event. At this early moment in the novel's plot of escalating calamities, Sidney is as committed as Holmes to the blamelessness of accidental harms, and to this end tries out three defenses for the hapless footman: 1) there has been no harm for which he could be blamed; 2) even if there was a harm, he has acted imprudently rather than culpably; and 3) his culpability is further vitiated by the fact that he is merely a cause, and not an agent, of the accident. As we saw in chapter 1, and as Holmes's account of the history of strict liability attests, the legal logic developing out of *Mitchell v. Allestry would* have held the footman— or rather the master in whose stead and for whose benefit he acts (is always acting)—accountable had Sidney been seriously injured. That she has not been alone indemnifies his actions. All Sidney needs to have said in the footman's defense is that she was not harmed. That she proceeds to ambiguate a harm that might easily have been disambiguated shows Sheridan beginning to think through questions of innocent culpability when they don't matter, preparing for when they do—when characters, Sidney included, are manifestly harmed by others' "undesigning" acts.

At first Sidney's tendency to want to exonerate others is positively contrasted with her mother's "despotic" tendency to want to blame them—in particular, to blame men. Mrs. Bidulph, Sidney reminds Cecilia, has a "partiality to her own sex, and where there is the least room for it, throws the whole of the blame upon the *man's* side; who, from her own early prepossessions, she is always inclined to think are deceivers of women" (50). Critics of *Sidney Bidulph* often emphasize this antimasculinist prepossession of Mrs. Bidulph's, blaming *her* for the vast tragic consequences of her refusal to allow Sidney to marry Faulkland once his prior connection to Miss Burchell has been revealed.[16] And yet, there's a clear sense in which Mrs. Bidulph is right to throw blame on men. The novel reveals a world in which women are all too ready to blame themselves (or other women) for things that go wrong and men are all too ready to let them. George's account of Faulkland's imbroglio with Miss Burchell is an important case in point. Faulkland gained the young woman's affections, George tells his mother and sister, "without seeking to do so; he never courted her, never attempted to please her, much less to win her heart, and least of all to ruin her virtue. I know that is an action he is not capable of committing." When Mrs. Bidulph asks—quite rightly, given that the girl is pregnant with Faulkland's child—"How comes it to pass then that he *did* so," George replies: "The *best* men . . . may fall into an error" (43). Mrs. Bidulph's use of the active voice is contrasted with George's use of the passive: she is interested in what Faulkland has done; George invokes active verbs only through negation ("not courted"; "never attempted"; "never ruined"), ultimately maintaining that Faulkland has not acted at all—he has fallen into error just as he has fallen, accidentally, into Miss Burchell's pliant body.

Faulkland too attempts to sway Mrs. Bidulph to his cause by emphasizing his lack of malign—or indeed any—intentions: "I never formed a thought of injuring that young lady," he avers, "till some unfortunate circumstances combined, and suddenly surprized me into the commission of a fault that had made us both unhappy" (46). "I was surprized into the fatal error," he pleads, and Mrs. Bidulph responds: "I don't pretend to know people's hearts, I can only judge of them from their actions" (46). George's and Faulkland's arguments echo the intentionalist logic of Sidney's defense of the footman, her willingness to see "undesigned" action as action for which one ought not to be held accountable (because one is accountable only for what one means to do). Mrs. Bidulph is ruthlessly skeptical about such arguments. "I think I talked pretty *roundly* to him," she says of her conversation with Faulkland. "He is an artful man, and I was resolved not to let him wind me about." "He would make a merit of having *formed no designs* upon the young lady," she complains, and George "impudently insinuated, that a man *must* not reject a lady upon these occasions" (50). (George's "must" makes Faulkland's seduction of Miss Burchell a question of etiquette: if a lady desires a man, he must find it in him to return her desire so as not to embarrass her with rejection. But as we have seen in Faulkland's account of the event, the presence of a lady's desire is less a social than a physiological obligation: if a lady desires a man he *must*—that is, he cannot help but—respond to her desire with a desire of his own.)

Mrs. Bidulph's contempt for Faulkland's emphasis on his lack of design is consistent with her interest in actions rather than hearts: she wants to hold people responsible for what they have done, even if what they have done is done "undesignedly." The problem with this misandrous stringency—and the reason *feminist* critics have been so hard on Mrs. Bidulph—is that it makes her hard on those who don't seem to deserve it, most frequently Sidney, whose marriage to Faulkland, her mother insists, "would make you as culpable as himself" (49). Mrs. Bidulph persists in believing that a union with Faulkland would be bigamous despite the fact that recent legislation had made irregular couplings like Falkland's and Miss Burchell's illegal. And it is here that the sexual politics of the novel—and its critical reception—become difficult to parse. Critics of the 1753 Marriage Act, from Henry Fox to Eve Bannet, fault its formalism—the way the controversial annulling clause invalidated consensual unions that failed to conform to prescribed norms of conjugation. Fox argued that the law put at risk women like Miss Burchell, who could no longer expect their sexual complaisance to translate into marital precontract, and Bannet reiterates the Whig opposition account of the act as "cruel" to the "fair sex" for the way it "changed the meaning of marriage by making the existence of marriage depend entirely on the couple's public observance of some purely ceremonial and procedural form." Attacks on the act later in the century by "egalitarians" such as Mary Wollstonecraft and Mary Hays, Bannet notes, ironically gave a "new name [to] a old way of doing things"; yet Bannet calls such revisionism "revolutionary," marking as feminist and implicitly progressive their commitment to a "sexual union based on a purely private, consensual agreement that derived its 'troth' not from its legality or its public solemnization but from that faith by which a man and a woman bind themselves to each other."[17]

This alignment of feminism with the superseded ecclesiastical law's valorization of verbal precontract is confusing, since it is Lady Bidulph who hews to the old line that purely private unions are indissoluble, and Bannet insists that her "obstinate championship of the cause of 'virtue' and of women in the person of Miss Burchell, and . . . her ruthless silencing of men" has "ruined

Sidney's life."[18] If Bannet is uncomfortable accepting Lady Bidulph as a feminist progenitor, it is perhaps because her strictness brings into focus something that is obscured when ecclesiastical consensualism is made identical with liberal consent theory, and liberal consensualism made identical with feminism: *ecclesiastical law was itself formalist.* There was no such thing, in the "old way of doing things," as *pre*marital sex, no space—temporal or conceptual—between the act of sex and the act of conjugation. Sex *was* marriage: to engage in the one was to have consented to the other, whether one consented or not. Ecclesiastical law is another species of strict liability, and Lady Burchell likes it because it binds men to consequences, and persons, they might otherwise abjure. It does this not by emphasizing "consensual agreement" but by subsuming individual assent under an act of heterosex that carries consent embedded in its form. Consent is an epiphenomenon (and not an antonym) of form. And before we agree that formalism is anathema to feminism, or to Sheridan, we must acknowledge that while the pathos of the novel might emerge from how much Lady Bidulph's strictness hurts, the ethos of the novel moves toward a theory of blame identical with hers.

Sidney is the first to see things in the same light as her mother—the light, that is, of strict liability:

> If Mr Faulkland feared the frailty of his virtue, why did he not fly when he was first alarmed with the knowledge of the lady's passion for him? . . . But since his evil fate urged him on, and the unhappy girl lost her honour, was he not bound to repair it? (86)

Like the men, Sidney deemphasizes Faulkland's agency—he is "urged on" by a "fate" identical with the irresistibility of heterosexual desire; the girl's honor is lost but not taken. But unlike them she sees him as responsible for what he cannot help but have done. When George writes to complain of Sidney's abandoning Faulkland, to "blame" her, he says, for submitting to her mother's will, Sidney responds: "[Mother] cannot but be sensible, that Miss B. is not without her share of blame in that affair which has so perplexed us all. But you know too that does not exculpate Mr Faulkland" (92). Sidney has admitted to Cecilia that "I have no will of my own. I never knew what it was to have one" (85) and says that she has objected to being treated by her mother "like a baby, that knows not what is fit for it to choose or to reject" (85). But when she searches her heart, trying to decide between Faulkland and her new suitor, Mr. Arnold, her choice follows on an account of the "perplexing affair" of Miss Burchell that is more like her mother's than George's: "An innocent child stigmatized; an amiable woman abandoned to shame and grief! I thank heaven I made not myself accessory to this" (87).

This anxiety about the liability of accessories for the acts of principals (Sidney has earlier worried that she is "in some measure accessory to" [33] Falkland's beating of the footman) is another of the ways *Sidney Bidulph* is indebted to "the author of *Clarissa*." As we saw in chapter 2, *Clarissa* explicitly invokes a model of strict liability concerned with principals and accessories in order to make the "unaccountable" Lovelace responsible for the effects of his own actions and the acts of those in his employ. If Sidney's self-inculpation threatens to shift the burden of responsibility away from Faulkland, this too comes from *Clarissa*. But both novels (and both paragons) ultimately come around to Lady Bidulph's position: that one need not be a paragon to be a victim; that one need not choose— as the men do, as the novel's feminist critics do—Faulkland over Miss Burchell. "As Miss Burchell's real character emerges in the course of the novel," Bannet asserts, "it becomes apparent that her 'artfulness,' deceitfulness, and promiscuity make her unworthy both of Lady Bidulph's championship and of Sidney's sacrifice."[19] Like George, Bannet seems to imagine that if one is not innocent, one has not been harmed, but for Lady Bidulph and her daughter, promiscuity does not obviate injury. What matters is who has been harmed, and women are the ones most often harmed by the "evil fate" of heterosexuality. "It is no longer of consequence to me, which was most to blame, the gentleman or the lady," Sidney tells Cecilia. "Miss Burchell is clearly the injured person" (103).

Sidney has come to realize that one might be, like Miss Burchell, blamable *and* injured; that one might have been, like Faulkland, harmed yet be responsible for repairing another, greater injury (the injury to women that is conception). This realization coincides with a turning point in the plot, and the story of Sidney and Mr. Arnold begins, as did the story of Sidney and Mr. Faulkland, with a running-down accident. Mr. Arnold's elder brother has died and Sidney's new husband stands to inherit the estate until news arrives that the brother's estranged widow is with child. "There was no mention of this at the time her husband died," Sidney recounts to Cecilia, "nor indeed any cause to suspect it; but the strongest presumptions in the world to the contrary, as her husband and she lived a-part" (105). The legal question of this child's legitimacy hovers over Sidney's relationship with her husband and over the remainder of the novel's plot. This is the story the widow tells of her improbable reunion with her husband:

She says, she had dined one day in the city, and was returning home to her lodgings in York-building in a hackney-coach; that the driver, by his carelessness in
coming along the Strand, had one of his forewheels taken off by a wagon, which accident obliged her to alight: the footboy, who was behind the coach, had by the jolt
been thrown off and received a hurt, which made it necessary to have him carried
into a shop for assistance. That the lady herself, being no otherwise injured than
by a little fright, found that she was so near home, that she did not think it worth
while to wait for another carriage, but pursued her way on foot. (109)

Sidney's transcription of the story for Cecilia takes the form, rhetorically, of a
deposition ("that the driver"; "that the lady herself"). And initially it looks as
though what is being described is the footboy's harm and the coach driver's—
perhaps the wagon's—responsibility: although the driver is described as careless, it is the *wagon* that is grammatically accorded agency in the scene as it
"takes off" the wheel of the coach and topples the footboy, all while seeming to
stand quite still. The narrative suddenly veers, however, from a tale of thing liability to a tale of rape. On her walk home the woman is "accosted by two gentlemen" who offer to see her safely home and then prevent her from acquiring that
safety by chasing her up the stairs of her lodgings to her rooms. Just as she is
about to be violated, the narrative veers once more from a tale of rape to a tale
of marital "unity." The woman is "surprised to find that one of [the rapists] was
her husband," who "congratulated them both on this fortunate mistake, and
saying, since the chance had been so propitious to Mr Arnold as to throw him
into the arms of so charming a woman, he hoped his discovering her to be his
wife would not render her the less agreeable to him; but that this unexpected
meeting might be a means of re-uniting them in their former amity" (109). Mr.
Arnold "advance[s] with open arms to embrace her," and the wife, "not declin-
ing," remains with her husband, as Sidney decorously puts it, "till late" (110).

Marriage performs its characteristic brand of magic here, as rape morphs
seamlessly into a second honeymoon—into the act of conjugation it always already was. Nor is this alchemy peculiar to the complex circumstances of the Arnolds' reunion: we have seen how the logic of sex as precontract, combined with
the instrumental assent of the desiring male body, makes it difficult for Faulkland to describe his imbroglio with Burchell as harmful. And as if to emphasize
the irrelevance of mental states to acts of sex and conjugation, Sheridan sets an
inanimate object at the center of this most recent tragedy. We are meant to re-
mark the extensive consequences of the wagon's inanimate yet causative activity: without its throwing of the footboy there would be no alighting at the shop,

no walk home, no attempted rape, no reconciliation, no conception, no child, no lawsuit, no dispossession of Mr. Arnold's brother, and no "cold, hard hand of poverty" (334) for Sidney and her children. It is as if the human agents intervening between the traffic accident and Sidney's penury are, like the wagon itself, moved rather than moving—irresistibly propelled by the person or event (the two are hardly distinguished) preceding them in a causal chain set in motion by the mindless collision of things.

Yet despite this suggestion, we are not initially prompted to blame the wagon for Sidney's predicament, and what looked to be a turning point moving us toward a model of liability detached from characterological depravity returns us, for the moment, to that excrescence of femininity, Mrs. Gerrarde. As the story of Sidney and Mr. Arnold progresses, so too does the frequency with which Sidney points to Mrs. Gerrarde as the final cause of the novel's catastrophes. "Into what hands am I fallen?" (137), Sidney wonders when she discovers her husband's affair with the same "determined gypsy" who'd helped to rape Faulkland. When Mr. Arnold sends Sidney away with a separate maintenance because he has been persuaded she is having an affair with Faulkland, Gerrarde is blamed for her lover's cruelty: "Oh that vile woman! 'tis she has done this" (145), Sidney complains. "Sure this woman was sent into the world for a scourge!" (147). When Sidney finally comes to tell Cecilia "by what means the widow Arnold carried her suit against us," it turns out that Mrs. Gerrarde's "career of iniquity" (148) extends there as well. "You may remember [the widow Arnold] had at the beginning threatened to produce a witness, who could prove, that her late husband had been with her on a particular night, a very little time before his death," Sidney reminds Cecilia:

> Who this witness was, had been kept an impenetrable secret. She did, however, produce him, when the cause came to be tried; and the witness proved to be Mrs. Gerrarde's brother. . . . This man it seems had been very intimate with [the widow] during her husband's life-time, while she was in a state of separation from him: . . . she was suspected of an intrigue with him, and in all human probability that child, which is to inherit the Arnold estate, is his. (243)

Sidney doesn't imagine that Mrs. Gerrarde is precisely "in this secret," but the fact that Sidney's husband has spent his capital to pursue his affair with Mrs. Gerrarde means that the loss of the lawsuit and thus of "900 pounds a year" plunges her family into "an abyss of misery" (242) for which Mrs. Gerrarde is somehow responsible.

It appears as though Sidney has repudiated her mother's example, her tendency to "throw all the blame on the man's side." But once again her indictment of women is compromised by an uncomfortable similarity with male characters' self-exculpating misogyny. Shortly after Sidney names Mrs. Gerrarde as the scourge of her marriage and her happiness, Faulkland sends Sidney a letter calling Gerrarde "the cause of Miss Burchell's misfortune; and therefore the remote cause of my losing Miss Bidulph" (170). "Had it not been for her, I should never have had the fall of that unhappy girl to answer for," he asserts, transposing onto a third party acts of penetration and impregnation that would seem unambiguously to be his own. This he accomplishes by removing his *self* (if not quite his body) from the scene of seduction: "*I* should not, I say (mark that); for the mercenary witch was determined to sell her to somebody, when my ill stars threw me in her way" (170). One encounters here the sentimental hero's trademark passive construction: the girl has fallen, but he has not felled her; indeed, he too has fallen, having been "thrown" in her way and presumably into her body. If Faulkland's claim that the act of penetration is not his act seems implausible, it invokes a familiar common-law example of unintentional, hence nonculpable, action. "You may show that there was no trespass," says Holmes, "by showing that the defendant did no act; as where he was thrown from his horse upon the plaintiff, or where a third person took his hand and struck the plaintiff with it. In such cases the defendant's body is the passive instrument of an external force, and the bodily motion relied on by the plaintiff is not his act at all" (68). Faulkland's penis, like the masculine subject for which it stands, is a passive instrument, wielded by others; it is Mrs. Gerrarde, not he, who has struck Miss Burchell to the quick. The first person does not factor into things at all ("*I* should not"): the proper name is a variable inserted as unknowingly and unwillingly as Faulkland's irrepressible body into someone's else's plot, but it could have been anyone—or anyone, at least, with the kind of body that cannot help but desire and deflower women.

Like Lovelace, Faulkland emphasizes the adventitiousness of his action in order to insist on his indemnity, and again indemnification is built on the logic of the subject. Not being able to help what one has done is to cease to be a man: it is to cease to be *hu*man in a culture in which (legal) personhood is synonymous with the capacity for reasoned action. This norm is what is at stake in Faulkland's strategic self-effacement: passivity, accidentality, instrumentality—these mark for him the subversion of masculine subjectivity and thus of subjectivity *tout court*. Unlike Sheridan, Faulkland highlights his lack of agency in order to insist on it, linking selfhood with *agential* action and disavowing attachment to those things (acts, others) to which he does not want, does not choose, and does not mean to be attached. Subjectivity is thus revealed as a rakish, masculinist norm tied to the practice and the philosophy of self-exculpation. Subjectivity is *limited* liability.

Sheridan emphasizes this point by moving immediately from this episode to an account of Faulkland's impressive capacity for premeditation. In a letter to George that occupies sixty-two pages of text and functions as a kind of inset narrative, Faulkland describes luring Mrs. Gerrarde away from Mr. Arnold and thus from her position as author of Sidney's financial and conjugal dispossession. The narrative is interesting, among other things, for what it does with *Clarissa*. Like a copycat Lovelace, Faulkland contrives to "carry Mrs Gerrarde away with the appearance of her own consent" (171):

> The measures I had to observe required some management. It would not answer the full extent of my purposes to rob Mr Arnold of his dear, if it did not appear at the same time that she had left him with her own consent. To bring about this, it was necessary that the flight on her part should seem premeditated. (173)

Sidney had described Mrs. Gerrarde as "one of the most artful of her sex"; "no woman was ever more formed to please and to deceive, than she" (137). But now Mrs. Gerrarde's premeditation is an effect of Faulkland's: the primum mobile has become moveable, has become *a* moveable indistinguishable from those Falkland uses to simulate a consent that "would not carry any face," he admits to George, "unless she took with her such of her moveables as were most valuable" (173). It is no longer Faulkland but Mrs. Gerrarde who is an "it."

Yet when Faulkland comes to describe to George his strategy concerning Mrs. Gerrarde—which is to made her think he intends to keep her for his mistress and in that way to persuade her to exonerate Sidney—he says he was "much more afraid of her than she was of me" (187), afraid that in his attempt to "keep up such an appearance of gallantry towards her, as she must naturally expect," he might not be able to avoid "all approaches which usually forerun the catastrophe of an amour" (187). Faulkland fears that simulated desire will produce authentic desire, that once again Mrs. Gerrarde will have seduced *him*, that gallantry—fond words, meaningful glances, a hand on the arm that rests a fraction too long—will prompt his body to respond in the way it must, and that that response will be as specious an index of his consent as the moveables that stand in for Mrs. Gerrarde's. Sheridan oscillates between describing Faulkland as a coercive agent on the model of Lovelace and describing him—quite seriously—as a passive victim of the supreme coercions of heterosexuality.[20] And that she does so makes it difficult to decide: is he guilty or innocent? The sentimental novel, the novel of "virtue in distress," requires us to pose the question in this way. But for *this* novel, the novel of distress-causing virtue, we are asked to simultaneously think the thought of Faulkland's victimization *and* his responsibility, his innocence and his guilt.

By shifting blame for the consequences of his encounter with Miss Burchell onto Mrs. Gerrarde, however—by continuing to tie culpability to agency—Faulkland exempts himself from the only context in which it makes sense to think of a person as innocent and at fault. Sheridan underscores this confusion in his thinking by having him explicitly invoke thing liability near the end of his letter to George. Describing how he has forced Gerrarde to choose between two equally unappealing options, Faulkland recounts himself saying that "you have no other choice to make; and so, madam, a husband or a convent; take which you like best" (213). Referring to an earlier letter he had written to George, he continues:

> When I mentioned the nunnery to you in a former letter, it was in mere gaiety of heart. . . . I knew the woman too well to suppose she would acquiesce; though, to confess the truth to you honestly, I think, if she refuses my other plan of accommodation, I must compel her to accept of this: nor ought it to be considered in any other light than that of confining a wild beast, who, having already done a great deal of mischief, would still do more, if left at liberty. (213)

Faulkland attempts to camouflage gendered violence in the language of animal liability, to make forced marriage and incarceration look like acts of public service. If this seems similar to Sheridan's own move from rape to deodand, the motivation, and the effect, is quite different. Gerrarde's inanimateness, or *mere* animation—her transubstantiation into a "moveable" and a "beast"—is not in Faulkland's hands, as it is in Sheridan's, a theory of (legal) personhood. Gerrarde's bestiality is meant to highlight Faulkland's humanity, her mindless toxicity meant to be distinguished from his moral condescension and volition. Faulkland's willingness to imagine that he might be responsible for the acts of others, like Tom Jones's "charitable" concealment and absorption of the Seagrams' faults, only resembles strict liability. As a burden he chooses for himself, Faulkland's liability for Mrs. Gerrarde signals his potency and autonomy—and also, paradoxically, his blamelessness. In this fantasy, Gerrarde remains the one to blame: the mischief her masculine owner condescends to contain is hers rather than his.

Faulkland's reading of the version of animal liability at work in his letter is highly idiosyncratic. In chapter 1, we saw how Defoe builds the new novel form around a model of responsibility emerging from, among other places, case law having to do with liability for "escapes," laws Sheridan self-consciously invokes. In *Mason v. Keeling* (1700), for example, the defendant's knowledge of his dog's dangerous propensities "fixed him with a strict liability for any damage which the animal caused, damage for which he would not otherwise be liable," a decision based on the precedent of Holmes's bête noir, *Mitchell v. Allestry* (1676), where the absent owner of a runaway horse was made to bear the burden of the animal's unforeseeable toxicity.[21] For Holmes the law of escapes is a way of limiting liability to categories of things (wild animals, natural objects such as wind, water, fire) whose dangerousness one is expected to foresee and thus to control and contain. Accidents, as he repeatedly insists, are unforeseeable and thus unimpeachable; with escapes one is in the realm of negligence rather than strict liability. But Defoe saw escapes as a category in which the nonidentity of liability and fault is made clear. Escapes are unambiguous accidents of fate: they say nothing about the character of the person to whom they are charged, but their radical adventitiousness does not make them unimpeachable. He who owns the field of wheat set ablaze by a lightening storm is responsible to the stranger burned when walking along the side of the road not because he has acted badly but because someone has been harmed. It makes no more sense to say that he is guilty than to say the wheat is guilty—both are *responsible* for causing injury, but responsibility is different from guilt. The owner of the wheat field might himself be a victim; he might have suffered burns; he might plausibly insist that there was nothing he could have done. Responsibility cannot be abjured by pointing to one's innocence.

In the law of escapes, as in deodand, the liability of a dangerous animal is transferred onto her owner "either because he is deemed to have been at fault in the control exercised over the animal or object, or because he is made strictly liable in order to encourage him to exercise proper care and control."[22] In neither case can the owner seal himself off from the animal's wrongdoing, as Faulkland attempts to do with the metaphor of Gerrarde's bestiality. As Holmes worries, seventeenth- and eighteenth-century applications of animal liability make persons liable for the unanticipated acts of others and the unanticipated consequences of their own acts. Faulkland's invocation of animal liability thus works against his own attempts to assure his immunity from blame. And from here on out, a language of *accidental* culpability—a language indifferent to the logic of the subject and its masculinist norms of self-exculpation—escalates in proportion to and as a means of comprehending the novel's escalating calamities.

When at an earlier moment in the plot Lady Bidulph learns of Sidney's forced separation from her husband, Mr. Arnold, she reflects: "You are a martyr to the crimes of others" (151). The "others" to whom she characteristically refers are the men in Sidney's life, and in an unusual alignment with Lady Bidulph's feminist invective, Faulkland agrees: "To be cast off by an undiscerning dolt! And I, though innocently, the accursed cause" (171). In Sheridan's hands, however, the argument for men's culpability very quickly becomes an account of the responsibility of *all* persons—and the person who is increasingly, though innocently, the accursed cause of harm is Sidney. One of the first harms for which Sidney blames herself is the death of her husband. After the couple is reconciled (the result of Faulkland's abduction of Mrs. Gerrarde) there is a break in Sidney's account of her restored marital happiness. Her servant, Patty Main, takes up her pen to describe for Cecilia the following tragic event:

> The day before yesterday my master was asked by some gentlemen in our neighborhood to go a hunting: he had no mind to go, for my lady was not very well, and he was unwilling to leave her; but she persuaded him, because she knew he loved hunting dearly: she has blamed herself for it ever since; but she could not know by enchantment what was to happen. He left my lady in bed, and went out about five o'clock in the morning. At eight, as my lady was sitting at breakfast, and I attending, the other maid called me out. Our man, who had gone abroad with my master, was in the kitchen, and looked as pale as death. I asked him what was the matter? The poor fellow could hardly speak; but at last said, my master has got a desperate fall in leaping a ditch, and I am afraid has hurt his skull. (283)

The wound is determined to be fatal, and within twenty-four hours Mr. Arnold has "breathed his last" (287).

In English law from at least the thirteenth through the eighteenth century, when a man fell from his horse the horse was deodand. "A source preserving the law of the fourteenth century provides that a fractious horse which throws and kills its rider is forfeit to the king," says MacCormack, and J. J. Finkelstein notes, "It is reported in the Warwickshire Eyre of 1221 that 'Simon of Coughton fell dead from his horse in drunkenness. . . . The horse's price is one mark, for which the sheriff must account.'"[23] Teresa Sutton has discovered a pattern of larger-than-normal deodand amounts in eighteenth-century cases "where a horse threw or kicked its victim," and though Sutton sees this as evidence for a movement toward negligence and away from absolute liability, she admits that most of these cases "illustrate the traditional principle that it was the death and normally the movement [of the horse] rather than any fault that necessitated the deodand."[24] This is the third time in the *Memoirs of Miss Sidney Bidulph* that someone is harmed by a fall from a horse.[25] And the accidents are clearly there because of Sheridan's interest in what Finkelstein calls the "distinctive feature" of cases of deodand—the "absoluteness of the criteria for forfeiture":

> The object which was the instrument of a human death was forfeit whether or not that object was animate and moved of its own accord (such as a horse or an ox), or inanimate (such as a cart or a boat, or even a tool), or fundamentally immobile (steps, beams, and the like). For it to be necessary that a deodand be declared it did not matter whether the victim was himself to blame for his death (through negligence, drunkenness, and so on). . . . The quintessential quality of the deodands . . . lay in the notion of "objective liability."[26]

Sheridan transfers the objective liability of things—and also their objecthood—onto human persons. As when Roxana sends her husband off without his usual valuables on his person, we are meant to see Sidney's sending her husband to the hunt as a possible factor in his death—as part of what Holmes calls the "environment" that alone makes actions culpable. ("Nothing would follow from the act except for the environment," Holmes says. "All acts, taken apart from their surrounding circumstances, are indifferent to the law" [46].) If her responsibility for that death seems implausible, Sidney's culpability is made less implausible by what happens next. Faulkland arrives back in England after a lengthy absence, during which he has, at Sidney's insistence, married Miss Burchell. He presents himself to his old friend with this piece of news: "You see a man, said he, whose life is forfeited to the law.—My wife is dead—and by my hand—" (421). It initially looks as though Faulkland uncharacteristically owns this act: Miss Burchell is dead and by his hand. Yet when he goes on to explain what has happened one begins to see what is at stake in "by my hand," for once again Faulkland's body has betrayed him—his *hand* has murdered Miss Burchell; he, himself, has not. "That wife," he explains to Sidney, "that woman whom you persuaded me to marry, I caught in adultery, and I punished the villain that wronged me with death. She shared in his fate, though without my intending it. For this act of justice, which the law will deem murder, I myself must die" (421). When George arrives, Faulkland elaborates: "I did not mean to stain my hands with her blood, perfidious as she was; her death be on her own head" (423). George's reply is a chilling example of the masculine self-exculpation his mother so detested: "That she is dead I rejoice, said he, but how, my dear Faulkland, were you accessory to it?" (423). And chilling, too, is Faulkland's most dramatic defense of his status as mere accessory: "I am come but to take a last look," he tells Sidney. "What recompence then can you make the man, whom you have brought to misery, shame, and death?" (421).

That Sidney accepts some kind of liability for what promises to be three deaths is discomfiting: "What recompence indeed can I make you," she replies (wringing her hands and "redoubling [her] tears"). "None, none, but to tell you that if you will fly this instant, my fortune shall be at your disposal" (421). But her sense of responsibility for Faulkland's rash acts is a persistent feature of the novel: it has been present since his beating of the footman and has been recently reinforced by the story George tells her of his own rape at the hands of the insatiable Miss Burchell. "Perhaps you meant well," he says of Sidney's role in persuading Faulkland to marry the female rake, "but it has ever been your peculiar misfortune I think to have your good intentions productive of nothing but evil" (328). "Oh, my dear, what a fatal wretch have I been to Mr. Faulkland! my best purposes, by some unseen power, are perverted from their ends," Sidney admits to Cecilia. "But I will calm my troubled mind with this reflexion, that I *meant* not to do evil" (391).

Sheridan makes it difficult for us to blame Sidney: we too want for it to matter that she "meant not to do evil." She also makes it difficult for us to blame Faulkland. The story Faulkland tells of his wife's death emphasizes in explicitly juridical terms his lack of premeditation, and this has made him seem, to many readers, sympathetic.[27] As Sidney recounts it, Faulkland surprises his friend Major Smyth in bed with his wife:

> The major instantly leaped out of bed, and though he saw Mr Faulkland was unarmed, he snatched up one of his own pistols, which lay on the table, and which his man had charged that night, as they were to go a short journey the next morning. Mr Faulkland, in the first transports of his rage, seized the other; the miserable woman, observing their fatal motions, threw herself out of bed. Mr Faulkland was too much distracted to be able to give a distinct account of this dreadful incident; all he can say is, that Major Smyth snapped his pistol at him, which, he thinks, missed fire, and he instantly discharged his with more fatal success; for Mrs Faulkland, who had in the instant rushed between them, shrieked out, and dropped on the ground; and the major, reeling a few steps, fell against one of the pillars of the bed, and cried out, He has killed us both. (430)

"After this dreadful action, without knowing what he did" Faulkland makes his way home. When his servant catches up with him there, Faulkland asks, "Have I killed any body?" and when he's told "you have killed my lady, and Major Smyth is mortally wounded," he replies, "I know not what I did . . . but I did not mean to hurt your mistress" (431).

For the next thirty pages, Sidney's family wrestles with the legal implications of this "dreadful action." George's first response—now that the obstacle of Miss Burchell has been violently removed—is to persuade Sidney to marry Faulkland. "Conscious as we both are of the innocence of your intentions," George tells Faulkland, "there will remain no bar to Mrs Arnold's giving you her hand" (436), and their kinsman Mr. Warner agrees: "Since he was guiltless in his intentions, it would be barbarous to make that an objection, and I dare answer for it, all mankind will acquit him, though the law perhaps may not, of that scoundrel's death, who so well deserved it at his hands" (433). Like George before him, Warner comes close to commending Faulkland for taking out the "scoundrel" Miss Burchell, and the men's sense that Faulkland's innocence is secured both by his not "knowing what he did" and by the moral turpitude of the victim is echoed by Faulkland himself, who says: "I was born to be the avenger of those crimes, into the commission of which I, perhaps, first led her" (450).

Faulkland's invocation of the earlier "crime" complicates any complacency about his innocence, however, as does the manner in which that criminal past is invoked. Is the first malfeasance *his* seduction or Miss Burchell's? Is it Miss Burchell's extralegal maternity? Is it her subsequent adultery? How can one vindicate a wrong he himself has caused? How can one be the avenging angel of one's own misdeed? Faulkland's tortured syntax makes it difficult to discriminate victim from perpetrator, here, and the syntactical ambiguity stands as an objective correlative for the novel's thematic preoccupation with the problem of agency and accountability. As he tells it, manslaughter is very similar in its contours to male rape (another form of man-slaughter): both are occasions of automatic action, of automaton agency. For him—as for George and Mr. Warner—not being in control of what one has done means not being responsible for it. But Sidney's response to the death of Miss Burchell stands as kind of chastisement to such evasions: "I own myself the unhappy cause of all your misfortunes" (435), she tells Faulkland. Echoing Faulkland's earlier insight that he has been an "innocent cause" of harm to her, Sidney accepts, in a way he does not, the consequences of that insight: that although she has acted unwittingly, ignorance is for her—as it is for the law—no excuse. "I beheld him now," she tells Cecilia, "in a light which I had never before viewed him": "I saw him as an exile, likely to be deprived of a noble fortune, his heart pieced with remorse for an involuntary crime" (451). Beholding Faulkland in the light of absolute liability, Sidney sees him as the novel, finally, sees him: as an involuntary criminal.

It might be objected that the blame Sidney imposes on herself and Faulkland is ethical rather than legal. Sheridan does not suggest that Sidney is guilty of a civil wrong for forcing Faulkland to marry Miss Burchell; she does not suggest that Faulkland is guilty of a criminal wrong either for seducing and impregnating Miss Burchell or for killing her. On the contrary, the legal questions surrounding Faulkland's role in the shootings are resolved in what I have called (in chapter 3) a "sentimental" rather than a "tragic" manner—in a manner that disambiguates his innocence and his good intentions. It turns out that Miss Burchell is not dead, though her lover is; that she has confessed "there was nothing premeditated in this fatal event, and that what Mr Faulkland did was in defence of his own life"; and that "there is no doubt of his being acquitted" (460). And so it turns out that the crime for which Sidney and Faulkland are to blame is not murder but bigamy.

There may be good reason, therefore, for seeing this as a novel preoccupied with marriage law and thus with questions of contractual rather than tortious obligation. As I've said, for Bannet the novel is concerned with the way desire, intention, consent—what she describes as indices of assent and agency—are thwarted by a legal formalism represented by the Marriage Act.[28] But although it's true that the pathos of the novel derives in part from Sidney's inability to find happiness with Faulkland, this is not where the characters or the editorial personae peopling the text locate its tragedy or its meaning. The novel does not end with the projected certainty of Faulkland's acquittal or with the revelation of the sentimental protagonists' bigamous union—does not end, in other words, with questions of intention or consent (questions clarified in the first instance, thwarted in the second). The novel ends, instead, with an event that returns us to the problem of agency and responsibility: Faulkland's death—at his own hands and Sidney's hands.

When Sidney receives the letter informing her of the first Mrs. Faulkland's survival, her narrative breaks off: "Adieu, my Cecilia," she writes, "nothing but my death should close such a scene as this" (457). The story picks up with Cecilia's "supplement" to Sidney's journal, a scene that closes not with Sidney's death but with Faulkland's. As George tells it, Faulkland responds to the news of his bigamy with surprising equanimity: "Knowing as we did the violence of his temper, we were apprehensive of sudden and dreadful consequences; but . . . after the first starts of passion were over, which though they shocked, did not alarm us, as we expected them, he assumed a clam resignation to his fate" (462). The calmness is shattered, however, once Faulkland receives a letter from Sidney repudiating him: "As their ill-fated marriage was an absolute secret to every one but the persons immediately concerned," Cecilia recounts Sidney as writing, "she hoped he would not suffer the thoughts of it to break in upon his future quiet; and concluded with beseeching him to forget her" (460). George reads Faulkland's response to the epistle as "tranquil," but the reader perceives its bitterness: "I admire your sister's stoicism," George recalls Faulkland saying. "This is true philosophy, laying his finger on the letter which he still held in his hand. *Her* heroic soul is still unmoved, and above the reach of adversity. Happy Mrs Arnold—What a vain fool was I to think that such a mind as *hers* could be subdued" (462). "We staid together till it was late," reflects George:

> He discoursed on a variety of subjects, but mentioned not my sister's name during the whole time. I thought I left him well, and his mind tolerably composed. . . . [B]ut an account was brought to me in the morning, that Mr Faulkland was found dead in his bed. There were no symptoms discovered on the body that could let us into the occasion of his death, but my own fears suggested too much. (464)

Despite George's conclusion, the question of whether Faulkland has "precipitated his own fate" that (462), the question of what Faulkland has done is never resolved. This is of course *the* question posed by this novel of male rape: has Faulkland acted? Has he harmed anyone? Is he responsible for his actions? Is he responsible for harm? When George sums up the life and death of his friend at the novel's close, he does so in the passive voice that has dominated descriptions of the sentimental hero: "Thus, proceeded Sir George, by a series of fatal events, each of which was occasioned by motives in themselves laudable, has one of the bravest and most noble minded men on earth been cut off in the prime of his youth" (464). George's way of seeing things, his relentless (and masculinist) intentionalism, has been met with skepticism throughout the text. Yet this sentence stands as an epitaph on the novel as well as its hero, and so we must pay close attention to what it says. The syntax of the sentence is convoluted but not ambiguous exactly: a "series of fatal events" has "cut off" Faulkland, George asserts. But if the events are themselves "fatal," is it they or their combination into a series that has led to Faulkland's demise? And what is the role of the human agent or agents with the "laudable" motives—motives that have "occasioned" these fatal events? Which of these—the series, the events, the motives—has precipitated Faulkland's fate? George's sentence plays out the tension between agentive and causal action that is the central preoccupation and governing logic of the *Memoirs of Miss Sidney Bidulph*. He means to establish an opposition between good intentions—Faulkland's but also, more importantly, *Sidney*'s—and an agentless fate that because it is agentless cannot be blamed.

Events might be said to be motivated, but *series* of events might not; for series come into view only retrospectively, their meaning obscure and hence unattributable to the actors whose motions constitute them. Yet the grammatical logic of the sentence works against George's desire to distinguish agentive and causal action and performs the discrepancy between intention and emplotment that is its subject.[29] The sentence implicates all causes, even remote ones, in the final, fatal outcome and in doing so implicates those who have acted unwittingly— even those who have acted well—in its tragic effects.

By blaming fate at the novel's close it might seem as though Sheridan gives up on the project of blaming persons. Even at the beginning of the tale, a providential rationale is twice offered by Cecilia as an explanation for Sidney's troubles. "My particular friend," she tells the man who will become the "editor" of the memoirs, "though a woman of most exemplary virtue, was, through the course of her whole life, persecuted by a variety of strange misfortunes. This lady . . . ought at last to have been rewarded even here—but her portion was affliction. What then are we to conclude, but that God does not estimate things as we do? It is ignorant as well as sinful to arraign his providence" (7). Cecilia's insistence on Sidney's innocence is less ambivalent than George's: she has preserved Sidney's journal, she says at the outset of the narrative proper, "to prove that neither prudence, foresight, nor even the best disposition that the human heart is capable of, are of themselves sufficient to defend us against the inevitable ills that sometimes are allotted, even to the best" (11–12). But Cecilia's exculpating providentialism—a providentialism that insists on the blamelessness of accidental harms—doesn't account for a novel obsessively concerned with the possibility of liability for accidents. Moreover, providentialism is ironized whenever it is invoked. When her friend Lord V., who has become the Arnolds' sole creditor, dies, Sidney reflects: "We can subsist upon the income which my mother is so good as to allow us; it is precarious it is true, but something may happen; I rely on that providence who has hitherto protected her" (280). It *is* to be relied on in this novel of crisis upon crises that "something may happen"—but what happens is never good. In the next journal entry we're told that the Arnolds are forced to sell Sidney's jointure and subsist on £50 per year. "Well may you call me a child of affliction," Sidney tells Cecilia, abandoning her belief that Providence will protect her or others. Providence might still be called on to explain Sidney's affliction, but that possibility, too, is ironized by the way the novel dwells on the more immediate causes of that affliction—on Mrs. Gerrarde's seduction of Mr. Arnold; on Mr. Arnold's uncontrollable desire. And it is finally repudiated in Sidney's heartbreaking response to her mother's deathbed quiescence:

"Tis strange, my Cecilia, that this best of parents, who has always so tenderly loved me, expresses now not the least uneasiness at the forlorn condition in which she must soon leave me. Her thoughts are employed on higher objects, and she seems to have weaned herself from all worldly attachments" (331).

To say that the *Memoirs of Miss Sidney Bidulph* blames Providence rather than persons is to overlook the challenge to our understanding of blame and personhood represented by Sheridan's inversion of the sentimental paradigm. Providential outcomes are ones for which no one is responsible: God may be the cause of providential events, but causality is emphatically distinguished from accountability. Sheridan consistently holds her characters accountable for the accidents of fate, however, which means that although she may possess a providentialist understanding of causation (causes are necessary and inscrutable), she eschews a providentialist understanding of responsibility. Sheridan asks us to see Faulkland as simultaneously a victim and a perpetrator of harm, simultaneously faultless and at fault. She asks us to see Faulkland in this way, and more uncomfortably she asks us to see Sidney, like Clarissa before her, in this way. In asking this, Sheridan is asking us to look at persons from the perspective of what they do rather than what they think (or think they do)—to look at them as causes *rather than* agents. I have been calling this way of thinking "objective liability," insisting more than a legal historian might do on the objecthood of the person under thing liability. For many, objecthood is itself an injury—the injury that is slavery, commodification, dehumanization. But for Sheridan, being thinglike is not a falling away from an ethico-ontological category implied by the conflation of humaneness with humanness. It is, rather, itself an ethics—a way of expanding the kinds of beings (even bad ones) and the kinds of actions (even good ones with bad consequences) for which one might be accountable. An early reviewer from the *Critical Review* seemed to understand this about the *Memoirs of Miss Sidney Bidulph:* "The design of this work is to prove that neither prudence, foresight, nor even the best disposition the human heart is capable of are of themselves sufficient," he says—reproducing Cecilia's providentialist reading of Sidney's story but shifting in midsentence to alter her sentence in important, insightful ways—"to defend us from the inevitable evils to which human nature is *liable*."[30]

☙

Sheridan is not the first to bring together deodand and rape. Andrew Marvell's "Nymph Complaining for the Death of Her Faun" begins with a complex (and still underanalyzed) allegory tying sexual seduction to the law of thing liability.

The wanton Troopers riding by
Have shot my fawn and it will dye.
Ungentle men! They cannot thrive
To kill thee. Thou neer didst alive
Them any harm: alas nor cou'd
Thy death yet do them any good.
I'me sure I never wish'd them ill;
Nor do I for all this; nor will:
But, if my simple Pray'rs may yet
Prevail with Heaven to forget
Thy murder, I will Joyn my Tears
Rather then fail. But, O my fears!
It cannot dye so. Heavens King
Keeps register of every thing:
And nothing may we use in vain.
Ev'n Beasts must be with justice slain;
Else Men are made their Deodands.[31]

"Why," Frank Kermode asked decades ago, "should the girl know about 'deo-dands,' which we have to look up?"[32] His answer—"we are listening to an intel-ligent child commenting on an adult situation"—has been less than satisfying to critics, and not only to feminist critics dismayed by the glib condescension of the claim. But even the most recent and sincere attempts to understand the allu-sion do little more than look the word up. Observes Daniel Jaeckle:

> The most obvious result of the word's use may be the creation of a bright young
> female who knows the word "deodand" and can reverse the creatures, making the
> human being the forfeit for the animal rather than the other way around. But the
> more important result of Marvell's insertion of this uncommon word is exposure
> of the severe limits of the language of pastoral complaint.

That the nymph "has to go all the way to British law" to settle her score with the troopers, he concludes, "is a most explicit indication that the traditional language of female complaint cannot cope with contemporary experience."[33] For Jaeckle, as for many of the poem's critics, the more important word in the opening lines is "trooper," which invokes marauding Covenanters and thus a civil war context that is now universally assumed to be the primary tenor of the poem's allegory.[34] The result is an odd literalism when it comes to the death of the nymph's fawn, which is often taken to *be* a fawn rather than an allegorical emblem of something else. Critics move quickly from sexual allegory ("female complaint") to the putatively more interesting political allegory as if the sexual allegory were self-evident and self-evidently a matter of a broken heart rather than a broken body.[35] But for me the question of what "deodand" means—and thus what the poem means—is tied to the question of what "fawn" means, a figure linked simultaneously to the predatory Sylvio *and* his complaining victim.

The alignment of Sylvio with the fawn immediately follows on the invocation of deodand, literalizing the fusion of man and beast that defines deodand in the first place:

> Unconstant Sylvio, when yet
> I had not found him counterfeit,
> One morning (I remember well)
> Tyd in this silver Chain and Bell,
> Gave it to me . . . (25–29)

The complex syntax of the nymph's periodic sentence initially makes it look as though *Sylvio* has arrived clad in a chain and bell, and while the "it" of line 29 seems to clarify things—only animals or objects typically receive the neuter pronoun—the antecedent is in fact quite obscure: we must look back to line 2 to determine for certain what "it" is: "The wanton Troopers riding by / Have shot my Faun and it will dye." (Thereafter, "faun" is replaced by second-person pronouns rather than the neuter pronoun: "thees," "thous," "thys.") The speaker's "I" in line 7 seems in comparison fairly unambiguous: "I'me sure I never wisht them ill," she reflects. Yet the line also echoes the preceding "Thou neer dist alive / Them any harm" (5–6), and all of sudden "thou" looks less like the second person than the first: the possibility arises that the nymph is the creature whom the troopers "cannot thrive to kill."

As the poem progresses, fawn and nymph are fused into an emblematic equivalence: "It seem'd to bless / Its self in me. How could I less / Than love it? (43–45); "It had so sweet a Breath! And oft / I blusht to see its foot more soft, / and white, (shall I say then my hand?) / NAY any Ladies of the Land" (59–62). This equivalence culminates in the final image of the two creatures cut into the marble of which their flesh and blood whiteness already partakes: "There at my feet shalt thou be laid, / Of purest Alabaster made: / For I would have thine Image be / White as I can, thou not as Thee" (119–22). Marvell ties the fawn to the female body understood as an aesthetic form or norm; less conventionally he makes the fawn the bloodied body *part* for which it also stands. How else are we to understand the bizarre series of images in which the fawn, bedded down in

the woman's "little wilderness" (74)—the garden overgrown with flowers marking at once passion, purity, martyrdom, and a martyred virginity—"rises" up to
feed on roses "until its Lips ev'n seem'd to bleed" (84)? The voracious and erect
animal poised over the diminutive bush once again calls to mind Sylvio, bringing into focus the hidden agenda of the lover's gift foreshadowed by his wry
pun, "look how your Huntsman here / Hath taught a Faun to hunt his *Dear*"
(31–32). But if the fawn is the phallus poised for destruction, he quickly mutates
into the flowers he consumes, becoming at once the subject and the object of
defloration. This oscillation between nymph and fawn, fawn and Sylvio, Sylvio
and nymph, man and woman, reflects the peculiar status of the animal in and
as deodand—as at once the harmer and the harmed, the creature who has destroyed another and must suffer destruction in return.[36]

Critics who, pointing to allusions to the Song of Solomon, would call this
"love" are rather too complacent about the poem's graphic metaphorics of harm:
the troopers washing their hands in the blood of the creature whose body has
been torn apart by their guns; the fawn printing the crimson stain of the roses
he's devoured on the nymph's lips; man reveling in the carnage that is reproductive heterosexuality for women.[37] One might object to calling it rape, wanting to read the nymph's "Smart" (35) as the pain of abandonment and betrayal
rather than sexual violence. But the story of her "beguilement" is quite a bit
more ambiguous than this makes it seem, since what Sylvio hides from the
nymph is not so much his promiscuity as his aggressivity: "But Sylvio soon had
me beguil'd. / This waxed tame; while he grew wild, / And quite regardless of
my Smart, / Left me his Faun, but took his Heart" (33–36). The temporality of
the lines suggests that the nymph's "Smart" precedes and is not identical with
Sylvio's inconstancy—that there is some other—prior—wound. And that "but"
suggests that what is beguiling is the fact that although Sylvio claims he has
taught the *fawn* to hunt—transposing his own status and aggression as "Huntsman" onto the conventional object of the hunt—it is he and not the creature
whose wildness has produced the "sharp, physical pain" conjured (historically
and onomatopoetically) by the word "smart."[38]

The allegory tying the smart of defloration to the murder of the fawn—indeed, Marvell's use of the term "murder," the most devastating category of harm
there is, to describe the physiology of heterosex—challenges any easy equanimity about the nymph's consent (an equanimity synonymous with pastoral lyric).
Can someone consent to an injury of such magnitude? And what does it mean
that Marvell insists on the injuriousness of sexual and poetic norms in the first
place? It is here that the question of what happens when we look up "deodand"

begins to be answered, and the answer turns on the conceptual and metaphysical work of allegory. Marvell ingeniously exploits the shared ontologic of allegory and deodand, producing descriptions of one thing in the image of another that continually traverse the line between subject and object, harmer and harmed, human and animal. Jaeckle is right to point out that Marvell "reverse[s] the creatures, making the human being the forfeit for the animal rather than the other way around."[39] But he doesn't notice that deodand itself *already reverses creatures* through a nested allegory that personifies the animal (making her a legal person) only to depersonify the human owner onto whom the animal's responsibility is ultimately transposed: the responsible person in deodand is not what many would call a person at all, emptied as she of the interiority that underwrites the distinction between persons and (mere) animals or things.

Marvell makes us look up deodand because deodand comes closest to his own nonanthropocentric brand of allegory. To imagine that men might be "*made* Deodands," that they might be forfeited to atone for harms they cause to animals, is to insist on an equivalence between animal harm and human harm— to insist, in the first instance, that animals *can* be harmed. (Even deodand does not properly accomplish this, calling the destruction of the animal "justice" *rather than* harm.) Marvell resists the de facto humanism of most versions of allegory—resists the animal's ephemeralization, its vehicularity, its conversion into a human tenor that alone possesses significance. Yet if animals quite literally *matter* to Marvell it is finally so that *women* might matter: so that *their* harm is not ephemeralized, translated into "eros" or into "love." To call defloration "murder" is to question the justice of heteronormativity and its presumed compensations. Marriage is the usual recompense for a loss (maidenhead) that is otherwise irrecoverable and that in any case can be recovered only once ("There is not such another in the World, / to offer for their Sin" [23–24]). But Marvell's feminist allegory is very far from an epithalamion. And if he makes deodand the remedy for sexual harm, this is because deodand continues to register harm *as* harm rather than as a benefit to which one retroactively and retrospectively consents.

Some might chafe at my calling "feminist" an allegory that turns on thing liability, on an alignment between humans (female humans in particular), animals, and things. "Objectification" has been a watchword of feminist criticism on allegorical poetry that follows Marvell in literalizing the in-humanity of the female body. The *Rape of the Lock,* for example, is anathema to many feminists for the pervasiveness with which it ties woman to thing: for the symbolic equation of Belinda with the global commodities that adorn her dressing table and her person; for the poem's formal commitment to synecdoche—the lock allegorizing a body part (maidenhead) that stands in for a greater whole (the female body) that stands in for an even greater whole (woman as such— reduced, through synecdoche, to an *equivalence* with the part that characterizes her kind).[40] This reduction is in one sense an effect of the formal operations of allegory, which, in its "naive" mode, transforms characters that in another mode would appear as (human) persons into abstractions: "Allegory," Goethe famously complained, "is where the particular serves only as an instance or example of the general."[41] In another sense it is an effect of the operations of history—commodification as allegory writ large, where (as Laura Brown puts it, speaking of the *Rape of the Lock*) "relations between things replace relations between people, [and] human beings themselves can come to be redefined as objects."[42] On this account, in which enfranchisement is equated with partic- ularity and particularity with depth, with being something more than (one's) form, not only would it not make sense to call Marvell's allegory feminist. On this account, it is impossible to regard allegory as such as anything but funda- mentally antifeminist and illiberal.

This is not how Benjamin sees allegory when he describes it as the "arma- ture of the modern."[43] For him, allegory is not synonymous with objectifica- tion conventionally understood; rather, allegory is a "devaluation of the world of objects" that takes place, paradoxically, through a devaluation of the world of persons. In its modern instantiation (in Baudelaire), it is a form of personi- fication, a "heroic" attempt to "humanize (*humanisieren*) the commodity," an attempt equivalent to "the simultaneous attempt of the bourgeoisie to personify the commodity (*vermenschlichen*): to give the commodity, like a person, hous- ing."[44] But this is not to say that Benjamin revalues allegory by aligning it with a depth model of personhood. The power of allegory—its "destructive," which is to say its progressive tendency—comes rather from the way "any person, any object, any relationship can mean absolutely anything else," the way it renders "details unimportant"—including, perhaps especially, those details we call "in- dividuals."[45] Benjamin loves the skeletal quality of allegory, its "renunciation of the natural," its "destruction of the organic and living," its "petrification."[46] This hollowness is, again paradoxically, what allows allegory to resist the distortions of an advertising culture that "seeks to veil the commodity character of things": in allegory the commodity "look[s] itself in the face," "celebrates its becoming human in the whore," acknowledges that if it is (like) a person, this is only be- cause persons are (like) things.[47]

For Benjamin, as for Jameson after him, allegory is a critical operation whose similarity with the ontologic of commodification helps demystify capitalism's commitment to the objecthood of human persons. For others, however, that similarity implicates allegory in the historical—and literary-historical—project of dehumanization. Alex Woloch begins *The One vs. the Many* by arguing that "the realist novel never ceases to make allegorical (or functional) use of subordinate characters" and that realism is a "ferocious" problematization of its allegorical impulses: "Allegorical characterization now comes at a price: the price of the human particularity that it elides."[48] Although he mobilizes the standard distinction between allegorization and particularity, Woloch also makes flatness "essential to realism": "Flatness simultaneously renders subordinate characters allegorical and, in its compelling distortions, calls attention to the subordination that underlies allegory."[49] For Woloch, as for Benjamin, allegory alerts one to the presence of a formal self-consciousness: allegory is the realist novel looking itself in the face. "The omniscient novel is particularly conscious of this narrative process [the flattening of subordinate characters], integrating its awareness into the narrative fabric," he says.[50] But because he yokes allegory to a pronounced rhetoric of instrumentalization, listing "exclusion, hierarchy and stratification, abstraction, utility, functionality and effacement" as the "formal terms of the socionarrative matrix," one sees in Woloch something Benjamin's more subtle dialectic escapes: if allegory brings into relief the distortions of capitalism, it also makes the proper form of the literary person the human being in all her complexity. Woloch is quite clear on this point: the problem with and for the minor character is that the "inwardness of a person—her presence, her 'personality'—gets expressed only through an exterior sign."[51] The minor character is a "roundness squared to a sharp edge," an "implied human being who gets constricted into a delimited role, but who has enough resonance with a human being to make us aware of this constricted position *as* delimited."[52] The pathos of minoritization is the fleeting presence of an inwardness that is synonymous with human being and whose actualization is the sacred charge of any humane politics or ethics.

In Marvell one encounters a different politics for flatness, a feminist politics preoccupied with questions of substantive harm rather than the harm of misrepresentation, a politics skeptical precisely of how signs of inwardness (consent, desire) are made signs that one has not been harmed—where, to the contrary, they are signs that one has been properly recognized (or recognized properly). Allegory is the necessary vehicle for this politics, and for a feminist poetics, not because it *demystifies* the objectifying effects of modernity, pointing to a future in which humans would recover a fullness of being peculiar to their kind. Allegory is necessary to a feminist poetics because it is safer for creatures whose interiority underwrites a reflexive practice of (self-) justification to be looked at from the outside—to be asked, as Lady Bidulph might put it, not what's in their hearts but what they have *done*.

I have suggested in this chapter, and throughout this book, that norms of interiority are masculinist norms: that the logic of the subject, as I put it above, is a logic of limited liability. The externalizing countergenealogy of liberalism offered in its stead gives us a new way of understanding why a poem about "rape"—a poem that follows Marvell in invoking a strident category of harm to describe the operations of heteronormativity—might be a poem about "locks." In the *Rape of the Lock*, accounts of states of mind are so relentlessly associated with objects that it is virtually impossible to pry the two apart. The toyshop where "Wigs with Wigs, with Sword-knots Sword-knots strive" (1.101) is an account of desire; spleen is the place where "living Teapots stand," "pipkins" walk, jars sigh, "Goose-pye's talk, and "Maids turn'd Bottles, call aloud for Corks" (4.49–54). Of the period's premier allegorist, Leopold Damrosch observes: "In [Bunyan's] *The Holy War* the heart is a structure, not a person, the interior castle that holds out even when the rest of the town has fallen, and whose doors are opened by faith to Christ"; this "creates a distance by representing the heart, the deepest self, as something *other*," he concludes.[53] For Bunyan the loss of self is meant to be "profoundly consoling"; "the body becomes dehumanized," according to Roger Sharrock, whom Damrosch quotes, "a thing done to, and in compensation the spirit creates a world of its own."[54] But one can see why being "done to" might be less than consoling to Pope's feminist critics, who worry about the way allegory turns body parts into objects, literalizing a dualism (so congenial to Bunyan) that makes even affect too embodied for, and thus detachable from, subjects. In the poem's development objects cease to be *part* of a subject/person and become synonymous with the person herself: synecdoche is superseded by a substitutional logic that is more than metaphorical. In synecdoche, the part is comprehensible in relation to a whole that it helps to underwrite: body parts are elements of persons who, although anatomized, remain ontologically intact. But in the *Rape of the Lock* there is no way for a person to be sure she is a person because there is no way to distinguish a state of mind, being mindfull, from the mindlessness of things.

This is only a problem, however, if one wants thinking and feeling to be something fundamentally distinct from moving; if one wants persons to be ontologically distinct from animate or inanimate things; if one wants allegory to "give way to characterization."[55] This is what recent critical work on objects tends to want: "Only by means of the grossest delusion," Jonathan Lamb insists, "is it possible to make . . . sentimental equations between the lives of humans and animals."[56] Lamb is speaking of Coetzee's *Disgrace*, which he reads as an allegory of the "limits of sympathy" that dismantles barriers between persons and animals, persons and things.[57] His interest in the personifying logic of slavery produces an understandable anxiety about Coetzee's inversions: "Slave and owner," he observes, "are metamorphosed by the same process and confront each other as animals, locked in a passionate enmity from which reason and humanity have been expelled" (165). For political and methodological reasons, Lamb wants to hang on to the special status of the human being as something more than a thing, and this desire underwrites most work on object narration, preoccupied as it is with the dehumanizing effects of a generalized commodification.

In the tradition of feminist allegory that moves from Marvell and Pope to Defoe, Richardson, and Sheridan, however, one sees what it looks like to make the equation Lamb descries, to offer the objecthood of human persons precisely as an *escape* from sentimental models of being and belonging, including the sentimentalism (and de facto humanism) of economic materialism. Objectification, externalization, allegorization, flatness—these come into focus as values once one shifts attention from the market to the law, from commodification to responsibility. The *Memoirs of Miss Sidney Bidulph* conflates subjects and objects, persons and things, in order to make deodand, quite explicitly, an answer to the problem of rape. By making states of mind irrelevant to the question of harm and compensation, deodand avoids the antifeminist depredations of consent theory so relentlessly anatomized in *Clarissa*. Sheridan understands rape law and the sentimental novel as it is conventionally conceived as genres whose emphasis on consent demands that victims be virtuous and villains perfidious in a way that obscures the complex relationship between character and action, fault and blame. I have called Sheridan's sense of this relationship "tragic" for the way persons discover who they are by discovering that they have acted in a way that inevitably goes against (and makes irrelevant as an account of who they are and what they have done) their own sense of themselves. To quote Bernard Williams again:

> The whole of the *Oedipus Tyrannus*, that dreadful machine moves to the discovery of just one thing, that *he did it*. . . . The terrible thing that happened to [Oedipus], through no fault of his own, was that he did those things. . . . [H]e is the person who did those things.[58]

Happened to; did it. As I've said before, Williams's rhetoric makes two things clear: that the tragic model of responsibility conceives of blame without fault—even, perhaps, without agency—and that character happens to and does not usher from persons.

A leitmotif of *Harm's Way* has been Williams's brief, enigmatic observation that "we" moderns retain, in the form of "offences of strict liability," this seemingly archaic commitment to "blam[ing] and sanction[ing] people for things that they did unintentionally." "We are thought not to do this," he says, "or at least to regard it as unjust."[59] Williams does not think that recognizing responsibility and recognizing what we call "people" in this way is unjust. Neither does Sheridan. If the tragic logic of absolute liability makes it harder to see persons as endowed with those qualities of mind we imagine are uniquely the property of human beings, it also allows us to see them more humanely. Criminals aren't bad people but material causes; victims aren't required to be virtuous (or passive or female) for their harm to count as harm. For Sheridan, this kind of "flattening" is a way of making harm—even harms complicated by the presence of affection, desire, or consent, even harms produced by good people and experienced by bad—*matter*. Pope famously ends the *Rape of the Lock* by imagining that like the eminently literary deodand, literature can best acknowledge persons by acknowledging their objecthood—their inescapable, irresistible vulnerability to (cause or suffer) harm. The lock (and the *Lock*), he assures Belinda, will survive long after "the self shall die." In exchange for the exigencies of embodiment, literature offers persons the compensations of form.

Bad Form

Not everything had a cause.

—Ian McEwan, *Atonement*

Charles Dickens's *Hard Times* is intrigued by, but ultimately rejects, a realist aesthetic underwritten by the logic of strict liability. On the one hand, Dickens excoriates the "injured men of Coketown" who consider themselves

> ruined, when inspectors were appointed to look into their works; they were ruined when such inspectors considered it doubtful whether they were quite justified in chopping people up with their machinery; they were utterly undone, when it was hinted that perhaps they need not always make quite so much smoke.[1]

"Surely there never was such fragile china-ware as that of which the millers of Coketown were made," his narrator complains:

> Whenever a Coketowner felt he was ill used—that is to say, whenever he was not left entirely alone, and it was proposed to hold him accountable for the consequences of any of his acts—he was sure to come out with the awful menace that he would "sooner pitch his property into the Atlantic." (145–46)

Ranked among these "fine gentlemen" is James Harthouse's older brother, whose suspect character is marked by his habit of entertaining the House of Commons with

his (and the Board of Director's) view of a railway accident, in which the most careful officers ever heard of, assisted by the finest mechanical contrivances ever de-
vised, the whole in action on the best line ever constructed, had killed five people
and wounded thirty-two, by a casualty without which the excellence of the whole
system would have been positively incomplete.

"Among the slain was a cow, and among the scattered articles unowned, a widow's cap," the narrator explains:

> And the honourable member had so tickled the House (which has a delicate sense
> of humour) by putting the cap on the cow, that it became impatient of any serious
> reference to the Coroner's Inquest, and brought the railway off with Cheers and
> Laughter. (158)

Clearly, bringing off—*letting* off—the railway with cheers and laughter is not
funny.[2] And yet, when Stephen Blackpool falls into an abandoned mining shaft
there is barely a hint that the "fragile" miller who left behind the unmarked
hazard might be accountable. "Ah, Rachel, aw a muddle! Fro' first to last, a muddle!" Stephen reflects on his injury:

> I ha' fell into th'pit, my dear, as have cost wi'in the knowledge o' folk now livin,
> hundreds and hundreds o' men's lives. . . . I ha' fell into a pit that ha' been wi' the'
> Fire-damp crueler than battle. I ha' read on't in the public petition, as onny one
> may read, fro' the men that works in pits, in which they ha' pray'n an pray'n the
> lawmakers for Christ's sake not to let their work be murder to 'em.

"When it were in work, it killed wi'out need; when 'tis done, it kills wi'out need,"
he concludes. "See how we die an no need, one way an another—in a muddle—
every day!" (289–90). It looks as though by calling industrial accidents "murder," Stephen means to indict the millers for their failure to take responsibility
for the safety of their employees and for the toxic byproducts of their industry.
And it even looks as though he is indicting Tom Gradgrind for *his* vicarious
responsibility for the accident:

> If aw th' things that tooches us, my dear, was not so muddled, I should'n ha' had'n
> need to coom here. If we was not in a muddle among ourseln, I should'n ha' been,
> by my own fellow weavers and workin' brothers, so mistook. If Mr Bounderby had
> ever know'd me right—if he'd ever know'd me at aw—he would'n ha' took'n of-
> fence wi' me. He would'n ha' suspect'n me. (290)

It looks this way, but he is not. For while the "poor, crushed human creature"
(289) lies "upon his back with one arm doubled under him" (288), the "muddle"
in his mind clears, and what he see is this:

If soom ha' been wantin' in unnerstan'in me better, I, too, ha' been wantin' in unnerstan'in them better. . . . . I ha' seen more clear, and ha' made it my dyin prayer that aw th' world may on'y coom together more, an get a better unnerstan'in o'one another. (290–91)

Rejecting liability in favor of "unnerstan'in," Stephen's solution, while it *feels* tragic, is profoundly comic—a commitment, at one with the novel's own, to the sentimental project of exculpation.[3]

What happens in the ninety-three years between Sheridan's *Memoirs of Miss Sidney Bidulph* and *Hard Times* that explains Dickens's preference for a realism in which, as Eagleton says of Eliot, *tout comprendre c'est tout pardonner?*[4] To a certain extent this is an effect of a fondness for Fielding, whose eschewal of tragic responsibility (which is to say, whose preference for comedy) is a model and source for Dickens's own. But there are other, darker, forces at work. Thinking of *Sidney Bidulph* and *Clarissa* as novels interested in the instrumentality of agency—in the ontological consequences of being *merely* animated—sends realism in a direction it has not generally been seen as going: in the direction of *The Castle of Otranto*, with its animated helmets, paintings, swords, and statues, and *Frankenstein*, with its animated and not-quite-human protagonist. The English gothic, that quintessential fiction of harm, is obsessed with the terror of producing and being held accountable for catastrophes. Put this way, its investments can be seen to represent an apotheosis and a literalization of the aims of realism as I have been describing them. In the realist novel, beings we are used to calling "persons" are made responsible for the effects of an agency that looks, and *is*, like the instrumentality of things; in the gothic novel, things *are* the effects for which persons are asked to be responsible. Placing a text like *Frankenstein* in the context of the literary and legal genealogies mapped out in this book allows us to see something we haven't seen about its famous interest in production. Namely, that the novel proleptically articulates a new logic of strict liability—products liability—that continually returns to *Frankenstein* itself to account for the way it conceives of responsibility.

"We were warned about the dangers of automation," begins a 1992 article in the *Harvard Journal of Law and Technology* called, "The Responsibility of Intelligent Artifacts: Toward an Automation Jurisprudence": "Over a hundred years ago, Dr. Frankenstein created and activated his monster, a conglomeration of human flesh and wire electrodes, the brainchild of a maniacal scientist. Can humanity, which considers itself the master, control its progeny?" "Mary Shelley's *Frankenstein* is symptomatic of this unease about mankind's ostensible control of science and technology," the author, Leon Wein, goes on to suggest, "an anxiety that things—animate things—might get out of hand."[5] The invocation of Shelley's *Frankenstein* is de rigueur in the contemporary literature on products liability. "Regulating Dr. Frankenstein: Money, Lax Ethics, and Clinical Trials" is the title of a *Legal Times* article covering *Gelsinger v. Trustees of the University of Pennsylvania*, a 2000 tort suit brought by the family of a young man who died during the course of gene-transfer therapy.[6] "It's funny but ephedra has become something of a modern-day Frankenstein monster. As in the Mary Wollestonecraft Shelley novel of the Victorian era [sic], our ephedra Frankenstein seems to be constantly pursued by an angry and fearful mob of ignorant peasants with burning torches who have not the faintest understanding of what they are seeking to destroy," muses Scott Tips, editor of *Heath Freedom News* and legal counsel for the National Health Federation, a conservative think tank devoted to among other things defending supplement producers from government regulation and tort action suits.[7] The debate over biotechnology and genetically engineered food is fair to bursting with references to Shelley's modern Prometheus: "Biotechnology and the Fear of Frankenstein" is the title of a recent essay in the *Cambridge Quarterly of Healthcare Ethics;* "More Faust than Frankenstein" insists an article on risk regulation for genetically modified crops in the *Journal of Risk Research;* "So Whose Afraid of Frankenstein Food?" asks an essay in the *Journal of Social Philosophy;* and a personal favorite in *Food Science and Technology Today* announces, as if in answer: "Enough of Frankenstein."[8]

For the scientists and ethicists concerned with the potentially deleterious effects of biotechnology, "Frankenstein" is shorthand for the overweening ambitions of what Marilyn Butler calls "radical" and Franco Moretti calls "modern" science.[9] For lawyers, however, what is important about the *Frankenstein* paradigm is less the actions of the novel's eponymous protagonist than the action of its plot—a plot, as Wein implies, preoccupied with what it means for human beings to be responsible for machines or, to put this another way, what it means for machines to be responsible for themselves. This question gets at something important about the novel, its interest in what Mark Hansen calls the "ontology of technological change" coincident with the advent of "machine automation."[10] For Hansen, *Frankenstein* tells the story of the emergence of a "technological product in a quite specific, postindustrial sense: a product of a process whose 'effects' are neither predetermined nor constrained by theoretical principles of science."[11] The unpredictability of "technology's autonomous functioning" is a key feature of the logic of the machine: it is, Hansen says, an *"inhuman"* logic.[12] The inhumanity of this logic, he argues, is nowhere more evident than in those scenes of legal judgment in which Frankenstein is implicated in the machine's effects. Frankenstein's escalating tendency to accept responsibility for these effects—to see himself as a "murderer" leaving bodies in his wake—signals, for Hansen, his "submission to pure machinism": having lost the ability "to distinguish his action from that of the monster, he has become the inhuman complement of the machinic."[13]

Hansen's emphasis on the creature as a machinic product resists the humanist allegoresis so prevalent in the traditional criticism on the novel, where the creature is woman, or the proletariat, or the "mass being" of human population but rarely a machine.[14] His work is thus crucial for understanding how *Frankenstein* comes to figure as a representative text in the history of products and their liability. But the suggestion that there is something "inhuman" and therefore inhumane about the novel's interest in the question of vicarious liability is one with which I disagree—and not only because it resurrects the humanism it had seemed to renounce. A reader steeped the tradition of tragic realism might be prompted to ask: isn't the "autonomous functioning" of what we call persons unpredictable as well? And if the logic of vicarious liability seems ethical when it requires Roxana or Lovelace be responsible for the acts of agents in their employ, why does it seem unethical when it asks Victor to be responsible for the machine that he has made? The answer, I think, has to do with a discomfort we've encountered before with making persons responsible for accidents—and accident, according to Hansen, is above all what machines produce. Shelley's text, he says, "suggests that technology cannot be thought in terms of 'ethicity,' even when—or especially when—it generates a (purely chance) event which (paradoxically) can easily be attributed to a human agent."[15] But *are* the effects generated by Frankenstein's product purely chance events? And even if they were, would this obviate his responsibility for them? Does ethics require a model of the subject who can predict or control the outcome of her acts? Does obligation require that the acts for which one is liable be one's own? Could being an "inhuman complement of the machinic" *constitute* an ethics?

Hansen's answer of "no" to this question is offered as an account of Shelley's position on the ethics of accidental responsibility. But *Frankenstein* seems to me obsessed with the problem, and the possibilities, of strict liability, and so I wonder if it isn't more accurate as a description of Hansen's own position than Shelley's. The first few pages of Victor Frankenstein's inset narrative, after all, are filled with accidents—benign acts or omissions leading "insensibly," he says, "to my after tale of misery."[16] When on vacation with his family, a chance "inclemency of weather obliged us to remain a day confined to the inn," where he similarly "chanced to find a volume of the works of Cornelius Agrippa" (21). Victor's father responds to this random enthusiasm of his son's "carelessly," without which carelessness, Victor reflects, "it is even possible, that the train of my ideas would never have received the fatal impulse that lead to my ruin" (21). This is the first of many occasions in which someone other than the creature looks as though she might be the final cause of the novel's calamities. But before we have time to contemplate Frankenstein père's responsibility, our attention is drawn to the lightning storm that usurps the authority of Cornelius Agrippa, the "strange fatality" that keeps Victor from the study of modern science, and the "accident" that prevents him from attending a course of lectures on natural philosophy, sending him instead, "from idleness," to M. Waldman—who, we're told, "decided my destiny" (23, 27–28). In between is the death of Victor's mother, who, in a scene straight out of the *Journal of the Plague Year,* is unwittingly destroyed as a consequence of her affection for another: "When she heard that her favourite was recovering," we are told, "she could no longer debar herself from [Elizabeth's] society, and entered her chamber long before the danger of infection was past" (24).

This series of misadventures leads directly into the central action, and most significant accident, of the book: the making of the creature. Intending to leave Ingolstadt for home—"I thought of returning to my friends and native town," Victor reflects—that intention is thwarted when "an incident happened that protracted my stay" (29). It's never entirely clear whether this "incident" is some unnamed occurrence that keeps Victor at his labors until the moment when he discovers, through stages "distinct and probable," the secret of animation or whether it is that moment itself, the fortuitous "pause" during which he examines "all the minutiae of causation . . . until from the midst of this darkness a sudden light broke in upon me" (30). In any case, Shelley takes pains to distinguish production from intention, both here and in the scene in which Victor forms what he calls his "determination" to begin "the creation of a human being." "As the minuteness of the parts formed a great hindrance to my speed," he tells us, "I resolved, contrary to my first intention, to make the being of a gigantic stature; that is to say, about eight feet in height, and proportionably large" (31–32). "Resolution," like "determination," sounds like intention, but it is a compensatory, contingent adjustment, an act explicitly distinguished from full (or "first") intentionality. It is a resolution that of all the uncertain acts contributing to this event has the most devastating consequences for the creature and the world in which he moves. For in making him "gigantic," Victor ensures the creature's exclusion from a model of species and obligation predicated on resemblance, and by exceeding the dimensions of human morphology, no matter what he does or means to do, the creature is seen as injurious.

I will return to this great tragedy of *Frankenstein*—the tragedy of shape or form. But for now I want to focus attention on *Victor's* injuriousness. While in the throes of creating his product it occurs to Victor that his father must be feeling neglected: "I then thought that my father would be unjust if he ascribed my neglect to vice, or faultiness on my part," he reflects, "but I am now convinced that he was justified in conceiving that I should not be altogether free from blame" (33). Victor's tortured syntax betrays his ambivalent relation to the question of his blameworthiness—an ambivalence that persists far longer than it ought ("now" marks his sojourn on Walton's ship, at some distance from the total annihilation of his extended family). This ambivalence is a consistent feature of the diegesis, even as evidence of Victor's complicity in the calamitous events it represents increases. Nowhere is this ambivalence more acute, or more alarming, than in the subplot concerning Justine Moritz and the murder of young William that immediately follows the "catastrophe" (34) of the creature's making. Asserting that "Justine, and indeed every human being, was guiltless of this murder," Frankenstein nonetheless proceeds to wonder "whether the *result* of my curiosity and lawless devices would *cause* the death of two of my fellow-beings" (52; emphases mine). The theory of causation Victor advances here is as contorted as his earlier self-recrimination: the creature is at once "result" and "cause," act and effect, alpha and omega of the plot's escalating harms. One registers that there are two separate actions at issue: the creature is a consequence of *Victor's* act; death is a consequence of the *creature's* act. But the syntactical structure of the sentence makes the creature the lone subject of it, concealing Victor's connection to William's murder and the "far more dreadful murder" of Justine. Victor might have asked: "Did my curiosity and lawless devices cause the death of William and Justine?" Yet a grammar of personification deflects agency and responsibility onto the creature ("result" as subject of the action), compromising the sincerity of Victor's express remorse: "All was to be obliterated in an ignominious grave; and I the cause!" (52). Although he briefly entertains owning this declaration—imagining he might exonerate Justine by taking responsibility for William's murder—he tells himself (and us) that such a confession would have been madness, for "I was absent when [the crime] was committed" (52).

Why does Victor feel indemnified against harms he admits he has somehow caused? Is this what it means to be "by birth a Genevese" (17) rather than an Englishman living under the constant threat of vicarious liability enshrined in the common law? As we've seen, the doctrine of agency established that a master, who before 1700 was liable for a servant's acts only if he had commanded them, "could be made vicariously liable for acts which he did not command"— acts whose effects became his even though he was ignorant of their being committed and not present when they were committed, even though he himself *had not moved*.[17] Agency emerged from cases involving traffic accidents, where the liability of common carriers (hackney coachmen, watermen) turned on an ancient standard of strict liability governing innkeepers. Over time this "custom of the realm" establishing the inescapable "common duty" of landlords to travelers was extended to include less proximate but still adventitious encounters between persons—those mediated by what the law calls "escapes," for example, dangerous forces such as fire, animals, and water, the negligent use of which occasioned "stricter liability than would otherwise attach."[18]

What interests me about custom of the realm and the doctrine of agency it helps to underwrite is the significant gap between agency as a legal principle and agency understood as a philosophical category (as roughly synonymous with volition).[19] Although the doctrine of agency often turns on formal relations such as those between masters and servants, conceptually, and precisely as a result of this formalism, it is a model of what legal scholars call "nonrelationship liability": relationship on this account is profoundly nonvolitional, emerging independently of any prior connection between the parties other than that brought about by accident, harm, injury. Injury *produces* relationship, enforcing obligations between those who have not chosen or wanted to belong to one another.

It may be that Victor's nationality protects him from such quintessentially English—and historically recent—forms of responsibility as the doctrine of agency. But before we concede that *Frankenstein* rejects such a doctrine, "revealing the inadequacy of the entire Western justice system, civil and criminal, to Frankenstein and the creature's predicament," we must take note of the fact that Victor's understanding of causation and liability is much more naive than the novel's own.[20] Victor is committed to the idea that proximity is necessary for responsibility; like Lovelace, he wants to imagine that action at a distance is no action at all, that although he has set the creature in motion its acts are solely its own: "I lived in daily fear," he muses, "lest the monster whom I had created should perpetrate some new wickedness" (60). The novel's relentless imagery of doubling and replication makes this a difficult position to maintain, however, and it is in response to this gothic logic of symbiosis that Victor begins to deploy the vocabulary of self-inculpation that for Hansen signals his submission to "pure machinism" and thus his exclusion from a model of ethics predicated on human being—that is, on being the kind of being who generates something more than "chance events."[21]

As in *Roxana*, the form this inculpation takes turns on the word "murder." "I the true murderer" (57), Victor thinks as Justine awaits execution. The phrase echoes his earlier "I the cause" and in doing so links murder with a merely causal agency distinct from its normative alignment with malicious mens rea. We have seen how often Defoe and Richardson use the term "murder" to describe fatal harms that lack the requisite intentionality to be considered criminal (plague-infected mothers "murdering" their nursing infants; Roxana "murdering" her daughter Susan; Lovelace "murdering" Clarissa). It is a gesture, I have been arguing, that is at once conceptual and formal—a way of marking a text as realist, as tragic, as what I have just called "gothic." It is a gesture Shelley self-consciously reproduces, as the rhetoric of homicide escalates alongside the novel's accumulating harms. "I, not in deed, but in effect, was [William's] true murderer" (61), Victor repeats. Victor is less inclined than Roxana to accede to his prosthetic attachment to others and their acts, however and when confronted with indictment for Cherval's death insists, "I was innocent; that could easily be proved" (128). "Justine, poor unhappy Justine was as innocent as I," he complains, "and she suffered the same charge; she died for it." One might think that Justine is considerably *more* innocent than Victor, and indeed, in midsentence he vacillates once again, making a charge against himself so rigorous that his father attributes it to "delirium": "I am the cause of this—I murdered her. William, Justine, and Henry—they all died by my hands" (128); "I am the assassin of those most innocent victims; they died by my machinations" (129). This tendency to describe himself as innocent despite feeling hyperbolically to blame is in one sense consistent with the logic of accidental responsibility, which, in the case of Clarissa for example, allows faultlessness to coincide with blameworthiness. But Victor's ambivalence about his responsibility is quite unlike Clarissa's self-immolating guilt and is in marked contrast with the alacrity with which the creature holds himself responsible for accidents and for the distant effects of his own actions. Victor's persistent refusal of the strictures of strict liability makes him a less tragic figure than Clarissa or Roxana—or indeed than his exquisitely compunctious creation—and if strict liability remains a model for thinking about obligation in *Frankenstein*, it is in tension with one better suited to Victor's ambivalence: negligence.

"Wretched devil! You reproach me with your creation; come on then, that I may extinguish the spark which I so negligently bestowed" (66), Victor threatens his progeny in the shadow of Mont Blanc. The creature has reproached Victor with having failed in his duties toward him, a failure most often understood in terms of filiation: "The novel is in part an examination of the responsibility of the father to the son," observes George Levine, a claim consistent with but also importantly revised by feminist readings of the novel as a "phantasmagoria of the nursery."[22] It is of course true that the novel allegorizes the depredations of reproduction: "For the first time, also, I felt what the duties of a creator toward his creature were," Victor reflects as he complies with the creature's demand that he "hear my tale" (67). Yet to emphasize what a parent owes his child is to miss the other way that Victor describes his responsibility—as a question not of cultivation but of negligent *making*. And the mistake he has made is not so much to have engaged in an inappropriate act of "technological production" in the first place but to have made the product too large—and thus, in the language of products liability, to have made an "inherently dangerous thing."[23]

For although the being declares himself "*thy* creature" (65–67; emphasis mine) five times in the space of one and a half pages, what is emphasized throughout the novel—and especially in the creature's inset narrative—are the ways he fails to be like Victor, and thus to *be* Victor's. "Remember, thou has made me more powerful than thyself," he reminds his maker. "My height is superior to thine" (66). In the Miltonic creation scene early in the novel, the creature's monstrosity appears to be an effect of a deformed visage: "I had selected his features as beautiful. Beautiful—Great God!" (34), Victor famously complains, the ensuing mock-blazon cataloging the being's yellowed skin, watery eyes, "shriveled complexion, and straight black lips" (34). But in subsequent encounters what is highlighted is a deviant morphology: "A flash of lightening illuminated the object, and discovered its shape plainly to me. . . . Nothing in human shape could have destroyed that fair child. He was the murderer! I could not doubt it" (48), Victor reflects, as he makes out the creature amid the storm on Mont Salêve. On the ice field under Mont Blanc he sees "the figure of a man, at some distance, advancing toward me with superhuman speed": "I perceived, as the shape came nearer, (sight tremendous and abhorred!) that it was the wretch whom I had created" (65), Victor explains, and although in both scenes he goes on to describe the "unearthly ugliness" (65) of the creature's face, what is most immediately abhorrent is that "his stature . . . seemed to exceed that of man" (65). "My form is a filthy type of yours," confirms the creature, "more horrid from its very resemblance" (88).

The tale the creature goes on to tell catalogues the tragic consequences of a model of obligation and belonging predicated on resemblance. Although his life "has been hitherto harmless," the creature explains to De Lacey père, those whom he wishes to aid "believe that I wish to injure them" (90). This belief we immediately see enacted, as Felix, encountering the massive creature with his arms around his father's knees, reads the kinesics of supplication as aggression and "dashed me to the ground, and struck me violently with a stick" (91). When the creature subsequently rescues a young girl from drowning—"she was sense-less; and I endeavoured, by every means in my power, to restore animation," he recounts—her father likewise reads the position of the creature's body vis-à-vis another, smaller being's, as harmful:

> On seeing me, he darted towards me, and tearing the girl from my arms, hastened towards the deeper parts of the wood. I followed, but when the man saw me draw near, he aimed a gun, which he carried, at my body, and fired. I sunk to the ground, and my injurer, with increased swiftness, escaped into the wood. (95)

Here it is the creature himself who is injured by Victor's failure to fashion him an appropriate shape. But these scenes are followed by the encounter with Wil-liam, which literalizes the risk of bodily harm projected onto the creature's out-sized form. Imagining the boy too young to presume the harmfulness of his frame, the creature attempts to befriend him. "I seized on the boy as he passed, and drew him towards me," we're told, but "as soon as he beheld my form, he placed his hands before his eyes, and uttered a shrill scream" (96). "I do not intend to hurt you," the creature tells the child, but the encounter goes horribly awry as, against his intention, the creature fulfills the instrumental logic of his form. "The child still struggled, and loaded me with epithets which carried despair to my heart: I grasped his throat to silence him, and in a moment he lay dead at my feet" (97).

The creature means only to quiet the child, not to throttle him. But so pow-erful a being grasps throats at his peril. It is an accident. And yet this is not how the creature describes his act: "I left the spot where I had committed the murder" (97), he concludes. Murder is the class of harms under which Justine is prosecuted for William's death in the creature's stead, and one might expect that in the portion of the narrative devoted to *his* point of view the indictment would be softened. "I didn't mean to kill him," the creature seems justified in saying. "It was manslaughter at best, really homicide *per infortunium*"—an un-fortunate killing lacking even the momentarily malign intent of manslaughter (for the creature is saddened, not enraged, by the child's speaking). That he does not excuse himself is what, far more than his shape, distinguishes the creature from his maker (a point to which I will return). Yet if he is strict with himself—

fastening on himself the most strident category of responsibility there is—he also insists on Victor's share of blame. "It is in your power to recompense me" (66), the creature tells Victor when they meet on Mont Blanc, and the ensuing tale serves as an account of what needs compensating—the injuriousness of his design, the fact that he is made in such a way that the most benign embrace looks like, and ultimately is, the kiss of death.

We have gotten used to thinking that there is some justice in the demands the creature makes on his creator, but we have not yet noticed how often those demands are framed in the language of injury and compensation. Compensation functions as an alternative to other models of justice at work in the novel: capital punishment, on the one hand, and the creature's vengeful rage, on the other. Indeed, these two are not easily kept apart, as Elizabeth's critique of judicial murder acknowledges:

> When one creature is murdered, another is immediately deprived of life in a slow torturing manner. . . . They call this *retribution*. Hateful name! When that word is pronounced, I know greater and more horrid punishments are going to be inflicted than the gloomiest tyrant has ever invented to satiate his utmost revenge. (56)

The bloodthirstiness of retribution is reinvoked in the creature's threat to "revenge his injuries" (98). And "recompense" is proffered as a surrogate retaliation, one designed to prevent future harms, including the harm of more vengeful comeuppance: "On you it rests," the creature tells Victor, "whether I quit for ever the neighborhood of man, and lead a harmless life, or become the scourge of your fellow-creatures, and the author of your own speedy ruin" (67).

The logic that the creature invokes to tie Victor to him sounds like, and has always been assumed to be, the logic of kinship: "You, my creator, detest and spurn me, *thy* creature, to whom thou art bound by ties only dissoluble by the annihilation of one of us" (65; emphasis mine). We have seen how profoundly the creature suffers under kinship regimes, however—under a resemblance model of belonging that ties obligation to kind-ness, to being another's kind. The presence of a language of compensation in the novel helps us to perceive another logic at work in the creature's claim that there is an indissoluble connection between a creator and the thing she has made—the logic of strict vicarious liability, which is profoundly *unkind* (or, one might say, gothic) in the way it binds persons to strange others and to the adventitious strangeness of their own acts.

I am tempted to describe the opposition between kinship and compensation in *Frankenstein* as an opposition between relationship and nonrelationship liability. And if the literature of products liability is obsessed with *Frankenstein*, it is perhaps because this same opposition underwrites the legal history of responsibility for things. Until the early years of the twentieth century, products liability was stymied by the precedent of *Winterbottom v. Wright* (1842), a case in which a postal service wagon driver injured by a fall occasioned by a faulty wheel attempted to sue the wagon's maker. The attempt failed because the courts invoked "privity of contract," arguing that there was no prior relationship, and thus no obligation, between the injured carrier and the manufacturer. The doctrine of privity of contract stood in the way of the full development of strict products liability until the landmark case of *MacPherson v. Buick Motor Co.* (1916), which also involved a defective wheel, and in which Benjamin Cardozo successfully argued for a "duty irrespective of contract" that he tied to the "liability of landlords."[24]

Products liability thus rejected privity—a doctrine refined and entrenched in nineteenth-century law—by turning to older forms of strict liability such as carrier liability and custom of the realm in which relationship was understood in noncontractual and nondisclaimable terms. Cardozo explicitly invokes custom of the realm (the liability of landlords), but for legal historians the most powerful influence on products liability was the law of deodand or thing liability.[25] As we saw in chapter 4, deodand was a technology for compensating harms to humans by nonhumans. Forfeiture of an object that caused harm was grounded in the sense that, as William Blackstone put it, "such misfortunes are in part owing to the negligence of the owner, and therefore he is properly punished by such forfeiture." But, as we've seen, "negligence" as Blackstone uses the term is not a culpable failure to foresee harm; it simply marks a person's relationship to a thing and to its effects. "It matters not whether the owner were concerned in the killing or not," Blackstone observes, "for if a man kills another with my sword, the sword is forfeited as an accursed thing."[26] ("As in modern strict liability," notes Anita Bernstein, "the owner of the injuring animal [like the manufacturer of a product] cannot escape responsibility even when the victim does not prove fault.")[27] In deodand, the animal's mental attitude is quite irrelevant, and that irrelevance is transferred to its owner, who is made strictly liable to urge him to be careful and take the necessary precautions. Bad form—being a cart whose wheel has come loose—is met by a good formalism that detaches responsibility from moral turpitude, making liability a description of the sheer phenomenology of an act and thereby (and *only* thereby) its ethics.

Frankenstein confirms and helps to articulate the importance of eighteenth-century innovations in strict liability to products liability. It does so by literalizing the logic of deodand with its simultaneous personification of animals and things and its depersonification of human beings. Shelley marks this logic in the creature's uncertain ontological status somewhere between human, animal, and thing. And if her novel is a phantasmagoria of the nursery, it is because the nursery is where stories about talking objects are read. *Frankenstein* shows us what it would look like if "accursed things" could give an account of themselves and their actions. But because the creature's tale finally does not absolve him of responsibility for what he has done, it also highlights the insignificance of cherished indices of human personhood (language, self-consciousness, self-justification) to strict liability—the way the legal persons of strict liability are "guilty in an objective, not a subjective sense," the way such legal entities are objects rather than subjects.

The object likeness of strictly liable persons—that they are blamed for what they did not mean to do, and no accounting of what they meant can exculpate them—is what critics dislike about deodand and products liability. It is also what Victor dislikes; for although Hansen feels that Victor loses the ability "to distinguish his action from that of the monster," what strikes me is how ruthlessly in the closing pages of the novel he does precisely that. "I felt as if I had committed some great crime, the consciousness of which haunted me," he muses, but, he continues, "I was guiltless" (112). "They were dead," he reflects of his annihilated circle, "and I lived; their murderer also lived, and to destroy him I must drag out my weary existence" (140). That "also" confidently separates Victor from the creature and his deeds, a separation reiterated in Victor's death-bed assessment of the novel's catastrophes: "I have been occupied in examining my past conduct; nor do I find it blameable" (151), he asserts. As if to emphasize the profound gulf between Victor's and the creature's relation to the question of accidental responsibility, on finding his maker dead of what appear to be natural causes, the creature declares: "That is also my victim! . . . [I]n his murder my crimes are consummated" (153). It is Victor and not the creature, it seems, who wants to be a subject, who wants for the story of his "conduct" to exonerate him. Victor's narrative seeks to prove that he has not acted "blamably" and that since he is not blamable he is not to blame. But the novel in which that narrative is embedded finally rejects a negligence model of responsibility that would let Victor off the hook if it could be shown that he was not at fault—rejects negligence in favor of the creature's more perfect "submission to pure machinism," or, in other words, his submission to strict liability.

I began by asking whether being an "inhuman complement of the machinic" might constitute an ethics. Shelley's answer is "yes," but Hansen is not alone in answering "no." It is difficult, knowing what we know about ourselves, being continually confronted with the complex richness of our thoughts and feelings, to imagine that we act with the random instrumentality of machines. And it is even more difficult to accept that when we do so we might be responsible for what we have done. The need to explain ourselves and for that explanation to excuse us is strong: we want to say, with Gradgrind, "I have meant to do right," and we want for others to answer, as Louisa does, "I have never blamed you, and I never shall" (244–45). "When I call over the frightful catalogue of my deeds, I cannot believe that I am he whose thoughts were once filled with sublime and transcendent visions of the beauty and the majesty of goodness," Frankenstein's creature reflects, and although this statement is a tragic one—"it is even so" (154), he insists—we want to read the passage comically, which is to say like a liberal: we want for there to be an exculpating distance between who he is and what he has done.

But before we accede to the comic version of what it means to be ethical, or liberal, we must consider the other reason for Dickens's abandonment of the realism of tragic responsibility. With the emergence the railroad and the momentary resurgence of deodand in the 1830s when coroner's juries imposed hefty damage suits on railway corporations, the costs of a culture of strict liability came to many to seem too steep. In 1846, Lord Campbell's Act (known colloquially as the "Act to Abolish Deodands") dispensed with this ancient technology of compensation. Historians of English railway capitalism note that while in the late 1830s and 1840s railway passengers and employees both engaged in legal actions for damages, common-law judges created a body of law that was "exceedingly generous to injured railway patrons, but almost intractably ungenerous to injured railway laborers"—this despite the fact that workers were five times more likely to be killed than passengers.[28] These choices, explains R. W. Kostal:

> involved the selective application of the old law of carriers' and employers' liability
> to the new world of industrial accidents. When confronted with the legal actions
> of injured passengers, the judges chose continuity: the broad vicarious liability
> of preindustrial carriers was applied with vigour. When injured railway workers
> claimed that their employers, on the maxim *respondeat superior*, were vicariously
> liable also for injuries caused by the negligence of one servant towards another,
> the maxim was not applied.[29]

Instead "the judges chose to elaborate a contractual conception of work-related accidents, and then to defend it fiercely against legal and extralegal attacks."[30]

Railway companies were as delighted by these developments as by Harthouse's joke about the cow in the widow's cap, and responded by calling for privity of contract to govern damages to passengers as well. In leading cases on both sides of the Atlantic (*Priestley v. Fowler* [1837], *Farwell v. Boston and Worcester Railroad* [1842]) judges engaged in a judicial activism designed to enshrine the tenets of possessive individualism. Recognizing that strict liability was a threat to market freedoms, these judges tied labor and commercial relations firmly to contractual liability. The victims' claims, one judge opined, "must be maintained, if maintained at all, on the ground of contract."[31]

Hard Times, set in the context of Lord Campbell's Act and published contemporaneously with the Limited Liability Act, which legislated that industrialization "could not be carried out except with limited liability," is a creature of its age.[32] It is a different age from the one I have been describing. Enlightenment writers committed to *harm*'s way, to a way of thinking about social obligation that acknowledges the seriousness of harm to any being, are very clear on the question of whose rights contract protects. As the example of Dickens suggests, this way of thinking about obligation as fundamentally impersonal, adventitious, and nondisclaimable goes into a kind of dormancy in the nineteenth century under the pressures of industrialization. Acts such as Lord Campbell's ensured that the nineteenth century would be an era of exculpation in marked contrast with the strictures of *Frankenstein*'s world.[33] The story I've been telling about the novel of tragic responsibility, therefore, might not account for the Victorian novel, whose characteristic interest in detection represents a movement away from accidental and toward criminal culpability that consolidates the genre's preoccupation with character. But it might explain naturalism as a revisionist attack on the intentionalism of nineteenth-century realism, one that looks to an earlier moment in the history of the novel for its formal and sociological interest in accidents.[34] Or it might describe the importance of inadvertency in James— for example, *The Europeans*, which is saturated in what looks like interiority but turns on a scene of anagnorisis that reveals the limits of thinking. Or it might help us understand the tragedy of *Native Son*, where the instrumentality of the masculine and racialized body produces fatal harms that are genuinely accidental and yet nonetheless culpable.[35] And once again, it might explain McEwan, whose great novel of accidental injury and the fantasy of compensation, *Atonement*, is quite self-consciously an *eighteenth-century* novel.

"Her wish for a harmonious, organized world denied her the reckless possibilities of wrongdoing," we are told of Briony, the thirteen-year-old heroine, whose desire for order and for indemnity is fulfilled by the practice of writing, in particular the practice of writing marriage comedy.[36] "Divorce," Briony reflects, "was a mundane unravelling that could not be reversed, and therefore offered no opportunities to the storyteller: it belonged in the realm of disorder. Marriage was the thing, or rather a wedding was, with its formal neatness of virtue rewarded" (8). This invocation of Richardson is not the novel's last: when we first encounter Briony's older sister, Cecilia, she is "read[ing] her way through Richardson's *Clarissa*" (20) and not much liking it. "How's Clarissa?" her childhood friend Robbie asks her, and when she pronounces it "Boring," the following exchange ensues: " 'We mustn't say so.' 'I wish she'd get on with it.' 'She does. And it gets better' " (24). When Cecilia announces, "I'd rather read Fielding any day," Robbie replies with an assessment straight out of Watt: " 'I know what you mean,' he said as they walked the remaining few yards to the fountain. 'There's more life in Fielding, but he can be psychologically crude compared to Richardson' " (24). Cecilia is as disappointed with this conversation as she is with *Clarissa:* "The last thing she wanted was an undergraduate debate on eighteenth-century literature. She didn't think Fielding was crude at all, or that Richardson was a fine psychologist, but she wasn't going to be drawn in, defending, defining, attacking" (25). Cecilia seeks escape from the Oxbridge ethos the scene clearly parodies, but she is drawn into its more significant referent: nonetheless the logic of genre, a genre wholly indebted to Richardson.

For the debate on eighteenth-century literature, presided over by the spectre of *Clarissa*, sets in motion a chain of events that sends these well-meaning characters hurting toward tragedy. It is a tragedy built on the exquisite edifice of accident. Irritated by what she perceives is Robbie's contempt for her preference for Fielding, Cecilia leans past him to fill a precious Meissen vase with water from a fountain; when he reaches out to help, "a section of the vase came away in his hand, and split into two triangular pieces which dropped into the water" (28). "She had the presence of mind to set the ruined vase back down on the step before letting herself confront the significance of the accident" (28), we're told; yet it takes the remainder of the novel for that significance to come into view, as the accident exfoliates outward from the shattering of eighteenth-century porcelain to the carnage of total war. For the moment, Cecilia understands the mishap as retribution for Robbie's obscure hauteur: "It was irresistible, she knew, even delicious, for the graver it was, the worse it would be for Robbie" (28). McEwan highlights here even as he deploys the perceived sadism of accidental responsibility: Robbie "looked into the water, then he looked back at her,

and simply shook his head as he raised a hand to cover his mouth. By this gesture he assumed full responsibility, but at that moment, she hated him for the
inadequacy of the response" (28). "Denying his help, any possibility of making
amends, was his punishment" (29), Cecilia reflects, and her reflection serves as
an emblem of the novel's plot and its meaning.

This accident, and the fountain that is its immediate setting, occupies an
eighteenth-century landscape: "An Adam-style house had stood here until destroyed by fire in the late 1880s," the narrator explains. "What remained was
[an] artificial lake and island" (18), whose Georgian temple "grieved for the
burned-down mansion": "Tragedy had rescued the temple from being entirely
a fake" (69). Nested within older tragedies, the accident foreshadows the more
catastrophic mistakes to come: Robbie's unintentionally sending the obscene
draft of his letter to Cecilia; Briony's opening the letter; her reading the consensual kiss between them as unwanted sexual aggression; the twins' running
away; Robbie's decision to go out searching for them alone, a "decision, as he
was to acknowledge many times, transformed his life" (135); Briony's decision to
head for the island—where she has her accidental encounter with Lola and her
shadowy rapist—rather than the comfort of her mother's arms. "She could have
gone in to her mother then and snuggled close beside her and begun a résumé
of the day," observes the second person narrator. "If she had she would not have
committed her crime. So much would not have happened, nothing would have
happened" (152). The nothing that would have happened, of course, is Briony's
fingering Robbie for the rape, the subsequent obliteration of his professional
and romantic prospects and finally of his life in the war to end all wars. Instead,
Briony

> came away, and as she did so her shoulder caught an edge of one of the open
> French windows, knocking it shut. The sound was sharp—seasoned pine on hard-
> wood—and rang out like a rebuke. To stay she would have had to explain herself,
> so she slipped away into the darkness. (152)

Earlier Briony has meditated on the accidental quality of even such actions
as seem quite deliberate:

> She bent her finger and straightened it. The mystery was in the instant before it
> moved, the dividing moment between not moving and moving, when her inten-
> tion took effect. . . . She brought her forefinger closer to her face and stared at it,
> urging it to move. It remained still because she was pretending, she was not en-
> tirely serious, and because willing it to move, or being about to move it, was not the

same as actually moving it. And when she did crook it finally, the action seemed to start in the finger itself, not in some part of her mind. (33–34)

If this account of the adventitiousness of action seems very familiar from the literature of tragic responsibility, there is a way that *Atonement*, like *Frankenstein*, might be said to be interested in negligence rather than strict liability. Cecilia, for one, blames what has happened on the sins and omissions of her family: on their choosing to "believe the evidence of a silly, hysterical little girl" and "giving her no room to turn back"; on the "snobbery that lay behind their stupidity" (196); on her father's workaholic indifference and her brother's spineless good nature; on her mother's invalid neutrality, her lazy, exculpating insistence that "not everything had a cause" (140). Briony, like a latter-day Quixote, blames her own misprisions on her saturation in romance and later on the mendacity of Lola and Paul Marshall. "And what luck that was for Lola—barely more than a child, prized open and taken—to marry her rapist" (306), Briony thinks with some bitterness. "The truth that only Marshall and his bride knew at first hand was steadily being walled up within the mausoleum of their marriage" (307). This reference to Lola's nuptials summons another fifteen-year-old girl whose sexual harm is repaired by marriage: Pamela. And the allusion suggests why negligence or complicity is not, finally, what is at stake in this novel of rape and its unintended consequences. For despite Cecilia's preference for Fielding, McEwan is not himself an anti-Pamelist: Lola *is* harmed, and the notion that marriage compensates that harm—a notion, we recall, to which Lovelace is thoroughly committed—is ironized by what Briony comes to understand about harm and compensation.

Wanting her novel to be "an atonement" (330) for what she has unwittingly done to Cecilia and Robbie, Briony asks: "Who would want to believe that they never met again, never fulfilled their love? Who would want to believe that, except in the service of the bleakest realism?" (350). The project of atonement, we see here, is self-consciously a comic project—a rejection of the tragedy of realism, a marriage comedy that restages the "Trials of Arabella" so that Briony's "spontaneous, fortuitous sister and her medical prince survive to love" (350). The novel of atonement is the one we are reading prior to the final chapter and its devastating peripeteia. And if *that* novel is comic, the novel in which it is embedded is not. Invoking the familiar desire for literature to function as an equitable readjustment of the inequalities and injustices of the real world, one that happens by paying attention to character, by making sure that good persons are given good ends, McEwan insists that although the realist novel might want to do this, it cannot. The novel is a *tragic* genre, whose only consolation is the pity so powerfully elicited by *Atonement*. Pity: the "least punitive acknowledgement of things done involuntarily"; an acknowledgment that persons who are not monsters might have done monstrous, unforgivable, unremediable things.[37] In defiance of her mother's quiescence and her own need for absolution, Briony comes to see that everything *does* have a cause: that like Oedipus, Roxana, Clarissa, Sidney Bidulph, Frankenstein's colossal creature, *she* is the person who has done this thing. Responsibility is not atonement.

INTRODUCTION. INJURING LOVE

1. Aphra Behn, *Oroonoko*, ed. Joanna Lipking (New York: Norton Company, 1997), 60–61.

2. In her preface to the Norton critical edition of *Oroonoko*, Joanna Lipking notes that the text has been assimilated to the tradition of heroic romance and epic drama and has been seen as "the first realistic novel, thirty years before Defoe" (xi). For a discussion of the gender politics of slavery and (implicitly) of sentimentalism, see Charlotte Sussman, "The Other Problem with Women: Reproduction and Slave Culture in Aphra Behn's *Oroonoko*," in *Rereading Aphra Behn: History, Theory, and Criticism,* ed. Heidi Hutner (Charlottesville: University Press of Virginia, 1993), 212–33. This quotation comes from the revised version of Sussman's essay reprinted in the Norton edition of *Oroonoko* (249).

3. D. A. Miller, *Jane Austen, or The Secret of Style* (Princeton: Princeton University Press, 2003), 75.

4. Miller, *Secret of Style*, 31–32, 28.

5. Ruth Perry, *Novel Relations: The Transformation of Kinship in English Literature and Culture, 1748–1818* (Cambridge: Cambridge University Press, 2004), 2. See also Patricia Meyer Spacks, who argues that "eighteenth-century England did not originate the concept of privacy, but the evidence indicates a new level of attention to it during the period," especially to "psychological privacy"—"the idea of privacy as authenticity, as a space of self-discovery" (*Privacy: Concealing the Eighteenth-Century Self* [Chicago: University of Chicago Press, 2003], 6, 8).

6. Perry, *Novel Relations*, 408, 406.

7. Michael McKeon, *The Secret History of Domesticity: Public, Private, and the Division of Knowledge* (Baltimore: Johns Hopkins University Press, 2005), 716–17.

8. McKeon, *Secret History of Domesticity*, 717; emphasis mine.

9. In the essay-length version of "The Secret History of Domesticity," the concluding emphasis falls rather on the persistence of "exteriority": "To a striking degree, the logic of modernity is the logic of progressive privatization and interiorization. . . . But if the logic of modernity is that of the journey inward, the coherence of this journey depends entirely on the dialectical rediscovery, at each successive stage, of a new outpost of exteriority. The modern relation between the private and the public is finally not a mutual exclusion, but a tool to think with" ("The Secret History of Domesticity: Private, Public, and the Division of Knowledge," in *The Age of Cultural Revolutions: Britain and France,*

1750–1820, ed. Colin Jones and Dror Wahrman [Berkeley: University of California Press, 2002], 188–89).

10. The argument that culture and the law progress from status to contract is found in Henry Sumner Maine's *Ancient Law: Its Connection with the Early History of Society and Its Relation to Modern Ideals* (1861; rpt., Gloucester, MA: Beacon Press, 1963), esp. chap. 5. So thoroughly was Maine wedded to this dictum that his biographer saw fit to use it in the title of his book; see George Feaver, *From Status to Contract: A Biography of Sir Henry Maine 1822–1888* (London: Longmans Green, 1969).

11. Bernard Williams, "The Liberation of Antiquity," in *Shame and Necessity* (Berkeley: University of California Press, 1993), 7.

12. Williams, "Recognising Responsibility," in *Shame and Necessity*, 63, 64.

13. Friedrech Nietzsche, *The Birth of Tragedy*, in *The Birth of Tragedy, and The Case of Wagner*, trans. Walter Kaufmann (New York: Vintage, 1967), 91, 84.

14. Nietzsche, *Birth of Tragedy*, 83–84, 86, 95.

15. Georg Lukács, *The Theory of the Novel: A Historico-Philosophical Essay on the Forms of Great Epic Literature*, trans. Anna Bostock (Cambridge, MA: MIT Press, 1971), 36.

16. Lukács, *Theory of the Novel*, 49, 35.

17. Lukács, *Theory of the Novel*, 48.

18. Lukács, *Theory of the Novel*, 35, 36.

19. Lukács, *Theory of the Novel*, 57–58.

20. Lukács, *Theory of the Novel*, 73. In calling the novel a "hazardous" genre, Lukács points to the risk involved in undertaking to *write* a novel, not to risk (or harm or accident) as essential to its form. The novel is a "dangerous" form, he later explains, because of the risk of its "being reduced to mere entertainment" (130).

21. Franco Moretti, *The Way of the World: The "Bildungsroman" in European Culture*, trans. Albert Sbragia (1987; rpt., London: Verso, 2000), 45–46.

22. Lukács, *Theory of the Novel*, 88–89.

23. Moretti, *Way of the World*, 55, 70.

24. Lukács, *Theory of the Novel*, 80, 99. Lukács is speaking here of the novel of "abstract idealism."

25. Moretti, *Way of the World*, 46.

26. Lukács, *Theory of the Novel*, 137.

27. Lukács, *Theory of the Novel*, 135. For Moretti, this security is ultimately purchased at the expense of freedom. "The classical *Bildungsroman* narrates how the French Revolution could have been avoided" by dramatizing the individual's renunciation of "the path of individuality." "Meaning in the classical *Bildungsroman* has its price, he concludes, "and this price is freedom" (*Way of the World*, 64, 59, 63).

28. Frederic Jameson, *The Political Unconscious: Narrative as a Socially Symbolic Act* (Ithaca: Cornell University Press, 1981), 102, 183.

29. Jameson, *Political Unconscious*, 179.

30. There is a temptation to imagine that Lukács, Moretti, and Jameson offer more sophisticated accounts of realism than does Watt, and in a sense this is true. And yet Watt himself argued that realist "personality" is compensatory: the novel "present[s] a picture of life in which the individual is immersed in private and personal relationships

because a larger communion with nature or society is no longer available" (*The Rise of the Novel: Studies in Defoe, Richardson, and Fielding* [Berkeley: University of California Press, 1957], 185).

31. Terry Eagleton, "Tragedy and the Novel," in *Sweet Violence: The Idea of the Tragic* (Oxford, UK: Blackwell, 2003), 201, 191. John Orr likewise sees the modern novel as a tragic form, but he continues to call novels in this tradition "realist" (*Tragic Realism and Modern Society: Studies in the Sociology of the Modern Novel* [London: Macmillan, 1989]).

32. Eagleton, "Tragedy and the Novel," 184. Eagleton is using Eliot to represent a particular view on the question of tragedy and the novel (Moretti's, for example); it is a view, as I've said, from which he distances himself, but he remains committed to the notion that realism such as Eliot's is largely inhospitable to the condemnatory logic of the tragic and that it is difficult "to think of many tragic novelists in England before Hardy, James and Conrad" (178).

33. Eagleton, "Tragedy and the Novel," 185, 187.

34. Stanley Cavell, "The Avoidance of Love: A Reading of *King Lear*," in *Must We Mean What We Say? A Book of Essays*, updated ed. (Cambridge: Cambridge University Press, 2002), 323.

35. Cavell, "The Avoidance of Love," 323.

36. Eagleton, "Tragedy and the Novel," 189. One thinks, for example, of Locke's preoccupation with the problem of habituation, or senility, in the *Essay* or of Hobbes's observation that "thought is quick"—that thinking becomes action with such alacrity that there is no space for what one might want to call "deliberation," or "intention" (*Leviathan* [New York: Norton, 1996], 95).

37. Moretti, *Way of the World*, 55.

38. Watt, *The Rise of the Novel*, 280.

39. Aristotle, *Poetics*, trans. Ingram Bywater, in *The Basic Works of Aristotle*, ed. Richard McKeon (New York: Random House, 1941), 1461; Aristotle, *Poetics*, trans. Malcolm Heath (London: Penguin, 1996), 12 (I prefer the succinctness of Heath's translation of the passage in which Aristotle offers a definition of tragedy).

40. Bernard Williams, "Recognising Responsibility," 69, 71.

41. G. W. F. Hegel, *Aesthetics: Lectures on Fine Art*, 2 vols., trans. T. M. Knox (Oxford: Clarendon Press, 1975), 2:1212; emphasis mine. For Lessing's character-driven theory of tragedy, see his *Hamburg Dramaturgy*, trans. Victor Lange (New York: Dover, 1962). Throughout *Hamburg Dramaturgy* Lessing describes Aristotelian probability in terms of characterological motivation: "The motives for every resolve, for every change of opinion or even thoughts, must be in accordance with the hypothetical character, and must never produce more than they could produce in accordance with strict probability" (8). Probability understood as depth psychology is what grounds Shakespeare's supremacy over French dramatists such as Voltaire and Corneille: "Voltaire's ghost is nothing else but a poetical machine that is only employed to help the unravelling of the plot; it does not interest us in the very least on its own account. Shakespeare's ghost, on the contrary, is a real active personage, in whose fate we take an interest, who excites not only our fear but our pity" (35). In example after example Lessing recommends the "domestic" quality of English tragedy, its interest in "real personages" and the passions that move them rather

than in (aristocratic) types. There is some debate about Lessing's commitment to character. Claudia Brodsky observes of Lessing's changes to his classical source in *Emilia Galotti* that "Emilia, as opposed to Virginia, is viewed as the heroine of a tragic plot not to the extent that she is essentially innocent of her fate, but because she is a character who decides to die and is the primary agent responsible for her death." But Brodsky goes on to contest this view of the play as a "tragedy of character" ("Lessing and the Drama of the Theory of Tragedy," *MLN* 98.3 [1983]: 430).

42. Hegel, *Aesthetics*, 2:1205.

43. Hegel, *Aesthetics*, 2:1214.

44. Hegel, *Aesthetics*, 2:1214.

45. Hegel, *Aesthetics*, 2:1215.

46. Hegel, *Aesthetics*, 2:1219–20.

47. Hegel, *Aesthetics*, 2:1215.

48. Walter Benjamin, "Allegory and *Trauerspeil*," in *The Origin of German Tragic Drama*, trans. John Osborne (London: Verso, 1998), 129. Benjamin distinguishes between "tragic poetry" (classical tragedy) and the "drama of fate" (*Trauerspiel*). In the latter, "it is the act and the act alone which, by malicious accident, throws the guiltless into the abyss of general guilt" (131). This opposition between the accidentally responsible hero and the self-conscious one who "discovers" and possesses his guilt helps to explain why "*Trauerspiel* therefore has no individual hero" (132).

49. Lukács, *Theory of the Novel*, 92.

50. Hegel, *Aesthetics*, 2:1199.

51. Williams, "Recognising Responsibility," 70.

52. Ian McEwan, *Enduring Love* (1997; rpt., New York: Anchor, 1999), 17, 59.

53. McEwan, *Enduring Love*, 58–59.

54. McEwan, *Enduring Love*, 17; emphasis mine.

55. McEwan, *Enduring Love*, 1.

56. McEwan, *Enduring Love*, 231.

57. McEwan, *Enduring Love*, 230.

58. McEwan, *Enduring Love*, 234–35.

59. Eagleton, "Tragedy and the Novel," 201.

60. Eagleton, "Tragedy and the Novel," 202.

61. Aristotle, *Poetics*, trans. Heath, 21, 23.

62. Samuel Richardson, *Clarissa; or, The History of a Young Lady*, ed. Angus Ross (1747–48; rpt., London: Penguin, 1985), 565–66.

63. Richardson, *Clarissa*, 568.

64. Eagleton, "Tragedy and the Novel," 184.

65. T. C. Duncan Eaves and Ben D. Kimpel, "An Unpublished Pamphlet by Samuel Richardson," *Philological Quarterly* 63.3 (1984): 402.

66. Bernard Williams, "Centres of Agency," in *Shame and Necessity*, 36; Williams, "Recognising Responsibility," 64.

67. Miller, *Secret of Style*, 32.

68. McKeon, "Secret History of Domesticity," 189; Miller, *Secret of Style*, 32. See also Catherine Gallagher, *Nobody's Story: The Vanishing Acts of Women Writers in the Market-*

place, 1670–1820 (Berkeley: University of California Press, 1995); Deidre Lynch, *The Economy of Character: Novels, Market Culture, and the Business of Inner Meaning* (Chicago: University of Chicago Press, 1998); and Alex Woloch, *The One vs. the Many: Minor Characters and the Space of the Protagonist in the Novel* (Princeton: Princeton University Press, 2003).

69. Gallagher is genuinely interested in the "possibilities of disembodiment" and strenuously distinguishes such abstraction from alienation: "anonymous" does not point to an authentic self oppressed and occluded by the demands of the print market. Yet if anonymity doesn't mark an identity, it continues to signal a kind of agency. Thus women writers "call attention to" their commodification and "openly link" authorship with signification as a "strategy for capitalizing on their femaleness" (*Nobody's Story*, xxi, xxiv). Lynch too is compelled by the way the impersonality of "typographical culture" reveals "unsuspected complexities and depths" (*Economy of Character*, 5, 13, 20). Individuation emerges through the practice of reading as a "profoundly social experience" (9). What this experience produces, however, is someone we would still have to call an *agent*—a pragmatic, though not a psychological, subject—even if we might no longer want to call her an individual.

70. Woloch, *One vs. the Many*, 13, 14, 20.

71. Woloch, *One vs. the Many*, 20.

72. Woloch, *One vs. the Many*, 31.

73. Woloch, *One vs. the Many*, 21, 31.

74. H. L. A. Hart, *Punishment and Responsibility: Essays in the Philosophy of Law* (Oxford, UK: Clarendon Press, 1968), 20.

75. For a recent survey of the problem of strict liability, see A. P. Simester, ed., *Appraising Strict Liability* (Oxford: Oxford University Press, 2005).

76. Hart, *Punishment and Responsibility*, 35.

77. Hart, *Punishment and Responsibility*, 39.

78. Hart, *Punishment and Responsibility*, 92.

79. Hart, *Punishment and Responsibility*, 139, 181.

80. Hart, *Punishment and Responsibility*, 226. "It is surely unjust to hold someone strictly liable for [an act] he did not commit intentionally, recklessly or negligently," agrees R. A. Duff (*Intention, Agency and Criminal Liability: Philosophy of Action and the Criminal Law* [Oxford, UK: Blackwell, 1990], 9). Recently Martin Stone has mounted a strong argument in defense of such a negligence model of liability, one that "attaches direct normative significance to the relation that exists between two persons whenever it appropriately can be said, concerning a certain injury, that one person 'did it' and the other 'suffered it' " ("The Significance of Doing and Suffering," in *Philosophy and the Law of Torts*, ed. Gerald J. Postema [Cambridge: Cambridge University Press, 2001], 131–32).

81. See Stanley Cavell, "Knowing and Acknowledging," in *Must We Mean What We Say?* esp. 263ff.

82. Cavell, "Knowing and Acknowledging," 251, 265.

83. Williams, "Recognising Responsibility," 68.

84. Williams, "Recognising Responsibility," 74.

85. Williams, "Recognising Responsibility," 102.

86. Miller, *Secret of Style*, 52.

87. Miller, *Secret of Style*, 53.

88. Miller, *Secret of Style*, 52.

89. Miller, *Secret of Style*, 25.

90. Miller, *Secret of Style*, 32, 33, 39.

91. Miller, *Secret of Style*, 42, 59, 68.

92. Miller, *Secret of Style*, 53.

93. Miller, *Secret of Style*, 76, 44, 67.

94. For an argument that the eighteenth-century moves not so much from status to contract as from "status to class," see Michael McKeon, *Origins of the English Novel, 1600–1740* (Baltimore: Johns Hopkins University Press, 1987), 162–67.

95. See, for example, Carole Pateman, *The Sexual Contract* (Stanford: Stanford University Press, 1988); Susan Staves, *Married Women's Separate Property in England, 1660–1833* (Cambridge, MA: Harvard University Press, 1990); Claudia Johnson, *Equivocal Beings: Politics, Gender, and Sentimentality in the 1790s: Wollstonecraft, Radcliffe, Burney, Austen* (Chicago: University of Chicago Press, 1995); Andrea Dworkin, *Pornography: Men Possessing Women* (New York: Perigee Books, 1981); Andrea Dworkin, *Intercourse* (New York: Free Press, 1987); Catharine MacKinnon, *Feminism Unmodified: Discourses on Life and Law* (Cambridge, MA: Harvard University Press, 1987); and Catharine MacKinnon, *Only Words* (Cambridge, MA: Harvard University Press, 1993).

96. Catharine A. MacKinnon and Andrea Dworkin, "The Roar on the Other Side of Silence," in *In Harm's Way: The Pornography Civil Rights Hearings*, ed. Catharine A. MacKinnon and Andrea Dworkin (Cambridge, MA: Harvard University Press, 1998), 3. It is hard to know just what to make of the connection between this book and an earlier volume on the work of legal philosopher Joel Feinberg, *In Harm's Way: Essays in Honor of Joel Feinberg*, ed. Jules L. Coleman and Allen Buchanan (New York: Cambridge University Press, 1994). Feinberg possesses a strongly libertarian bent, and the editors of the festschrift position him as an eloquent defender of a liberalism presently under attack by "communitarians" (vii)—later clarified to include "feminists, critical race theorists, and critical legal theorists" (Thomas Morawetz, "Liberalism and the New Skeptics," 130). But he is also someone for whom the harmfulness of an action alone justifies restrictions on free action. See Joel Feinberg, "Sua Culpa," in *Doing and Deserving* (Princeton: Princeton University Press, 1970), 187–221. It is likely that MacKinnon and Dworkin's title is simply an earnest description of women's vulnerability within the pornographic industrial complex. And yet, given their commitment to invective as a rhetorical mode, it is not outside the realm of possibility that the title parodies the liberal apologetics of Coleman's volume as well as Feinberg's own blindness to sex discrimination as a fault.

97. For an argument that takes seriously MacKinnon and Dworkin's structuralist account of (hetero)sexuality but observes, quite rightly, that "redemptive" political investments vitiate the skepticism and structuralism of their own claims, see Leo Bersani's 1987 "Is the Rectum a Grave?" reprinted in *AIDS: Cultural Analysis, Cultural Activism*, ed. Douglas Crimp (Cambridge, MA: Harvard University Press, 1988), 197–222. See also Leo Bersani, *The Culture of Redemption* (Cambridge, MA: Harvard University Press, 1990).

98. Wendy Brown, *States of Injury: Power and Freedom in Late Modernity* (Princeton: Princeton University Press, 1995), 18, 21.

99. Brown, *States of Injury*, 21, 27.

100. Brown, *States of Injury*, 27.

101. Brown, *States of Injury*, 27.

102. Lauren Berlant makes a similar—though more satisfying—argument in her recent work on sentimental citizenship. "The object of the nation state," Berlant argues, "is to eradicate systemic social pain, the absence of which becomes the definition of freedom"; trauma liberalism promotes "a dubious optimism that the law and other conspicuous regimes of inequality can be made accountable (the way persons are) to remedy their own taxonomizing harms" and "overidentifies the eradication of pain with the achievement of justice" ("The Subject of True Feeling: Pain, Privacy, and Politics," in *Cultural Studies and Political Theory*, ed. Jodi Dean [Cornell: Cornell University Press, 2000], 45). This seems to me right as an account of sentimentalism, which throughout *Harm's Way*, and particularly in chapter 3, I describe as a "comic" mode committed to the reparation if not the total elision of harm. But I disagree that laws that "make persons accountable" for harm inevitably do so in the expectation of ameliorating future harms. Compensation is *compensatory*, a "remedy" underwritten by the assumption that harm is in an important sense irremediable. And although negligence may be a form of corrective justice, strict liability, emphatically, is not.

103. Patchen Markell, *Bound by Recognition* (Princeton: Princeton University Press, 2003), 7.

104. Markell, *Bound by Recognition*, 63, 65.

105. Markell, *Bound by Recognition*, 38; emphasis mine.

CHAPTER I. MATRIMONIAL MURDER

1. Daniel Defoe, *Conjugal Lewdness; or, Matrimonial Whoredom: A Treatise concerning the Use and Abuse of the Marriage Bed* (1727; rpt., Gainesville: Scholars' Facsimiles and Reprints, 1967), 34, 376.

2. See, for example, G. A. Starr, *Defoe and Spiritual Autobiography* (Princeton: Princeton University Press, 1965); Leopold Damrosch, *God's Plot and Man's Stories: Studies in the Fictional Imagination from Milton to Fielding* (Chicago: University of Chicago Press, 1965); and J. Paul Hunter, *The Reluctant Pilgrim: Defoe's Emblematic Method and Quest for Form in "Robinson Crusoe"* (Baltimore: Johns Hopkins University Press, 1966).

3. Everett Zimmerman, "H. F.'s Meditations: A Journal of the Plague Year," *PMLA* 87.3 (1972): 417.

4. Michael Witmore, *Culture of Accidents: Unexpected Knowledges in Early Modern England* (Stanford: Stanford University Press, 2001), 17, 41, 39, 44, 39. For a related argument that modernity makes accident central to "new knowledge," see Ross Hamilton, *Accident: A Philosophical and Literary History* (Chicago: University of Chicago Press, 2007), 127.

5. Martin C. Battestin, *The Providence of Wit: Aspects of Form in Augustan Literature and the Arts* (1974; rpt., Charlottesville: University Press of Virginia, 1989), viii.

6. Christian Thorne, "Providence in the Early Novel, or Accident If You Please," *MLQ* 64.3 (2003): 330, 334, 339, 347.

7. Daniel Defoe, *The Fortunes and Misfortunes of the Famous Moll Flanders*, ed. David Blewett (Middlesex, UK: Penguin, 1989), 121–22.

8. Defoe, *Moll Flanders*, 41.

9. Defoe, *A Journal of the Plague Year*, ed. Paula Backscheider (New York: Norton, 1992), 11; hereafter cited parenthetically by page number.

10. John Richetti, *Defoe's Narratives: Situations and Structures* (Oxford, UK: Clarendon Press, 1975), 234, 238.

11. John Bender, *Imagining the Penitentiary: Fiction and the Architecture of Mind in Eighteenth-Century England* (Chicago: University of Chicago Press, 1987), 82. I don't mean that Bender himself is an optimist, only that he sees Defoe as an enthusiastic proponent of managerial foresight and oversight.

12. Cavell emphasizes the futility of such a hermeneutics: "Epistemology will demonstrate that we cannot know, cannot be certain of, the future; but we don't believe it. We anticipate, and so we are always wrong. Even when what we anticipate comes to pass we get the wrong idea of our powers and of what our safety depends upon, for we imagine that we knew this would happen, and take it either as an occasion for congratulations or for punishments, of ourselves or others. Instead of acting as we can and remaining equal to the consequences" ("The Avoidance of Love: A Reading of *King Lear*," in *Must We Mean What We Say? A Book of Essays*, updated ed. [Cambridge: Cambridge University Press, 2002], 322).

13. J. H. Baker argues that although in theory a principle of automatic liability could be "applied to the man whose conduct killed another, even if he had no guilty mind," this did not in fact happen. The grant of a pardon in the case of accidental or excusable killings was a matter of course; from the late fourteenth century onward, many who killed by accident "were probably not arraigned at all," and in the eighteenth century, general verdicts of not guilty were applied in cases of misadventure and self-defense. By the early sixteenth century the status of "murder" as a crime of "malice aforethought" was consolidated, as the line between murder and manslaughter was "judicially discussed and refined" (*An Introduction to English Legal History*, 4th ed. [London: Butterworths, 2002], 529–30).

14. For an interesting version of comic determinism, see Damrosch, who argues that "a thoughtful Puritan knew very well that he or she was unfree, and longed to exchange a corrupting and destructive unfreedom for the special form of freedom known as Christian liberty" (*God's Plots and Man's Stories*, 26).

15. Maximillian Novak, "Defoe and the Disordered City," *PMLA* 92.2 (1977): 250, 252.

16. Novak, "Defoe and the Disordered City," 252.

17. Bernard Williams, "Recognising Responsibility," in *Shame and Necessity* (Berkeley: University of California Press, 1993), 71–72.

18. Williams, "Recognising Responsibility," 74.

19. Bernard Williams, "The Liberation of Antiquity," in *Shame and Necessity*, 7.

20. Williams, "Recognising Responsibility," 64.

21. Williams, "Recognising Responsibility," 63.

22. Williams, "Recognising Responsibility," 64, 57.

23. Daniel Defoe, *An Essay upon Projects* (London: Thomas Cockerill, 1697), 118.

24. Defoe, *Essay*, 125.

25. Defoe's actuarial tables here are based on statistics from William Petty's *Political Arithmetick* (1683). Ian Hacking describes Petty as a "man who wanted to put statistics to the service of the state" (*The Emergence of Probability: A Philosophical Study of Early Ideas about Probability, Induction and Statistical Inference* [Cambridge: Cambridge University Press, 1975], 105); and indeed, he campaigned as early as 1671 for a central statistical office to determine life expectancy in various communities and to locate health risks so as to be able to legislate proper measures for preventing future injury, illness, or contagion (in this, Petty would seem to have been an influence on Defoe's *Due Preparations for the Plague* as well).

26. Defoe, *Essay*, 321.

27. Defoe, *Essay*, 328.

28. Defoe, *Some Considerations on the Reasonableness and Necessity of Encreasing and Encouraging the Seamen* (London: J. Roberts, 1728), quoted in Paula Backscheider, *Daniel Defoe: His Life* (Baltimore: Johns Hopkins University Press, 1989), 197. Backscheider says this project was "typical of Defoe's authoritarian, centralized schemes" (198).

Defoe's recommendations here and in the *Essay* are in part derived from statute law already in place: in 1695, two years prior to the publication of the *Essay*, the Act for the Increase and Encouragement of Seamen (7 and 8 Will. III) had stated that seamen "who by Age, Wounds, or other Accidents, shall become Disabled for future Service at Sea, and shall not be in a condition to maintain themselves Comfortably" would henceforth be "supported at the publick Charge." Initially the statute makes it look as though William is dispensing benefits (disbursing pensions, endowing a veterans' hospital in Greenwich), but as one reads on it becomes clear that on the contrary he's withholding wages unless seamen agree to be impressed into military service: "And to the Intent that such Mariners, Watermen, Seamen, Fishermen, Lightermen, Bargemen and Keelemen, as shall voluntarily come in and Register themselves, in and for his Majesties Sea-Service, as hereafter is mentioned, may have and receive the privileges, Benefits and Advantages following."

Defoe is obviously familiar with the statute—the title of his 1728 pamphlet explicitly invokes it—and aware of the irony of that "voluntarily." His own project, he asserts, "wou'd reduce the Seamen to better Circumstances, at least 'twou'd have them in readiness for any Publick Service much easier than by all the late methods of Encouragement by registering Seamen, &c" (*Essay*, 328). The difference is subtle and hinges on what it means to be the king's "hired *servant*." If the king functioned more like a merchant than a lord, the "sundry ill circumstances" that result from "violent dragging men into the Fleet" would be avoided: "Oppressions, Quarrelings, and oftentimes Murthers"; men's "Kidnapping people out of the Kingdom, robbing Houses, and picking Pockets"; and "various Abuses of the like nature, some to the King, and some to the Subject" (323). But there are benefits to sovereignty and impressment: if, under the terms of 7 and 8 Will. III, a seaman "who Enters himself, or is Press'd into the King's Service be by any Accident Wounded or Disabled, to Recompense him for the Loss, he receives a Pension during Life, which the Sailors call *Smart-Money*, and is proportioned to their Hurt, as for the Loss of an Eye, Arm, Leg, or Finger." Such compensation is "but reasonable," says Defoe; yet "if you come to the Seamen in the Merchants Service, not the least Provision is made" (126). His solution is to transform merchants back into lords so as to extend the feudal logic of impressment—the king's unlimited liability to those under his awe—to mercantile relations and by doing so avoid another kind of "ill circumstance": the unremediated loss of eye, limb, life, and livelihood that attends freedom of contract.

29. Manuel Schonhorn, *Defoe's Politics: Parliament, Power, Kingship, and "Robinson Crusoe"* (Cambridge: Cambridge University Press, 1991), 3.

30. Ian Watt, *The Rise of the Novel: Studies in Defoe, Richardson and Fielding* (Berkeley: University of California Press, 1957); J. G. A. Pocock, *The Machiavellian Moment: Florentine Political Thought and the Atlantic Republican Tradition* (Princeton: Princeton University Press, 1975), 433–34; Richard Ashcraft, *Revolutionary Politics and Locke's "Two Treatises of Government"* (Princeton: Princeton University Press, 1986), 565. Pocock of course argues that liberal contractarianism does not emerge until the late eighteenth or early nineteenth century; but when it *does* emerge, modernity looks much the way Defoe looks.

31. This skepticism is in large part a consequence of the Foucauldian turn in criticism of the novel, which revealed the idea of autonomy that Defoe is invested in to be compatible with, indeed to work through, authoritarian mechanisms of power. See Nancy Armstrong, *Desire and Domestic Fiction: A Political History of the Novel* (Oxford: Oxford University Press, 1987); D. A. Miller, *The Novel and the Police* (Berkeley: University of California Press, 1988); and Bender, *Imagining the Penitentiary*. When attention turned to Defoe's interest in conduct rather than autonomy, a similar structure was seen to emerge. David Blewett argued in 1981 that Defoe was "one of the most important moralists . . . in the early eighteenth century" and that his conduct books provide a corrective "commentary on the often-disputed morality of his novels" ("Changing Attitudes toward Marriage in the Time of Defoe: The Case of Moll Flanders," *Huntington Library Quarterly* 44.2 [1981]: 82, 83). Critics influenced by Bender, Armstrong, and Miller approached those conduct books through the late-Foucauldian concept of "biopower," which functions in a less overtly repressive way than the "sovereign power" of *Discipline and Punish* to structure and limit a subject's "field of action" by stipulating a range of possibilities "in which [only] several ways of behaving, several reactions and diverse comportments may be realized" (Hubert L. Dreyfus and Paul Rabinov, *Michel Foucault: Beyond Structuralism and Hermeneutics* [Chicago: University of Chicago Press, 1982], 214, 221). See, for example, Carol Houlihan Flynn, who argues that Defoe's texts articulate an "ideology of conduct" in which regulation is designed to appear voluntary and natural ("Defoe's Idea of Conduct: Ideological Fictions and Fictional Reality," in *The Ideology of Conduct: Essays on Literature and the History of Sexuality*, ed. Nancy Armstrong and Leonard Tennenhouse [New York: Methuen, 1987], 73–95).

32. John P. Zomchick, *Family and the Law in Eighteenth-Century Fiction: The Public Conscience in the Private Sphere* (Cambridge: Cambridge University Press, 1993), 33; Sandra Sherman, *Finance and Fictionality in the Early Eighteenth Century: Accounting for Defoe* (Cambridge: Cambridge University Press, 1996). For a similar argument about Defoe's anxiety over credit, see Anne Louise Kibbie, "Monstrous Generation: The Birth of Capital in Defoe's *Moll Flanders* and *Roxana*," *PMLA* 110.5 (1995): 1023–34.

33. For example, Zomchick's nuanced analysis follows closely that of Watt, who distinguishes *Moll Flanders* from picaresque novels because it is "rooted in the dynamics of economic individualism . . . [where] the individual's orientation to life is determined, not by his acceptance of the positive standards of the community, but by his own personal aims which are restrained only by the legal power of authority" (*Rise of the Novel*, 94–95).

34. The epithet "conservative = royalist" comes is from Schonhorn, *Defoe's Politics*, 8. James Thompson similarly argues that Defoe's novels move from primitive accumulation to mercantilism rather than to full-blown capitalism (and thus modernity) (*Models of Value: Eighteenth-Century Political Economy and the Novel* [Durham: Duke University Press, 1996], 88–89).

35. Dror Wahrman, *The Making of the Modern Self: Identity and Culture in Eighteenth-Century England* (New Haven: Yale University Press, 2004), 168.

36. Wolfram Schmidgen, *Eighteenth-Century Fiction and the Law of Property* (Cambridge: Cambridge University Press, 2002), 5.

37. To my mind the most persuasive critique of the "interiority thesis" is Deidre Lynch's. Lynch resists consigning what she calls "typographical culture"—a culture committed to a materialist understanding of character—to "premodernity." On her account, impersonality is central to the way in which modernity conceives of character and individuality. To this extent our arguments are similar, for I too am interested in an "impersonal" model of personhood. But because of her emphasis on commodification, Lynch is more inclined to see impersonality as a problem to which the idea of "roundness" and "interiority" is a compensatory response (*The Economy of Character: Novels, Market Culture, and the Business of Inner Meaning* [Chicago: University of Chicago Press, 1998], 3).

38. Wahrman, *Making of the Modern Self*, 276, xiii. For a related argument that the eighteenth century witnesses a shift to "internal markers of states of mind" in the law, see Nicola Lacey, *Women, Crime, and Character—From Moll Flanders to Tess of the D'Urbervilles* (Oxford: Oxford University Press, 2008), 52.

39. Schmidgen, *Eighteenth-Century Fiction and the Law of Property*, 4. In noting the interpenetration of subjects and objects, he is referring to the work of Bruno Latour and Donna Haraway, who have "prominently argued that we need to account for the mixtures of the human and the material that increasingly govern our lives."

40. Schmidgen, *Eighteenth-Century Fiction and the Law of Property*, 4; emphasis mine.

41. Revisionists include those skeptical about the "modernity" of post-Revolution England (Jonathan Clark, Jonathan Scott) and those skeptical about the progressiveness of contract theory (Carole Pateman); revisionists of the revisionists tend to follow Lois Schwoerer in arguing that although the change that comes about after the Reformation, Civil War, and Glorious Revolution is neither as dramatic nor as progressive as whig historians would have it, change did occur. See, for example, Alan Houston and Steven Pincus, eds., *A Nation Transformed: England After the Restoration* (Cambridge: Cambridge University Press, 2001).

42. As does Schonhorn, *Defoe's Politics*, 3, 8, and Backscheider, *Daniel Defoe*, 198.

43. Daniel Defoe, *Every-Body's Business is No-Body's Business; or, Private Abuses, Pub-*

lick Grievances: Exemplified in the Pride, Insolence, and Exorbitant Wages of our Women-Servants, Footmen, &c, in *Robinson Crusoe, and Other Writings*, ed. James Sutherland (New York: New York University Press, 1977), 368, 370, 371.

44. Giles Jacob, *The Compleat Parish-Officer*, 4th ed. (London: Bernard Lintot, 1726), 106.

45. J. H. Baker, *An Introduction to English Legal History*, 3rd ed. (London: Butterworths, 1990), 71.

46. M. J. Prichard, *Scott v. Shepherd (1773) and the Emergence of the Tort of Negligence* (London: Selden Society, 1976), 25; Baker, *Introduction to English Legal History*, 3rd. ed., 374. Grant Gilmore argues that under the common law there was no clear distinction between contract and tort until nineteenth-century theorists insisted on drawing the line; the writ of assumpsit, from which theories of contract derive, had its origins in the tort action of trespass. According to Gilmore, after a brief period of prominence (primarily influenced by Oliver Wendell Holmes), during which time the attempt was made to limit a contractor's liability to what was expressly stipulated in an agreement, contract was again absorbed into the theory of tort: "Classical contract theory," Gilmore concludes, "might well be described as an attempt to stake out an enclave within the general domain of torts" (*The Death of Contract* [Columbus: Ohio University Press, 1974], 140 n. 228, 87). If Gilmore sees contract as but a moment in the long history of tort, Prichard sees tort as a product of the long eighteenth century: "We find 'Tort' used as a contrast to 'Assumpsit' in the classification of pleadings in Books of Entries from the Restoration onwards" (Prichard, *Scott v. Shepherd*, 24).

47. Blackstone describes action on the case as a "universal remedy, given for all personal wrongs and injuries without force" or "unaccompanied by force"; trespass is "trespass vi et armis, this being an inchoate, though not an absolute, violence" (*Commentaries on the Laws of England*, 4 vols. [1765–69; rpt., Chicago: University of Chicago Press, 1979], 3:122, 3:120). See also Prichard, *Scott v. Shepherd*, 72. There is a great deal of debate among legal historians about the relationship between "trespass" and "case," but Baker asserts that "we now know that the distinction between trespass and case was the result of the jurisdictional accident that the royal courts [in which writs of trespass were adjudicated] entertained complaints of forcible breaches of the peace before they let in other wrongs" (*Introduction to English Legal History*, 3rd. ed., 464). The distinction between the two was "an accident of history . . . elevated into a principle of law" (*Introduction to English Legal History*, 3rd. ed., 75).

48. Baker, *Introduction to English Legal History*, 3rd. ed., 75; Prichard, *Scott v. Shepherd*, 13.

49. Baker, *Introduction to English Legal History*, 3rd. ed., 462.

50. J. H. Baker and S. F. C. Milsom, *Sources of English Legal History: Private Law to 1750* (London: Butterworths, 1986), 370–77.

51. Baker and Milsom, *Sources of English Legal History*, 376.

52. Baker, *Introduction to English Legal History*, 3rd. ed., 464; Prichard, *Scott v. Shepherd*, 15.

53. Prichard, *Scott v. Shepherd*, 16.

54. Baker, *Introduction to English Legal History*, 3rd. ed., 464–65.

55. Baker, *Introduction to English Legal History*, 3rd. ed., 465, 466.

56. Baker, *Introduction to English Legal History*, 3rd. ed., 462.

57. Public Record Office, *Coram Rege Rolls*, 27, quoted in Baker and Milsom, *Sources of English Legal History*, 572. The case named James as plaintiff because under coverture Mary had no legal existence from which to sue for damages. The case named Allestry rather than Scrivener as defendant for a related reason: a lack of legal existence predicated on the strict liability of masters for the actions of their servants.

58. Peyton Ventris, *Reports*, 2 vols. (London: printed by the assigns of Richard and Edward Atkins, 1701), 295. I am grateful to the Huntington Library for allowing me to consult its copy of Ventris's report.

59. Baker, *Introduction to English Legal History*, 3rd. ed., 465.

60. Baker, *Introduction to English Legal History*, 3rd. ed., 465.

61. Raynsford's statement on the case is transcribed in a manuscript at Exeter College, Oxford, but does not show up in reporting on the case. See Baker and Milsom, *Sources of English Legal History*, 574.

62. Baker, *Introduction to English Legal History*, 3rd. ed., 465.

63. Prichard, *Scott v. Shepherd*, 31, 15. Prichard doesn't mean that cases involving custom of the realm weren't cases of trespass in the loose sense of cases of civil liability; only that they were pleaded as actions on the case rather than actions of trespass.

64. Baker and Milsom, *Sources of English Legal History*, 332.

65. Baker and Milsom, *Sources of English Legal History*, 333.

66. Oliver Wendell Holmes, *The Common Law*, ed. Mark DeWolfe Howe (1881; rpt., Boston: Little, Brown, 1963), 65.

67. Holmes, *The Common Law*, 126. About the case Holmes observes: "If the place where the owner tries to break [a horse] is a crowded thoroughfare, the owner knows an additional circumstance which, according to common experience, makes this conduct dangerous, and therefore must take the risk of what harm may be done" (125).

68. Holmes, *The Common Law*, 71.

69. See, for example, *Dickinson v. Watson* (1682), where finding was for the plaintiff despite the defendant's claim that "the plaintiff accidentally wandered into the way as [his pistol] was discharging" and that "if any harm thereby befell the plaintiff it was inevitable, and against the defendant's will"; *Gibbon v. Pepper* (1695), where decision was again for the plaintiff even though the defendant, Thomas Pepper, argued that his horse was "frightened (*terrificatus*) so that the aforesaid horse then and there violently ran away with the same Thomas Pepper, and the same Thomas Pepper could not then and there govern the aforesaid horse; whereupon the same Thomas Pepper then and there in a loud voice gave notice to the passersby in the aforesaid street to take care of themselves; but nevertheless, the aforesaid Thomas Gibbon at that time remaining there in the aforesaid street, the aforesaid horse ran upon the same Thomas Gibbon against the will of the selfsame Thomas Pepper" (Baker and Milsom, *Sources of English Legal History*, 334–35, 335–37); and *Scott v. Shepherd* (1773), where the defendant was held responsible for throwing a lighted squib from the street into a crowded market house despite the fact that two other men threw it away from themselves ("to prevent injury to himself") before it struck the plaintiff in the face and put out his eye (Prichard, *Scott v. Shepherd*, 4).

70. Holmes, *The Common Law*, 72.

71. Holmes, *The Common Law*, 72.

72. Holmes, *The Common Law*, 82; emphasis mine. Frances Ferguson likewise argues that the eighteenth century's contribution to legal reform occurred primarily in the development of a law of torts "to supplement the criminal law" and that the paradigmatic early cases of tortious liability involved establishing a "law of the road" according to which individuals were held accountable even for damages they might "unwillingly and unwittingly commit against others" ("*Justine;* or, The Law of the Road," in *Aesthetics and Ideology*, ed. George Levine [New Brunswick: Rutgers University Press, 1994]), 115).

73. I think Holmes is right about this. Although Baker and Prichard tie the body of case law I have been invoking to the "rise" of negligence, they also admit that negligence is more properly a concern of nineteenth-century jurisprudence (such as Holmes's).

74. For persons as object lessons, see H. F.'s account of the "dismal Objects which represented themselves to me as I look't thro' my Chamber Windows" (86).

75. William Hawkins, *A Treatise of the Pleas of the Crown*, 2 vols. (1716–21; rpt., Abingdon, UK: Professional Books, 1980), 1:66; emphasis mine.

76. For example, in John Kelyng's account of Grey's case, in which a master was indicted for murder for having accidentally killed his servant in the process of chastising him with an iron bar to the head. Kelyng begins by observing that "if an Officer or other Person kill another in preserving the Peace, or a Parent, Master, or Schoolmaster kill his child, Servant or Scholar in chastising or correcting him, this shall be said to be *per Infortunium*." "They must do it," however, "with such things as are fit for Correction, as not with such Instruments as may probably kill them"; "and a bar of Iron is no Instrument for Correction. It is all one as if he had run him through with a Sword." The plea of *per infortunium* doesn't initially work for Grey; but Kelyng frets about the case at length, and the reader is later told that Kelyng convinced the king to grant Grey a pardon: "I did Certiue the King, that tho' in strictness of Law, his Offence was Murder; yet it was attended with such Circumstances as might render the Person an Object of his Majesty's Grace and Pardon . . . and upon this the King was pleased to grant him his Pardon" (*A Report of Cases in Pleas of the Crown, Adjudged and Determined, in the Reign of the Late King Charles II* [London: printed for Isaac Cleave, 1708], 64–65). The pardon would have involved accepting that the death was *per infortunium*. I am grateful to the Huntington Library for access to its copy of Kelyng's report.

77. Blackstone, *Commentaries*, 1:291.

78. Holmes, *The Common Law*, 24. Holmes's source for this observation is the entry under "Deodand" in Giles Jacob's *The New Law Dictionary*, 4th ed. (London: H. Lintot, 1748), 258.

79. Jacob, *New Law Dictionary*, 258.

80. Defoe, *Moll Flanders*, 227–28.

81. Defoe, *Moll Flanders*, 233–34.

82. Defoe, *Roxana, the Fortunate Mistress*, ed. John Mullan (Oxford: Oxford University Press, 1996), 70–80; hereafter cited parenthetically by page number.

83. Terry Castle, "'Amy Who Knew My Disease': A Psychosexual Pattern in Defoe's

Roxana," in *The Female Thermometer: Eighteenth-Century Culture and the Invention of the Uncanny* (Oxford: Oxford University Press, 1995), 55.

84. Castle, "'Amy Who Knew My Disease,'" 46.

85. Castle, "'Amy Who Knew My Disease,'" 53.

86. Zomchick, *Family and the Law in Eighteenth-Century Fiction*, 57.

87. Zomchick argues that Roxana wants "obligation-free autonomy" (*Family and the Law in Eighteenth-Century Fiction*, 34); Castle makes a different, obverse, claim: that Roxana wants obligation-free (infantile) subjection ("'Amy Who Knew My Disease,'" 52).

88. Baker, *Introduction to English Legal History*, 3rd. ed., 464–65.

89. In addition to Castle, who implicitly describes Roxana as "hysterical" ("'Amy Who Knew My Disease,'" 52), see Geoffrey Sill, "*Roxana's* Susan: Whose Daughter Is She Anyway?" *Studies in Eighteenth-Century Culture* 29 (2000): 261–72; Kibbie, "Monstrous Generation"; and Veronica Kelly, "The Paranormal Roxana," in *Postmodernism Across the Ages*, ed. Bill Readings (Syracuse, NY: Syracuse University Press, 1993), 138–49.

90. This, in violation of Castle's argument that by becoming her "instrument," Amy "preserves Roxana's security" ("'Amy Who Knew My Disease,'" 53).

91. Castle, "'Amy Who Knew My Disease,'" 49.

92. Blackstone, *Commentaries*, 4:196; Holmes, *The Common Law*, 54.

93. Hawkins, *Treatise of the Pleas of the Crown*, 1:34.

94. Baker, *Introduction to English Legal History*, 4th ed., 527.

95. Castle, "'Amy Who Knew My Disease,'" 53.

96. P. J. Fitzgerald, *Criminal Law and Punishment* (Oxford, UK: Clarendon Press, 1962), 109.

97. Or, as Prichard puts it, in terms of "consequentiality" rather than "immediacy" (*Scott v. Shepherd*, 374).

98. Castle, "'Amy Who Knew My Disease,'" 49.

99. This is true of Christian Thorne's reading of *Roxana* as well. Thorne's claim that Defoe's narratives are "a single-minded onslaught on providence" derives from his sense that although Roxana worries about Providence, she "never gets what's coming to her." To think so, however, is to ignore both the return of Providence in the form of her daughter Susan, and the final paragraph in which Roxana takes responsibility for Susan's murder, a paragraph Thorne embeds in a footnote ("Providence in the Early Novel," 334, 335).

100. Cavell, "The Avoidance of Love," 323, 310.

101. Cavell, "The Avoidance of Love," 323.

CHAPTER 2. THE ENCROACHMENTS OF OTHERS

1. Samuel Richardson, *Clarissa; or, The History of a Young Lady*, ed. Angus Ross (London: Penguin, 1985), 142; hereafter cited parenthetically by page number.

2. Frances Ferguson, "Rape and the Rise of the Novel," *Representations* 20 (Autumn 1987): 88.

3. For a historical account of the consolidation of murder as a crime of "malice afore-

thought," see J. H. Baker, *An Introduction to English Legal History*, 4th ed. (London: Butterworths, 2002), 529–30. Philosopher R. A. Duff explains: "'*Actus non facit reum nisi mens sit rea*' runs the traditional maxim: an act does not make a person guilty unless his mind is also guilty. . . . The *actus reus* of murder is the killing (an act which has as a consequence the death) of a human being; its *mens rea* is an intention to cause death or serious injury" (*Intention, Agency and Criminal Liability: Philosophy of Action and the Criminal Law* [Oxford, UK: Basil Blackwell, 1990], 7–8).

4. Ian Watt, *The Rise of the Novel: Studies in Defoe, Richardson and Fielding* (Berkeley: University of California Press, 1957), 135.

5. Bernard Williams is paraphrasing Nietzsche ("Recognising Responsibility," in *Shame and Necessity* [Berkeley: University of California Press, 1993], 68).

6. Joan I. Schwarz, "Eighteenth-Century Abduction Law and *Clarissa*," in *Clarissa and Her Readers: New Essays for the "Clarissa" Project*, ed. Carol Houlihan Flynn and Edward Copeland (New York: AMS Press, 1999), 271.

7. Defoe, *Conjugal Lewdness; or, Matrimonial Whoredom: A Treatise concerning the Use and Abuse of the Marriage Bed* (1727; rpt., Gainesville: Scholars' Facsimiles and Reprints, 1967), 380.

8. Baker, *Introduction to English Legal History*, 4th ed., 411–12.

9. Baker, *Introduction to English Legal History*, 4th ed., 529.

10. Edward Coke, *The Third Part of the Institutes of the Laws of England* (London: W. Rawlins, 1680), 56.

11. "William Jackson and Others, 1748" (18 State Trials 1069), reprinted in *State Trials: Political and Social*, ed. H. L. Stephen, 2nd ser., vol. 4 (London: Duckworth, 1902), 126. For information on Richardson's printing of the state trials, see T. C. Duncan Eaves and Ben D. Kimpel, "An Unpublished Pamphlet by Samuel Richardson," *Philological Quarterly* 63.3 (1984): 401–9, and Schwarz, "Eighteenth-Century Abduction Law and *Clarissa*."

12. Michael Foster, *Discourse of Homicide*, in *Report of Some Proceedings on the Commission of Oyer and Terminer . . . to Which Are Added Discourses upon a Few Branches of the Crown Law* (1762; rpt., Abingdon, UK: Professional Books, 1982), 351–52.

13. Ferguson, "Rape and the Rise of the Novel," 108.

14. Ferguson, "Rape and the Rise of the Novel," 101, 109.

15. Ferguson, "Rape and the Rise of the Novel," 106.

16. Ferguson, "Rape and the Rise of the Novel," 108.

17. Ferguson, "Rape and the Rise of the Novel," 96, 105, 109.

18. The poststructuralist moment in *Clarissa* criticism was invaluable for making the problem of intentions—having them, comprehending them, adjudicating them—central to Richardson's literary project. Having raised the question of intentionality, however, critics such as Terry Eagleton, William Warner, and Terry Castle went on to assume that if intentionality was a problem, so, necessarily, was accountability: if language is "entirely free with regard to referential meaning," they reasoned, then an individual cannot be accountable for the accidental effects of what she says or does. This notion is crystallized in the title of *Limited Inc*. Derrida describes language users as a limited liability corporation: such corporations are grounded in the assumption that

accidents will and must happen, and a similar assumption—that signification is fundamentally accidental and (therefore impervious to the formalist containment imagined
by Austin)—grounds the deconstructive enterprise. For critics steeped in *Limited Inc,*
Clarissa's drive to establish her own innocence and Lovelace's guilt rests on a miscon-
ception about the nature of (linguistic) agency and of the agent: because the subject of
language is subject to language, her liability (as well as her innocence) is limited. See
Terry Castle, *Clarissa's Ciphers: Meaning and Disruption in Richardson's "Clarissa"* (Ithaca:
Cornell University Press, 1982); Terry Eagleton, *The Rape of Clarissa: Writing, Sexuality
and Class Struggle in Samuel Richardson* (Minneapolis: University of Minnesota Press,
1982); William Warner, *Reading "Clarissa": The Struggles of Interpretation* (New Haven:
Yale University Press, 1979); and Jacques Derrida, *Limited Inc,* trans. Samuel Weber and
Jeffrey Mehlman (1977; rpt., Evanston: Northwestern University Press, 1988).

19. George P. Fletcher, "Reflections on Felony-Murder," in *Philosophical Problems in
the Law,* 2nd ed., ed. David M. Adams (Belmont, CA: Wadsworth, 1996), 365.

20. Justice Fitzgerald in *People v. Aaron* (Michigan Supreme Court, 1980), in *Criminal Law: Cases, Materials and Texts,* 3rd ed., ed. Phillip E. Johnson (St. Paul, Minn.: West,
1985), 243; emphasis mine.

21. Nelson E. Roth and Scott E. Sundby, "The Felony-Murder Rule: A Doctrine at a
Constitutional Crossroads," *Cornell Law Review* 70.3 (1985): 455, 456 457.

22. Roth and Sundby, "The Felony-Murder Rule," 457 n. 63.

23. Fletcher, "Reflections on Felony-Murder," 365.

24. Fletcher, "Reflections on Felony-Murder," 367.

25. Fletcher, "Reflections on Felony-Murder," 367; emphasis mine.

26. Roth and Sundby, "The Felony-Murder Rule," 492, 486–87.

27. In two recent articles, legal scholar Guyora Binder has challenged the consensus
on felony murder outlined here. Calling the account of felony murder as a strict liability offense "unanimous," he insists that this obscures the "necessary role of normative
judgment in ascriptions of culpability" ("The Culpability of Felony Murder," *Notre Dame
Law Review* 83.3 [2008]: 973). He agrees that a strict liability rationale for the crime
would be "morally primitive" and argues that it is grounded instead in common sense
notions of criminal negligence aggravated by felonious motive. He acknowledges that "a
broad felony murder rule was proposed in some eighteenth-century treatises, and discussed favorably in some eighteenth-century English cases," but the paucity of case law
on the issues proves for him that the rule "was not applied" (967, 966). This leads him
to the most polemical of his claims: that the cherished notion that "this harsh rule long
prevailed as the common law rule in England" is untrue (969). It is not within the scope
of this chapter to confront Binder's objections in any detail, except to register some perplexity about what counts as historical evidence. Although the other essay, "The Origins
of American Felony Murder Rules" (*Stanford Law Review* 57.1 [2004–5]: 59–108), is offered as legal history, there is no analysis of *Lord Dacre's Case* or the work of eighteenth-
century English reporters, despite the fact that the article purports to prove the historical insignificance of felony murder doctrine prior to the later nineteenth century. (He
admits, for example, that "in the eighteenth century," "a few English courts extended
accomplice liability to murder committed in the course of crime to those who had agreed

only to the crime and not to the fatal wounding" [63, 64] but remains uninterested in what this does to his "expressive" theory of responsibility, which says that offenders can be inculpated only for having made, and acted on, bad choices.)

28. According to Bruno Latour, there is not. Latour does not register the countergenealogy of modernity traced in *Harm's Way,* one that anticipates the ontological conflation of humans and things that he assimilates to the new, not-yet-existent, "nonmodern" constitution (*We Have Never Been Modern,* trans. Catherine Porter [Cambridge, MA: Harvard University Press, 1993], 130).

29. William Hawkins, *A Treatise of the Pleas of the Crown,* 2 vols. (1716–21; rpt., Abingdon, UK: Professional Books, 1980), 1:74.

30. Hawkins, *Treatise of the Pleas of the Crown,* 1:74.

31. Matthew Hale, *The History of the Pleas of the Crown,* 2 vols. (1736; rpt., Abingdon, UK: Professional Books, 1980), 2:475. Although Hale's history wasn't published until 1736, its existence was well known from at least 1678.

32. *Rex v. Plummer,* in John Kelyng, *A Report of Divers Cases in Pleas of the Crown, Adjudged and Determined, In the Reign of the late King Charles II* (London: printed for Isaac Cleave, 1708), 117.

33. Kelyng, *Report of Divers Cases,* 117; emphasis mine.

34. Kelyng, *Report of Divers Cases,* 117.

35. Foster, *Discourse of Homicide,* 258.

36. Hawkins, *Treatise of the Pleas of the Crown,* 1:80.

37. Hawkins, *Treatise of the Pleas of the Crown,* 1:80.

38. Foster, *Discourse of Homicide,* 256.

39. Foster, *Discourse of Homicide,* 257.

40. Foster, *Discourse of Homicide,* 297.

41. I am grateful to Luke Wilson for this observation.

42. Hawkins, *Treatise of the Pleas of the Crown,* 1:81.

43. Oliver Wendell Holmes, *The Common Law* (1881; rpt., Boston: Little, Brown, 1963), 65.

44. Anonymous, "Felony Murder: A Tort Reconceptualization," *Harvard Law Review* 99.8 (1986): 1919–20.

45. Anonymous, "Felony Murder," 1922. Binder, as observed in n. 27, disagrees that felony murder is a strict liability offense.

46. Holmes, *The Common Law,* 73. "The rule of absolute responsibility is inconsistent with admitted doctrines and sound policy," argues Holmes, and he insists that "the common law has never known such a rule, unless in that period of dry precedent" he associates with Restoration and eighteenth-century case law (71).

47. Holmes, *The Common Law,* 77, 76.

48. Hawkins, *Treatise of the Pleas of the Crown,* 1:82.

49. Foster, *Discourse of Homicide,* 353–54.

50. The details of *People v. Stamp* are cited, among other sources, in David Crump and Susan Waite Crump, "In Defense of the Felony Murder Doctrine," *Harvard Journal of Law and Public Policy* 8.2 (1985), 383 n. 83; emphasis mine. The case argues what Lord M. argues when Lovelace demands "is death the natural consequence of a rape?" (1439):

that "if by committing an unlawful act, a capital crime is the consequence, you are answerable to both" (1438).

51. Crump and Crump, "In Defense of the Felony Murder Doctrine," 383 n. 83, 371.

52. Crump and Crump, "In Defense of the Felony Murder Doctrine," 383.

53. H. L. A. Hart and Tony Honoré, *Causation in the Law*, 2nd ed. (Oxford, UK: Clarendon Press, 1985), 99.

54. Hart and Honoré, *Causation in the Law*, 328.

55. Hart and Honoré, *Causation in the Law*, 99, 328.

56. Hart and Honoré, *Causation in the Law*, 329.

57. Hart and Honoré, *Causation in the Law*, 328.

58. Hart and Honoré, *Causation in the Law*, lxix–lxx.

59. Hart and Honoré, *Causation in the Law*, lxxviii.

60. Hart and Honoré, *Causation in the Law*, lxxiv, lxxv.

61. Hart and Honoré, *Causation in the Law*, lxxx–lxxxi.

62. Sandra Macpherson, "Lovelace, Ltd.," *ELH* 65.1 (1998): 99–121. In this essay I argue that *Clarissa* is centrally concerned with a conflict between intentionalist and consequentionalist accounts of responsibility. In making Richardson a consequentialist, I missed the important insight of "Rape and the Rise of the Novel": that consequentialism is a *species* of intentionalism in which actions are understood to emblematize latent mental content, which means that consequentialism is therefore identical with the constructive intent that allows Lovelace to make it appear as though Clarissa has consented to what is happening to her. My further research into the legal history behind Lord M.'s (and Richardson's) indictment of Lovelace brought to light felony murder's complex brand of consequentialism, which at its most extreme (in the merger doctrine, for example) eschews constructive intent, yoking agents to the consequences of acts that are clearly not theirs and thus undermining the antifeminist project of reading actions as signs of motive.

63. Ferguson, "Rape and the Rise of the Novel," 104.

64. Judith Wilt, "He Could Go No Farther: A Modest Proposal about Lovelace and Clarissa," *PMLA* 92.1 (1977): 19–32; 19.

65. Wilt, "He Could Go No Farther," 27.

66. Wilt, "He Could Go No Farther," 30.

67. Ferguson, "Rape and the Rise of the Novel," 101.

68. Ferguson, "Rape and the Rise of the Novel," 110, 106, 108.

69. I also wonder if the negation Ferguson invokes as constituting Clarissa's resistance and her personhood—as constituting personhood per se—doesn't remain agentive. This isn't true of the negative represented by Clarissa's unconsciousness during the rape, which "provides that Clarissa's nonconsent continues even in her absence, even in her unconsciousness." But when she turns to discuss Clarissa's actions following the rape, the language of agency returns in Ferguson's argument: the "mimesis of distinction" thus "represents in formal terms the negative that Clarissa continually *deploys* against what comes to look like Lovelace's complacent acceptance of forms"; "Clarissa *makes* her body, the body that Lovelace had hoped to convert into a form of consent, into a slowly wasting sign of the inability of form to carry mental states in anything but exces-

sively capacious (that is, ambiguous) or potentially self-contradictory stipulated forms";
"Clarissa thus *responds* with her own persistent *impersonation* of stipulated nonconsent"
("Rape and the Rise of the Novel," 100, 106, 107; emphases mine).

70. J. H. Baker, *An Introduction to English Legal History*, 3rd ed. (London: Butterworths, 1990), 464–65.

71. The pathology is Clarissa's for a body of psychoanalytically inflected criticism on
the novel. See, for example, Laura Hinton, "The Heroine's Subjection: Clarissa, Sado-
masochism, and Natural Law," *Eighteenth-Century Studies* 32.3 (1999): 293–308; Peggy
Thompson, "Abuse and Atonement: The Passion of Clarissa Harlowe," *Eighteenth-Century Fiction* 11.3 (1999): 255–70; Victor Lams, *Anger, Guilt and the Psychology of Self in
"Clarissa"* (New York: Peter Lang, 1999); and Daryl S. Ogden, "Richardson's Narrative
Space-Off: Freud, Vision, and the (Heterosexual) Problem of Reading *Clarissa*," *Literature and Psychology* 42.4 (1996): 37–52. For others the pathology is more broadly cultural. See, for example, Jayne Lewis's essay on the sadism of eighteenth-century moral
thinking, "Clarissa's Cruelty: Modern Fables of Moral Authority in the *History of a Young
Lady*," in *Clarissa and Her Readers: New Essay for the "Clarissa" Project*, 45–68, and He-
lene Moglen's *"Clarissa* and the Pornographic Imagination," in *The Trauma of Gender:
A Feminist Theory of the English Novel* (Berkeley: University of California Press, 2001),
57–85.

72. Eaves and Kimpel, "An Unpublished Pamphlet by Samuel Richardson," 402.

73. William Blackstone, *Commentaries on the Laws of England*, 4 vols. (1765–69; rpt.,
Chicago: University of Chicago Press, 1979), 4:240.

74 See E. P. Thompson's *Whigs and Hunters: The Origin of the Black Act* (New York:
Pantheon, 1975), and Douglas Hay, *Albion's Fatal Tree* (New York: Penguin, 1988).

75. Indeed, in the conclusion, in which he dispatches Lovelace and his agents, Richardson stages a scene of felony murder of the kind Hawkins discusses—one in which
an accessory to a duel is indicted for murder. "After the death of the profligate Sinclair,"
we're told, Polly Horton and Sally Martin "kept on the infamous trade with too much success; till an accident happened in the house—a gentleman killed in it in a fray, contend-
ing with another for a new-vamped face. Sally was accused of holding the gentleman's
arm, while his more favoured adversary run him through the heart, and then made off.
And she being tried for her life, narrowly escaped" (1491). If Sally is not expressly tried
for Clarissa's death, then, she is tried for a death that resembles it.

76. See, for example, Martha Nussbaum, *Poetic Justice* (Boston: Beacon Press, 1995).

77. Watt, *Rise of the Novel*, 175–76.

78. Watt, *Rise of the Novel*, 134.

79. Terry Eagleton, *Sweet Violence: The Idea of the Tragic* (Oxford, UK: Blackwell,
2003), 202.

80. Aristotle, *Poetics*, trans. Malcolm Heath (London: Penguin, 1996), 21, 23.

81. The entry under "hamartia" in Wikipedia notes that although the term is usually
translated as "tragic flaw," there is "debate as to what exactly hamartia means in Aristotle's *Poetics*. The word, in *Homeric Greek*, refers to a warrior who has missed his mark.
If an archer or a spear thrower misses, ἅμαρτες has occurred." "It has been suggested
by some," the entry continues, "that the modern idea of the 'tragic flaw' is a mistransla-

tion of the Greek. An alternative translation is 'tragic mistake'" (http://en.wikipedia.org/wiki/Ancient Greek). For the debate over hamartia, see Jan Bremer, *Hamartia: Tragic Error in the "Poetics" of Aristotle and in Greek Tragedy* (Amsterdam: Adolf M. Hakkert, 1969); Richard Sorabji, *Necessity, Cause, and Blame: Perspectives on Aristotle's Theory* (Ithaca: Cornell University Press, 1980); Stephen Halliwell, *Aristotle's "Poetics"* (Chapel Hill: University of North Carolina Press, 1986); and Kathy Eden, *Poetic and Legal Fiction in the Aristotelian Tradition* (Princeton: Princeton University Press, 1986).

82. This claim is to an extent at odds with Leopold Damrosch's sense that at the heart of the tragedy of *Clarissa* "lies the ancient truth embodied in Heraclitus's maxim that character is destiny." Damrosch aligns tragedy with Puritan providentialism and in the process makes tragedy what I have been calling "comic" (or felicitous). This leads him to a conclusion quite incongenial to my interest in the irrecuperable harmfulness of harm, viz., that "from Richardson's point of view, tragedy offered a reliable model for explaining and *justifying* human suffering" (*God's Plots and Man's Stories: Studies in the Fictional Imagination from Milton to Fielding* [Chicago: University of Chicago Press, 1985], 251, 257; emphasis mine).

83. Friedrich Nietzsche, *The Birth of Tragedy*, in *The Birth of Tragedy, and The Case of Wagner*, trans. Walter Kaufmann (New York: Vintage, 1967), 95.

84. Latour, *We Have Never Been Modern*, 84.

85. Latour, *We Have Never Been Modern*, 138.

86. Latour, *We Have Never Been Modern*, 85.

87. Latour, *We Have Never Been Modern*, 136–37.

CHAPTER 3. FIGHTING MEN

1. R. S. Crane, "The Concept of Plot and the Plot of *Tom Jones*," in *Critics and Criticism*, ed. R. S. Crane (Chicago: University of Chicago Press, 1952), 78, 79, 83.

2. Crane, "The Concept of Plot and the Plot of *Tom Jones*," 87, 86.

3. Henry Fielding, *The History of Tom Jones, a Foundling*, ed. Martin C. Battestin (Middletown, CT: Wesleyan University Press, 1975), 297–98; hereafter cited parenthetically by page number.

4. Ian Watt, *The Rise of the Novel: Studies in Defoe, Richardson and Fielding* (Berkeley: University of California Press, 1957), 264.

5. Susan Staves, "Fielding and the Comedy of Attempted Rape," in *History, Gender, and Eighteenth-Century Literature*, ed. Beth Fowkes Tobin (Athens: University of Georgia Press, 1994).

6. Henry Fielding, *Joseph Andrews and Shamela*, ed. Judith Hawley (London: Penguin, 1999), xxiii.

7. Staves, "Fielding and the Comedy of Attempted Rape," 106.

8. Staves, "Fielding and the Comedy of Attempted Rape," 107.

9. Staves, "Fielding and the Comedy of Attempted Rape," 106.

10. Staves, "Fielding and the Comedy of Attempted Rape," 108.

11. Mark Spilka, "Comic Resolution in Fielding's *Joseph Andrews*," *College English* 15.1 (1953): 11–19, reprinted in *Joseph Andrews, with Shamela and Related Writings*, ed. Homer

Goldberg (New York: Norton, 1987), 404–12. For Parson Adams's "harmlessness," see 408, 410; for the description of Slipslop's beating, see 409; for Fielding's comic method, see 408.

12. Christopher Johnson, "'British Championism': Early Pugilism and the Works of Fielding," *Review of English Studies* 47.187 (1996): 339.

13. Johnson, "'British Championism,'" 339. Johnson turns to handbills advertising the services of "Professor of Athletics" and boxing champion John Broughton, as well as to Steele's *Tatler*, for evidence of the idea "that boxing encouraged and indeed embodied the principles of 'magnanimity'" (332).

14. Johnson, "'British Championism,'" 338.

15. "Lovelace keeps insisting, almost to the end," observes William Park, "that their story is actually a comedy" ("Clarissa as Tragedy," *Studies in English Literature* 16.3 [1976]: 466).

16. Staves, "Fielding and the Comedy of Attempted Rape," 106–7. Staves is citing Antony E. Simpson, a leading authority on eighteenth-century rape law. See Simpson, "The 'Blackmail Myth' and the Prosecution of Rape and Its Attempt in Eighteenth-Century London: The Creation of a Legal Tradition," *Journal of Criminal Law and Criminology* 77.1 (1986): 101–50, 123.

17. Henry Fielding, *Joseph Andrews*, ed. Martin C. Battestin (Middletown, CT: Wesleyan University Press, 1967), 118; hereafter cited by page number.

18. Jill Campbell, *Natural Masques: Gender and Identity in Fielding's Plays and Novels* (Stanford: Stanford University Press, 1995), 84.

19. Campbell, *Natural Masques*, 114.

20. Campbell, *Natural Masques*, 103.

21. Frederick Pollock and Frederic William Maitland, *The History of English Law before the Time of Edward I* (1895; rpt., Cambridge: Cambridge University Press, 1968), 1:46, 1:47.

22. Pollock and Maitland, *The History of English Law before the Time of Edward I*, 2:449.

23. Pollock and Maitland, *The History of English Law before the Time of Edward I*, 2:450, 2:451.

24. William Blackstone, *Commentaries on the Laws of England*, 4 vols. (1765–69; rpt., Chicago: University of Chicago Press, 1979), 4:12–13.

25. Blackstone, *Commentaries*, 2:438; Theodore Sedgwick, *A Treatise on the Measure of Damages*, 3rd ed. (1847; rpt., London: Allen and Green, 1858), 17.

26. Sedgwick, *Treatise on the Measure of Damages*, 16.

27. Sedgwick, *Treatise on the Measure of Damages*, 16–17.

28. Why his system of damages would be any less arbitrary than any other is never addressed by Sedgwick, and the argument, on this score, is quite unpersuasive.

29. Johnson, "'British Championism,'" 351. Fielding's alignment of fighting with *caritas* rather than *eros* may provide another way of thinking about friendship than the one that has dominated the study of early modern literary history. There friendship is a species of homoeroticism and as such is implicitly tied to a transgressive or "utopian" politics. But in Fielding's hands friendship is linked with a sentimental homosociality

that is deeply normative. See Laurie Shannon, *Sovereign Amity: Figures of Friendship in Shakespearean Contexts* (Chicago: University of Chicago Press, 2001). For an account of friendship that ties its eighteenth-century instantiations to the philosophies of "moral benevolence," see Alan Bray, *The Friend* (Chicago: University of Chicago Press, 2003).

30. "Fault" seems to do double duty here: as an index of wrongdoing and as a technical term registering the specific form that wrongdoing takes (the failure of a dog to follow the exact line of a quarry in a hunt). See also Tom Jones, book 12, chapter 2: "The Master of the Hunt, however, often saw and approved the great Judgment of the Stranger [Squire Western] in drawing the Dogs when they were at a Fault" (624). This judgment is what Joseph apparently lacks.

31. The "scene recalls the parable of the Good Samaritan," observes J. Paul Hunter, and "its larger ramifications for the reader mark the shift in thematic emphasis from chastity to charity" (*Occasional Form: Henry Fielding and the Chains of Circumstance* [Baltimore: Johns Hopkins University Press, 1975], 107, 110). "The parable of the Good Samaritan," Ronald Paulson agrees, "stands firmly behind the episode of Joseph, the robbers, and the coachload of Pharisees and Levites with its one Good Samaritan." The paradigm is an obvious choice for Fielding in 1742, says Paulson, invoking as it does Bishop Hoadley's sermons on charity and Hogarth's murals for St. Bartholomew's Hospital ("Models and Paradigms: Joseph Andrews, Hogarth's Good Samaritan, and Fénelon's *Télémaque*," *MLN* 91.6 [1976]: 1190, 1191). The paradigmatic articulation of this account of book 1, chapter 12, of Joseph Andrews is Martin Battestin's: "The major thematic motif of *Joseph Andrews*, the doctrine of charity, principally informs Part II of the novel (Book I, chapter 11, through Book III)," he argues. "The theme of Christian charity is sounded at the start of Joseph's journey by the dramatic recasting of the Good Samaritan parable" in book 1, chapter 12 (*The Moral Basis of Fielding's Art: A Study of "Joseph Andrews"* [Middletown, CT: Wesleyan University Press, 1959], 95).

32. Hunter, *Occasional Form*, 110.

33. Oliver Wendell Holmes, *The Common Law*, ed. Mark DeWolfe Howe (1881; rpt., Boston: Little, Brown, 1963), 145.

34. Holmes, *The Common Law*, 145.

35. J. H. Baker, *An Introduction to English Legal History*, 3rd ed. (London: Butterworths, 1990), 465; Holmes, *The Common Law*, 65.

36. For the tradition of distinguishing Richardson and Fielding, see Allen Michie's indispensable, *Richardson and Fielding: The Dynamics of a Critical Rivalry* (Lewisburg, PA: Bucknell University Press, 1999); the quotes from Johnson are found on 68–69. It is an interesting irony that the opposition Fielding establishes in book 1, chapter 12, between Samaritanism and carrier liability breaks down in the legal history of what are now called "Good Samaritan laws." "Because of [its] reluctance to countenance 'non-feasance' as a basis of liability, the law has persistently refused to recognize the moral obligation of common decency and common humanity, to come to the aid of another human being who is in danger, even though the outcome is to cost him his life," legal historian William Prosser observes. "The remedy in such cases is left to the 'higher law' and the 'voice of conscience,' which in a wicked world, would seem to be singularly ineffective either to prevent the harm or to compensate the victim." Prosser made these

observations in the 1940s, when Anglo-American jurisprudence was developing Good Samaritan laws, laws that Prosser notes are derived from common-law actions such as those covering common carriers: "This process of extension [of the law of common carriers] has been slow, and marked with extreme caution; but there is reason to think that it may continue until it approaches a general holding that the mere knowledge of serious peril, threatening death or great bodily harm to another, which an identified defendant might avoid with little inconvenience, creates a sufficient relation, recognized by every moral and social standard, to impose a duty of action" (*Handbook of the Law of Torts*, 4th ed. [1941; rpt., St. Paul, MI: West, 1971], 340, 343). See also W. J. Curran, "Legal History of Emergency Medicine from Medieval Common Law to the AIDS Epidemic," *American Journal of Emergency Medicine* 15.7 (1997): 658–70. Although Prosser sounds very Fieldingesque in his indictment of failures of "common decency and humanity," Fielding would surely object to the juridicalization of Samaritanism for enforcing duties that ought to be spontaneously expressed.

37. I am grateful to Neil Chudgar for pointing out to me that some women in Fielding are good natured in precisely this way. But those women are also masculinized, and for me this confirms the alignment of goodness with a retaliatory masculinity even as it makes masculinity a structural rather than biological position.

38. Battestin, *History of Tom Jones*, 121 n. 1.

39. John Allen Stevenson, *The Real History of Tom Jones* (New York: Palgrave Macmillan, 2005), 201 n. 14; *Tom Jones*, ed. John Bender and Simon Stern (Oxford: Oxford University Press, 1996), 882 n. 142.

40. "Trespass for taking away goods (*de bonis asportatis*) was the civil counterpart of larceny," J. H. Baker observes. Robbery "had the same ingredients as trespass *de bonis asportatis*, with the addition of mens rea, an intent to steal" (*An Introduction to English Legal History*, 4th ed. [London: Butterworths, 2002], 394, 533). In *Joseph Andrews*, book 4, chapter 5, Fielding again mocks this "kind of felonious larcenous thing" (289)—this conversion of mere trespass into felony burglary. Joseph and Fanny stand accused of a trespass for "walking on the Grass out of the said Path in the said Felde" belonging to Lawyer Scout and cutting from said field a twig. " 'Jesu!' said the Squire, 'would you commit two Persons to *Bridewell* for a Twig?' 'Yes,' said the Lawyer, 'and with great Lenity too; for if we had called it a young Tree they would have been both hanged' " (290).

41. Henry James, *The Princess Casamassima* (1886; rpt., New York: Penguin Books, 1997), 15. The term "eclectic" is Watt's: "Fielding's technique was too eclectic to become a permanent element in the tradition of the novel," he says, pointing to what he has earlier described as Fielding's failure to break with typological conventions (*Rise of the Novel*, 288, 19). Fielding's commitment to typology receives nuanced attention in Michael McKeon's *Origins of the English Novel, 1600–1740* (Baltimore: Johns Hopkins University Press, 1987), Deidre Lynch's *The Economy of Character: Novels, Market Culture, and the Business of Inner Meaning* (Chicago: University of Chicago Press, 1998), and Wolfram Schmidgen's *Eighteenth-Century Fiction and the Law of Property* (Cambridge: Cambridge University Press, 2002) among other places.

42. Matthew Hale, *Historia placitorum coronae*, 2 vols. (1736; rpt., London: Professional Books, 1971), 1:452.

43. Hale, *Historia placitorum coronae*, 1:453. Hale's account of the murder/manslaughter distinction is derived from and closely follows sixteenth-century precedents. For a survey of these precedents, which emphasizes the conceptual importance of temporality to the (legal) representation mental states, see Luke Wilson, "Renaissance Tool Abuse and the Legal History of the Sudden," in *Literature, Politics, and Law in Renaissance England*, ed. Lorna Hutson and Erica Sheen (Basingstoke, UK: Palgrave Macmillan, 2005), 121–45.

44. Michael Foster, *Crown Law* (1762; rpt., Abingdon, UK: Professional Books, 1982), 297. Interestingly, in the preface, Foster calls into question the authenticity of the 1738 edition of Hale's *The History of Pleas of the Crown* (iv–v).

45. Foster, *Crown Law*, 297.

46. William Hawkins, *A Treatise of the Pleas of the Crown*, 2 vols. (1716–21; rpt., Abingdon, UK: Professional Books, 1980), 1:81.

47. Hawkins, *Treatise of the Pleas of the Crown*, 1:81.

48. I'm grateful to Erik Gunderson for help with this neologism.

49. Campbell, *Natural Masques*, 101–6. Campbell reads this episode as an allegory centering on gender and form in which the important form is satire. This seems right to me, but I want to suggest that on top of this is another allegory linking gender and speciation in which the important form is the novel.

50. Alexander Welsh, *Strong Representations: Narrative and Circumstantial Evidence in England* (Baltimore: Johns Hopkins University Press, 1992), 76.

51. Welsh, *Strong Representations*, 73.

52. Welsh, *Strong Representations*, 76.

53. John Loftis, "Trials and the Shaping of Identity in *Tom Jones*," *Studies in the Novel* 34.1 (2002): 8.

54. Loftis, "Trials and the Shaping of Identity in *Tom Jones*," 10.

55. Loftis, "Trials and the Shaping of Identity in *Tom Jones*," 11.

56. Frances Ferguson, "Rape and the Rise of the Novel," *Representations* 20 (Autumn 1987): 101, 109.

57. Ferguson, "Rape and the Rise of the Novel," 106.

58. See Hawley's note on Rich in Fielding, *Joseph Andrews and Shamela*, 351 n. 3.

59. Katherine M. Rogers, "Sensitive Feminism v. Conventional Sympathy: Richardson and Fielding on Women," *Novel* 9 (1976): 267, 257. Rogers's dissatisfaction with the novel's comic resolution is widely shared. April London reads the marriage in book 18 as a "subsumption of the female by the male through the agency of the 'natural' right of property and the 'affections it engages'" ("Controlling the Text: Women in Tom Jones," *Studies in the Novel* 19 [1987]: 331), and John Zomchick objects to the way in which "Tom can engage in morally questionable sexual relations with Molly Seagrim and Lady Bellaston without suffering disabling consequences from those relations" ("'A Penetration Which Nothing Can Deceive': Gender and Juridical Discourse in Some Eighteenth Century Narratives," *Studies in English Literature* 3 [1989]: 537).

60. Adam Smith, *The Theory of Moral Sentiments* (1759; rpt., New York: Prometheus, 2000), 104.

61. There is some work on Hume and responsibility—for example, Paul Russell's

Freedom and Moral Sentiment: Hume's Way of Naturalizing Responsibility (New York: Oxford University Press, 1995)—but the critical tradition on Smith tends to focus on sympathy, spectatorship, and "das Adam Smith problem" (how nineteenth-century German scholars referred to the conceptual tensions between the *Theory of Moral Sentiments* and the *Wealth of Nations*). For a discussion of Smith on guilt, see, R. F. Brissenden, "Authority, Guilt, and Anxiety in The Theory of Moral Sentiments," *Texas Studies in Literature and Language* 11.2 (1969): 945–62.

62. Smith, *Theory of Moral Sentiments*, 151.

63. Smith, *Theory of Moral Sentiments*, 149, 157, 151, 155; emphasis mine.

64. Smith, *Theory of Moral Sentiments*, 155–57.

65. Horace, *Satires, Epistles, and Ars Poetica*, trans. H. Rushton Fairclough (Cambridge, MA: Harvard University Press, 1926), 255.

66. Parson Williams cites the Latin original: "Nil conscire sibi nullae pallescere culpae" (*Joseph Andrews and Shamela*, 32).

67. See, for example, Ronald Paulson's suggestion (embedded in a complex account of Fielding's relationship to eighteenth-century moral philosophy before Smith) that *Tom Jones* centers on "the understanding of [a] single act" (*The Life of Henry Fielding: A Critical Biography* [Oxford, UK: Blackwell, 2000], 260).

68. Smith, *Theory of Moral Sentiments*, 134. For other recent work on Fielding and Scottish moral philosophy, see James Lynch, "Moral Sense and the Narrator of *Tom Jones*," *Studies in English Literature* 25.3 (1985): 599–614, and Adam Budd, "Moral Correction: The Refusal of Revision in Henry Fielding's *Amelia*," *Lumen* 20 (2001): 1–17.

69. Watt, *Rise of the Novel*, 269.

70. Watt, *Rise of the Novel*, 268, 276, 279.

71. Watt, *Rise of the Novel*, 280.

72. Jill Campbell, "Fielding's Style," *ELH* 72.2 (2005): 428.

73. Ferguson, "Rape and the Rise of the Novel," 108.

74. Frances Ferguson, "Jane Austen, *Emma*, and the Impact of Form," *MLQ* 61.1 (2000): 158.

75. Ferguson, "Jane Austen, *Emma*, and the Impact of Form," 159.

76. Ferguson, "Jane Austen, *Emma*, and the Impact of Form," 163, 165.

77. Ferguson, "Jane Austen, *Emma*, and the Impact of Form," 180.

78. Ferguson, "Jane Austen, *Emma*, and the Impact of Form," 180.

79. Ferguson, "Jane Austen, *Emma*, and the Impact of Form," 178.

80. Schmidgen, *Eighteenth-Century Fiction and the Law of Property*, 103.

81. Sedgwick, *Treatise on the Measure of Damages*, 30.

CHAPTER 4. THE RAPE OF THE COCK

1. R. F. Brissenden, *Virtue in Distress: Studies in the Novel of Sentiment from Richardson to Sade* (London: Macmillan, 1974). Admittedly, this formulation of the paradigm doesn't account for the complexities of Brissenden's argument. There *are* male sentimental protagonists, and some of these men are "in distress" (as in the chapter on the *Vicar of Wakefield*, *The Man of Feeling*, and *Werther*, subtitled "Comic, Pathetic and Tragic

Versions of the Distressed and Virtuous Hero"). But male virtue is under stress in a different way from female virtue: it is only women's virtue that comes under stress in the form of threats of sexual violation.

2. See, for example, Claudia Johnson's pathbreaking *Equivocal Beings: Politics, Gender, and Sentimentality in the 1790s: Wollstonecraft, Radcliffe, Burney, Austen* (Chicago: University of Chicago Press, 1995); Julie Ellison, *Cato's Tears and the Making of Anglo-American Emotion* (Chicago: University of Chicago Press, 1999); Glenn Hendler, *Public Sentiments: Structures of Feeling in Nineteenth-Century American Literature* (Chapel Hill: University of North Carolina Press, 2001); and Paul Kelleher, "Men of Feeling: Sentimentalism, Sexuality, and the Conduct of Life in Eighteenth-Century British Literature" (PhD diss., Princeton University, 2003).

3. Frances Sheridan, *The Memoirs of Miss Sidney Bidulph*, ed. Jean Coates Cleary and Patricia Koster (1761; rpt., Oxford: Oxford University Press, 1995), 306; hereafter cited parenthetically by page number. For President Clinton's rakish self-inculpation, see www.youtube.com/watch?v=KiIP_KDQmXs.

4. Marquis de Sade, *Justine; or, Virtue Well-Chastized*, in *Justine, Philosophy in the Bedroom, and Other Writings*, trans. Richard Seaver and Austyn Wainhouse (New York: Grove, 1990), 538–39.

5. In his chapter on Sade, Brissenden argues that pornographic sadism is what happens when sentimentalism fails: "The Marquis de Sade, although he is a literary figure of major importance, is not a great novelist, and the image of humanity presented in his writings can hardly be called balanced." Sade's "aberrations," he concludes, "led him into direct conflict with that complex of ideals, fantasies and theories about the nature of man and society which can be called sentimental" (283–84). Fielding and anti-*Pamelist* critics after him, however—Ian Watt, William Warner, James Grantham Turner, Sade himself—know sadism is what happens when sentimentalism succeeds. See Watt, *The Rise of the Novel: Studies in Defoe, Richardson and Fielding* (Berkeley: University of California Press, 1957), 29, 204, for the suggestion that Richardson's erotic scenes are more affecting than Boccaccio's and that, like a pornographer, he is committed to eliciting the reader's desire. In *Licensing Entertainment: The Elevation of Novel Reading in Britain, 1684–1750* (Berkeley: University of California Press, 1998), William Warner shows that Richardson is quite self-conscious about the eroticism of his form and about his relation to an earlier generation of amatory novelists such as Behn, Manley, and Haywood. Bradford K. Mudge argues in *The Whore's Story: Women, Pornography, and the British Novel, 1684–1830* (Oxford: Oxford University Press, 2000) that *Justine* is the "most devastating" anti-*Pamela* of them all (199, 265 n. 2). James Turner's strenuous review of *The Whore's Story* (*Studies in the Novel* 33.3 [2001]: 358–64) points, quite rightly, to an essay of his own ("The Whore's Rhetoric: Narrative, Pornography, and the Origin of the Novel," *Studies in Eighteenth-Century Culture* 24 [1995]: 297–306) for the claim that pornography is intimately tied to the rise of the novel in England.

6. Susan Sontag, "The Pornographic Imagination," in *Styles of Radical Will* (New York: Farrar, Straus and Giroux, [1969]), 149.

7. William Blackstone, *Commentaries of the Laws of England*, 4 vols. (1765–69; rpt., Chicago: University of Chicago Press, 1979), 1:291.

8. Edward Coke, *The Third Part of the Institutes of the Laws of England concerning High Treason and Other Pleas of the Crown and Criminal Causes* (1628; rpt., London: W. Clarke and Sons, 1809), 57–58.

9. J. J. Finkelstein has argued that thing liability functions historically as a rudimentary "vehicular traffic code" and that it is therefore connected to legal developments concerning the liability of human beings such as those discussed in previous chapters (carrier liability, felony murder, trespass), where states of mind are similarly irrelevant in adjudicating responsibility ("The Ox That Gored," *Transactions of the American Philosophical Society* 71.2 [1981]: 1–89).

10. For an argument about sentimental fiction's devotion to "vehicularity"—the use of figural and sometimes literal vehicles to describe affective states—see James Chandler, "Moving Accidents: The Emergence of Sentimental Probability," in *The Age of Cultural Revolutions: Britain and France, 1750–1820,* ed. Colin Jones and Dror Wahrman (Berkeley: University of California Press, 2002), 137–70. Chandler has also written an unpublished essay on the subject ("Sentimental Journeys, Vehicular States").

11. Geoffrey MacCormack, "On Thing Liability (*Sachhaftung*) in Early Law," *Irish Jurist* 19.2 (1984): 322.

12. MacCormack, "On Thing Liability (*Sachhaftung*) in Early Law," 332–33.

13. MacCormack, "On Thing Liability (*Sachhaftung*) in Early Law," 332.

14. Oliver Wendell Holmes, *The Common Law,* ed. Mark DeWolfe Howe (1881; rpt., Boston: Little, Brown, 1963), 12; hereafter cited parenthetically by page number. For a fascinating development of Holmes's alignment of tort law and personification, see Elaine Scarry, *The Body in Pain: The Making and Unmaking of the World* (New York: Oxford University Press, 1985). Scarry's account of the ethics of liability law is the reverse of mine: that it asks a harmful object "to be an object that knew better," and "if like an object." Ethics and aesthetics serve the world's "sentient inhabitants," restructuring "the naturally existing external environment to be laden with humane awareness." Scarry, 297, 294, 28, 305.

15. An exception to this line of analysis is Helen Thompson's; she sees the *Memoirs of Miss Sidney Bidulph* as concerned with the moral philosophical burdens of the sentimental novel as a form: "Lacking the sentiment that makes up *Pamela*'s inextricably virtuous and passionate letters, the text produced by *Memoirs*' loveless wife materializes as pure duty lacking the sanction of any original instinct whatsoever." "Frances Sheridan's 'disingenuous girl': Ingenuous Subjection and Epistolary Form," in *Ingenuous Subjection: Compliance and Power in the Eighteenth-Century Domestic Novel* (Philadelphia: University of Pennsylvania Press, 2005), 177.

16. "Sidney's life is ruined," argues Eve Tavor Bannet, "because she obeys her mother's directives rather than her brother's" (*The Domestic Revolution: Enlightenment Feminisms and the Novel* [Baltimore: Johns Hopkins University Press, 2000], 114). Margaret Anne Doody also attributes the novel's tragedies to Lady Bidulph, blaming her for imposing her own psychological (and marital) trauma onto Sidney in a manner that reproduces that trauma. The novel, Doody concludes, is about "patterns of action that affect the lives of a number of people in the next two generations." Doody calls this pattern

of action "psychological," but she also acknowledges Sidney continues to think she has done wrong despite knowing her intentions were good, a fact that contravenes "much of the dominant eighteenth-century morality, which insisted on the satisfactions of virtue" ("Frances Sheridan: Morality and Annihilated Time," in *Fetter'd or Free? British Women Novelists, 1670–1815,* ed. Mary Anne Schofield and Cecilia Macheski [Athens: Ohio University Press, 1986], 346, 339).

17. Bannet, *Domestic Revolution,* 111.

18. Bannet, *Domestic Revolution,* 114.

19. Bannet, *Domestic Revolution,* 114.

20. The inset narrative seems to reverse the tendency of the male characters to align themselves with Clarissa. Faulkland theatrically invokes Lovelace when describing his final success with Mrs. Gerrarde—his forcing her to marry a French valet named Pivet, whom he pays to keep her (using, it is hinted, "harsh measures" [224]) from returning to England. "Congratulate me, Sir George," he demands of his Belford:

> Honour me, as the first of politicians, the greatest of negotiators! Let no hero of romance compare himself to me, for first making difficulties, and then extricating myself out of them; let no giant pretend to equal me in the management of captive beauties in inchanted castles; let no necromancer presume to vie with me in skill for metamorphosing tigresses into doves, and changing imperious princesses into plain country nymphs! All this have I brought to pass, without the assistance of inchanted sword or dwarf, in the compass of a few days. (214–15)

On the other hand, what Faulkland is celebrating here is as much his own escape from Mrs. Gerrarde's seductions as Mrs. Gerrarde's capture.

21. J. H. Baker, *Introduction to English Legal History,* 3rd. ed. (London: Buttersworth, 1990), 462.

22. MacCormack, "On Thing Liability (*Sachhaftung*) in Early Law," 332.

23. MacCormack, "On Thing Liability (*Sachhaftung*) in Early Law," 328; Finkelstein, "The Ox That Gored," 76.

24. Teresa Sutton, "The Deodand and Responsibility for Death," *Legal History* 18.3 (1997): 48.

25. We are also told of the death of a man who "was drowned in crossing a deep water on horseback which he thought was fordable" (394). This story occurs in an inset narrative about the worthy but impecunious clergyman Mr. Price. The victim of the fall is Mr. Price's benefactor, and his death precipitates the clergyman's financial ruin, just as Mr. Arnold's death precipitates the ruin of Sidney and her children.

26. Finkelstein, "The Ox That Gored," 76–77.

27. According to readers who blame Lady Bidulph for the novel's tragic outcomes (see n. 16), Faulkland is as much a victim of her obstinacy as Sidney.

28. For an account of the Marriage Act that sees its formalism as progressive (or at least plausibly feminist), see Sandra Macpherson, "Lovelace, Ltd.," *ELH* 65.3 (1998): 99–121.

29. Thanks to Luke Wilson for help with this reading of George's epitaph.

30. *Critical Review* II (March 1761): 195; emphasis mine. Quoted in Jean Coates Cleary's introduction to the Oxford edition of the *Memoirs,* xii–xiii.

31. Andrew Marvell, "The Nymph Complaining for the Death of Her Faun," in *Miscellaneous Poems* (London: 1681), 1–17; hereafter cited parenthetically by line number.

32. Frank Kermode, introduction, *Andrew Marvell: Selected Poetry,* ed. Frank Kermode (New York: New American Library, 1967), xxv.

33. Daniel Jaeckle, "Marvell's Dialogized Nymph," *Studies in English Literature* 43.1 (2003): 142. Thanks to Joshua Scodel for help in understanding the intricacies of Marvell criticism.

34. As Geoffrey Hartman notes, an earlier generation of critics saw the love of the nymph for the fawn as a "reflection of the love of the Church for Christ" (*Beyond Formalism: Literary Essays, 1958–1970* [New Haven: Yale University Press, 1970], 173).

35. Hartman, for example, suggests that the poem's allegory derives from a pastoral tradition that "may show the beginnings of passion in an innocent mind, the obliquities of a young girl prey to her first love" (*Beyond Formalism,* 175). He goes on to read this obliquity as an allegory of "the intrusion of a historical into a pastoral world" in which history is "set fatally against poetry" (189).

36. Hartman observes that *"fawn,* a young deer, and *faun,* a semi-deity part animal part human, are homophones, and interchangeably spelled 'fawn' or 'faun' in the seventeenth century. . . . Faunus, in turn, is often associated with Sylvanus, a wood-god (Sylvae, Sylvio)" (*Beyond Formalism,* 188). Because he does not notice the word "deodand," he does not notice that it replays this philological metamorphosis of animal and human.

37. Hartman, *Beyond Formalism,* 173–41, 187–88.

38. The *Oxford English Dictionary*'s first definition of "smart" is "sharp physical pain, esp. such as is caused by a stroke, sting, or wound."

39. Jaeckle, "Marvell's Dialogized Nymph," 142.

40. On Pope and the objectification of women, see Felicity Nussbaum, *The Brink of All We Hate: English Satires on Women, 1660–1750* (Lexington: University of Kentucky Press, 1984); Ellen Pollack, *The Poetics of Sexual Myth: Gender, Ideology in the Verse of Pope and Swift* (Chicago: University of Chicago Press, 1985); Christa Knellwolf, *A Contradiction Still: Representations of Women in the Poetry of Alexander Pope* (Manchester, UK: Manchester University Press, 1998); Laura Brown, *Ends of Empire: Women and Ideology in Early Eighteenth-Century English Literature* (Cornell: Cornell University Press, 1993); and Tita Chico, "Arts of Beauty: Women's Cosmetics and Pope's Ekphrasis," *Eighteenth-Century Life* 26.1 (2002): 1–23.

41. I am quoting Benjamin's translation in "Allegory and *Trauerspiel,*" in *The Origin of German Tragic Drama,* trans. John Osborne (London: Verso, 1998), 161.

42. Laura Brown, *Fables of Modernity: Literature and Culture in the English Eighteenth Century* (Ithaca: Cornell University Press, 2001), 65.

43. Walter Benjamin, "Central Park," trans. Lloyd Spencer and Mark Harrington, *New German Critique* 34 (Winter 1985): 49.

44. Benjamin, "Central Park," 34, 42.

45. Benjamin, "Allegory and *Trauerspiel,*" 175.

46. Benjamin, "Central Park," 35, 41, 40.

47. Benjamin, "Central Park," 42. The question of gender in Benjamin's reading of Baudelairean allegory is complicated, and it is not within the scope of the present work to pursue the issue in much detail. There is a sense in which Benjamin sees allegory as a feminist mode in its resistance to norms of (re)productivity. This remains true despite his sense (derived from Adrienne Monnier) that "Baudelaire's readers are men. Women are not fond of him" (43).

48. Alex Woloch, *The One vs. the Many: Minor Characters and the Space of the Protagonist in the Novel* (Princeton: Princeton University Press, 2003), 20.

49. Woloch, *One vs. the Many*, 20.

50. Woloch, *One vs. the Many*, 20.

51. Woloch, *One vs. the Many*, 24.

52. Woloch, *One vs. the Many*, 42, 40.

53. Leopold Damrosch, *God's Plot and Man's Stories: Studies in the Fictional Imagination from Milton to Fielding* (Chicago: University of Chicago Press, 1985), 144.

54. Damrosch, *God's Plot and Man's Stories*, 162; Roger Sharrock, *John Bunyan*, new ed. (London: Macmillan, 1968), 70.

55. Damrosch, *God's Plot and Man's Stories*, 183. Although Damrosch objects to Wolfgang Iser's "breezy claim" that in *Pilgrim's Progress*, "mere allegory is surpassed through the sheer aliveness of the characters" (170), he concludes that Bunyan's text shares "affinities" with the novel in its "recognition of the differentness of different persons" (179) and that the movement from allegory and personification to characterization in literary form "reflects the larger movement of Puritanism from dogmatic clarity to ethical complexity" (183). It has been the point of this book to break precisely this alignment of ethics with an attention to particularity.

56. Jonathan Lamb, "Modern Metamorphoses and Disgraceful Tales," *Critical Inquiry* 28.1 (2001): 166. Most of the critical work on object narration follows Lamb in assuming that to tie a human being to a nonhuman thing or animal is to degrade the human. See, for example, Brown, *Fables of Modernity*; Aileen Douglas, "Britannia's Rule and the It-Narrator," *Eighteenth-Century Fiction* 6.1 (1993): 65–82; Christopher Flint, "Speaking Objects: The Circulation of Stories in Eighteenth-Century Prose Fiction," *PMLA* 113.2 (1998): 212–26; and Felicity Nussbaum, *Limits of the Human: Fictions of Anomaly, Race, and Gender in the Long Eighteenth Century* (Cambridge: Cambridge University Press, 2003). Pope's "moving Toyshop of [the] Heart" has not been seen as an instance of object narration despite the fact that, as Christopher Flint points out, "object tales" are "more extensive" than Aileen Douglas's groundbreaking "Britannia's Rule and the It-Narrator" allowed (212). Recent work by Jonathan Lamb suggests that he, at least, is moving in this direction. See Jonathan Lamb, *"The Rape of the Lock* as Still Life," in *The Secret Life of Things: Animals, Objects, and It-Narratives in Eighteenth-Century England*, ed. Mark Blackwell (Lewisburg, PA: Bucknell University Press, 2007), 43–62.

57. Lamb, "Modern Metamorphoses and Disgraceful Tales," 138.

58. Bernard Williams, "Recognising Responsibility," in *Shame and Necessity* (Berkeley: University of California Press, 1993), 69, 70, 71.

59. Williams, "Recognising Responsibility," 64.

CONCLUSION. BAD FORM

1. Charles Dickens, *Hard Times*, ed. David Craig (1854; rpt., New York: Penguin, 1969), 204, 145; hereafter cited parenthetically by page number.

2. I find Dickens's attack on the limited liability of railway companies immensely funny; but recently, Catherine Gallagher has argued that *Hard Times* is entirely mirthless, characterized by a "melancholic aimlessness," an "almost complete lack of narrative hope" ("*Hard Times* and the Somaeconomics of the Early Victorians," in *The Body Economic: Life, Death, and Sensation in Political Economy and the Victorian Novel* [Princeton: Princeton University Press, 2006], 70). I see *Hard Times* as comic rather than tragic, sentimental rather than hopeless.

3. Exculpation extends to Gradgrind père, whose plaintive explanation to Louisa—"I have proved my—my system to myself, and I have rigidly administered it; and I must bear the responsibility of its failures. I only entreat you to believe, my favourite child, I have meant to do right"—is met by the narrator's reflection that "to do him justice he had" and by Louisa's generous (in the technical, Fieldingesque sense) response: "I know you have intended to make me happy. I have never blamed you, and I never shall" (244–45). The plot of the novel is devoted to Gradgrind's learning, as he explains to Bounderby, "we are all liable to mistakes" (261)—but despite the proximity of the two terms, "mistake" is not synonymous with "liability." Mistake demands sympathy; it is what militates against responsibility. "Atone, by repentance and better conduct, for the shocking action you have committed, and the dreadful consequences to which it has led" (301), Gradgrind enjoins Tom, but the only atonement that is made is made by Gradgrind, in language that in one gesture exonerates himself and his son: "Broadsides in the streets," Louisa sees, "signed with her father's name, exonerating the late Stephen Blackpool, weaver, from misplaced suspicion, and publishing the guilt of his own son, with such extenuation as his years and temptation (he could not bring himself to add, his education) might beseech" (312).

4. Terry Eagleton, "Tragedy and the Novel," in *Sweet Violence: The Idea of the Tragic* (Oxford, UK: Blackwell, 2003), 184.

5. Leon E. Wein, "The Responsibility of Intelligent Artifacts: Toward an Automation Jurisprudence," *Harvard Journal of Law and Technology* 6.1 (1992): 103. Despite invoking Mary Shelley, Wein, like many of the lawyers and scientists who refer to *Frankenstein*, has a tenuous grasp of the novel's publication date and the details of its plot. As the allusion to "wire electrodes" suggests, references to *Frankenstein* in legal and biotechnology circles is largely influenced by visual culture (Gene Wilder's *Frankenstein* rather than Mary Shelley's).

6. Ronald Collins, "Regulating Dr. Frankenstein: Money, Lax Ethics, and Clinical Trials," *Legal Times*, 16 October 2000, 83. Republished on the Center for Science in the Public Interest website; www.cspinet.org/integrity/regulate_frank.html.

7. Scott Tips, "Ephedra Decision is a Mixed Blessing," *Health Freedom News*, July 2005; www.thenhf.com/ephedra_issues_02.html.

8. Courtney S. Campbell, "Biotechnology and the Fear of Frankenstein," *Cambridge Quarterly of Healthcare Ethics* 12.4 (2003): 342–52; Joyce Tait, "More Faust than Franken-

stein: The European Debate about the Precautionary Principle and Risk Regulation for Genetically Modified Crops," *Journal of Risk Research* 4.2 (2001): 175–89; D. R. Cooley, "So Who's Afraid of Frankenstein Food?" *Journal of Social Philosophy* 33.3 (2002): 442–63; J. R. Blanchfield, "Enough of Frankenstein," *Food Science and Technology Today* 13.4 (1999): 179–81.

9. Marilyn Butler, "*Frankenstein* and Radical Science," *Times Literary Supplement*, 4 April 1993; Franco Moretti, "Dialectic of Fear," in *Signs Taken for Wonders: On the Sociology of Literary Forms*, 2nd ed. (London: Verso, 2005), 85.

10. Mark Hansen, "'Not thus, after all, would life be given': Technesis, Technology and the Parody of Romantic Poetics in *Frankenstein*," *Studies in Romanticism* 36.4 (1997): 580, 586.

11. Hansen, "'Not thus, after all, would life be given,'" 582. Hansen's reading of the text is to my mind more satisfying than Moretti's, which sees Frankenstein's invention as an allegory of "the process of capitalist production" without accounting for the specificity of the product in question ("Dialectic of Fear," 87).

12. Hansen, "'Not thus, after all, would life be given,'" 606.

13. Hansen, "'Not thus, after all, would life be given,'" 608.

14. Moretti, "Dialectic of Fear," 85; Maureen McLane, "Literate Species: Populations, 'Humanities,' and *Frankenstein*," *ELH* 63.4 (1996): 979.

15. Hansen, "'Not thus, after all, would life be given,'" 605.

16. Mary Shelley, *Frankenstein*, ed. J. Paul Hunter (New York: Norton, 1996), 21; hereafter cited parenthetically by page number.

17. J. H. Baker, *Introduction to English Legal History*, 3rd. ed. (London: Buttersworth, 1990), 464–65.

18. Baker, *Introduction to English Legal History*, 3rd. ed., 462.

19. As in the first entry for the term in the *Oxford English Dictionary*: "The faculty of an agent or of acting; active working or operation; action, activity." The *OED*'s examples include Sir H. Slingsby's *Diary*, written in 1658 ("Privacy . . . if your Hours in it are not well employed, may become as dangerous as a place of agency"), Jonathan Edwards's 1762 *Freedom of the Will* ("The moral agency of the Supreme Being . . . differs in that respect from the moral agency of created intelligent beings"), and Samuel Taylor Coleridge's 1830 *On the Constitution of the Church and State* ("The State shall leave the largest portion of personal free agency to each of its citizens, that is compatible with the free agency of all").

20. Jonathan H. Grossman, "Mary Shelley's Legal *Frankenstein*," in *The Art of Alibi: English Law Courts and the Novel* (Baltimore: Johns Hopkins University Press, 2002), 75. Grossman is interested in legal questions surrounding custody, which leads him to argue that Shelley is more concerned with Victor's responsibility for his own actions toward his progeny than with his responsibility for "the human creature's actions, over which he has no control" (77). The problem of the novel is neither Victor's actions nor the creature's, he says, though we "continually attempt with varying success to affix blame on one or the other"; the problem, rather, is that "the relationship itself . . . is monstrous" (78–79). To my mind, however, the question of relationship is one and the same as the question of blame, and to think otherwise is to assume, as Victor does, that individuals can only be blamed for acts that are their own.

21. "Redoublings," observes George Levine, "are characteristic of the whole novel. Not only all the major characters, but the minor characters as well seem to be echoes of each other. Every story seems a variation on every other" (*"Frankenstein* and the Tradition of Realism," in Shelley, *Frankenstein,* 211).

22. Levine, *"Frankenstein* and the Tradition of Realism," 211. Ellen Moers, "Female Gothic: The Monster's Mother," in Shelley, *Frankenstein,* 224.

23. Hansen, "'Not thus, after all, would life be given,'" 582. For one of many accounts of the history of the "inherently dangerous" rule, see Edward H. Levi, *An Introduction to Legal Reasoning* (Chicago: University of Chicago Press, 1949).

24. *Reports of Cases in the Court of Appeals of the State of New York,* 217 New York 382 (1916): 382–401.

25. See Anita Bernstein, "How Can a Product Be Liable?" *Duke Law Journal* 45.1 (1995): 42.

26. Blackstone, *Commentaries on the Laws of England,* 4 vols. (1765–69; rpt., Chicago: University of Chicago Press, 1979), 1:291.

27. Bernstein, "How Can a Product be Liable?" 43.

28. R. W. Kostal, *Law and English Railway Capitalism, 1825–1875* (Oxford, UK: Clarendon Press, 1994), 255.

29. Kostal, *Law and English Railway Capitalism,* 256.

30. Kostal, *Law and English Railway Capitalism,* 257.

31. The quotation is from Chief Justice Shaw's decision in *Farwell v. Boston and Worcester Railroad* (1842), cited in Kostal, *Law and English Railway Capitalism,* 269. Kostal that the precedents in *Priestley* and *Farwell* were expanded in the 1850s, in the "fellow-servant" rule (which announced that workers "unwilling to accept the risk that they might be injured by a co-worker's negligence . . . were free to make a better bargain elsewhere" and which allowed that risk would be compensated only once, in the form of wages), and in *Bartonshill Coal Company v. Reid* (1858), which, he says, "eradicate[d] from employer liability the last British vestige of the old legal paternalism" (270–72).

32. *Hansard's Parliamentary Debates,* 3rd. ser., vol. 139 (1855), col. 2031.

33. Two wonderful books on nineteenth-century law and literature confirm this association of the period with negligence, at least in the context of American literary history: Nan Goodman's *Shifting the Blame: Literature, Law, and the Theory of Accidents in Nineteenth-Century America* (Princeton: Princeton University Press, 1998) and Stacey Margolis's *The Public Life of Privacy in Nineteenth-Century America* (Durham, NC: Duke University Press, 2005). The role of negligence in the literary history of the Victorian novel has yet to be written, but an important start was made in Andrew Miller's "Subjectivity Ltd: The Discourse of Liability in the Joint Stock Companies Act of 1856 and Gaskell's *Cranford," ELH* 61.1 (1994): 139–57.

34. Although it is not within the scope of *Harm's Way* to pursue this insight in much detail, naturalist adventitiousness seems to me distinct from the adventitiousness of early realism. In Zola, for example, the forms that determine a character's action—class most particularly—have become so ossified as to cease to function accidentally. As a result, Zola's murderers are not accidental murderers like Roxana or Lovelace, but murderers who, as Stephen Kern has recently noted, "kill because of an irresistible heredi-

tary taint or overwhelming biological, psychological, or social forces" (*A Cultural History of Causality: Science, Murder Novels, and Systems of Thought* [Princeton: Princeton University Press, 2004], 5). The differences between naturalist and realist adventitiousness come into stark relief at the conclusion of Frank Norris's superb final novel, *The Pit*. The book ends by surveying the consequences of Curtis Jadwin's ruinous bid to corner the market in wheat: "The great corner was a thing of the past; the great corner with the long train of disasters its collapse had started. The great failure had precipitated smaller failures, and the aggregate of smaller failures had pulled down one business house after another. For weeks afterward, the successive crashes were like the shock and reverberations of undermined buildings toppling to their ruin. An important bank had suspended payment, and hundreds of depositors had found their little fortunes swept away. The ramifications of the catastrophe were unbelievable" (*The Pit: A Story of Chicago* [New York: Grove, 1956], 419). One of these ramifications is the suicide of Jadwin's best friend, Charles Cressler, about whose death Jadwin reflects: "I've killed him, Sam. I might as well have held that pistol myself" (365). About the "great failure" of the corner, which the preceding third-person narrative voice does not assign to any one agent, Jadwin similarly insists: "I have been to blame for everything" (417). If *The Pit* had ended with chapter 10—with the tableau of Jadwin and his wife, Laura, holding one another as a "prolonged and wailing cry rose suddenly from the street, and passed on through the city under the stars and the wide canopy of the darkness. 'Extra, oh-h-h, extra! All about the Smash of the Great Wheat Corner! All about the Failure of Curtis Jadwin!'" (412)—it would have read as a novel of tragic responsibility similar in kind to *Clarissa* or *Frankenstein*. But the concluding chapter, which deviates from the typography of the rest of the book by being *called* "Conclusion," raises the possibility of Jadwin's liability only to deflect it onto the wheat he has attempted to master: "Laura would not admit her husband was in any way to blame. He had suffered, too. She repeated to herself his words, again and again: 'The wheat cornered itself. I simply stood between two sets of circumstances. The wheat cornered me, not I the wheat.' And all those millions and millions of bushels of Wheat were gone now. The Wheat that had killed Cressler, that had ingulfed Jadwin's fortune and all but unseated reason itself; the Wheat . . . had passed on, resistless, along its ordered and predetermined courses from West to East, like a vast Titanic flood, had passed, leaving Death and Ruin in its wake, but bearing Life and Prosperity to the crowded cities and centres of Europe" (420). If *The Pit* remains tragic, it is a different order—a different *magnitude*—of tragedy than is found in Richardson or Defoe. "For a moment, vague, dark perplexities assailed her, questionings as to the elemental forces, the forces of demand and supply that ruled the world," the narrator continues, picking up the thread of Laura's thought in the third person: "This huge resistless Nourisher of the Nation— why was it that it could not reach the People, could not fulfil its destiny, unmarred by all this suffering, unattended by all this misery?" Jadwin's self-inculpation, it seems, is properly understood as the inverse of his earlier grandiosity: for if one cannot hope to corner wheat—or, in other words, capital—one cannot be responsible for its "resistless" effects. Norris makes this point with a memorable final image of the Chicago Board of Trade, "black, monolithic, crouching on its foundations like a monstrous sphinx with blind eyes, silent, grave—crouching there without a sound, without sign of life, under the night and the drifting rain" (421). In Shelley, personification works to bind human beings to the animate and inanimate things they use and manufacture; but here, personification turns the commodity into a superior being distinct from the homely human person who can only be its victim. This distinction turns *The Pit* into a tragicomedy: for if the sociological plot sends naturalist determinism (at least in its American incarnation) back to a providentialism that in the 1720s may have been comic but in the wake of the Gilded Age is inescapably tragic; the romance plot sends Jadwin and his forgiving wife to a new life—and a new business venture—in the West: "'The world is all before us where to choose,' now, isn't it?" Laura asks, quoting Milton's fallen and yet favored pair. "And this big house and all the life we have led in it was just an incident in our lives—an incident that is closed" (414).

35. Consider, for example, the harrowing account of Bigger's accidental suffocation of Mary Dalton, which bears an uncanny resemblance to the creature's killing of William in *Frankenstein:*

> He looked at the shadowy bed and remembered Mary as some person he had not seen in a long time. She was still there. Had he hurt her? He went to the pillow. His hand moved toward her, but stopped in mid-air. He blinked his eyes and stared at Mary's face; it was darker than when he had first bent over her. Her bosom, her bosom, her—her bosom was not moving! He could not hear her breath coming and going now as he had when he had first brought her into the room! He bent and moved her head with his hand and found that she was relaxed and limp. He snatched his hand away. Thought and feeling were balked in him; there was something he was trying to tell himself, desperately, but could not. Then, convulsively, he sucked his breath in and huge words formed slowly, ringing in his ears: *She's dead.* . . .

Although the slowness with which it dawns on Bigger that he has killed Mary works to emphasize the adventitiousness of the killing, like Frankenstein's creature he immediately considers himself a murderer: "She was dead and he had killed her. He was a murderer, a Negro murderer, a black murderer. He had killed a white woman" (*Native Son* [New York: HarperCollins, 2005], 87). And as in Shelley's novel, where the creature's fatality is an effect of his shape—his being too big—Bigger's fatality is a consequence of his color—his being (too) black. I am grateful to Melissa Barton for turning my attention to Wright's novel. She offers a different account of the question of accidental responsibility in *Native Son* in an unpublished essay titled "Taking Credit, Not Blame, or What Bigger Killed For: Responsibility and Personhood in Richard Wright's *Native Son.*"

36. Ian McEwan, *Atonement* (2001; rpt., New York: Anchor Books, 2003), 5; hereafter cited parenthetically by page number.

37. Bernard Williams, "Recognising Responsibility," in *Shame and Necessity* (Berkeley: University of California Press, 1993), 72.